Contents Table

Welcome & What You'll Learn

Selecting the correct web element within a complex web page structure is the foundation of any effective web automation project. Without being able to accurately pinpoint and interact with elements, your scripts and tests will be unable to perform as designed. Mastering the art of element location is a pivotal skill for testers and developers working in the web automation space.

The Journey Ahead

This book, "Conquer Web Element Location with XPath and CSS Selectors", aims to transform you into an expert at crafting precise and robust locators for all types of web elements. We'll begin by solidifying the building blocks – delving into the world of HTML and how web browsers translate this code into the visual displays on your screen.

Using your newfound knowledge, you'll learn how to harness browser developer tools to dissect the anatomical makeup of a webpage. This ability will allow you to unlock the secrets of how individual elements are identified and the various properties that define them.

Two Essential Tools: XPath and CSS Selectors

As you progress through the book, we'll turn our attention to the two primary weapons in your element location arsenal:

- **XPath:** XPath, short for XML Path Language, is a language designed for navigating XML documents. Its flexibility and features make it incredibly powerful for identifying elements on the complex terrain of modern web pages, which are built with the HTML markup language (essentially a subset of XML).
- **CSS Selectors:** Cascading Style Sheets (CSS) define the way web pages are presented and styled. CSS selectors provide a concise and often more intuitive way to target elements based on their styles, classes, and structural position within the document.

Unleashing Your Skills

'Conquer Web Element Location with XPath and CSS Selectors' isn't simply a theoretical exploration. We'll dive deep into real-world scenarios and tackle the challenges frequently encountered during web automation projects. You'll learn:

- **Best practices for handling complex page layouts:** How to find the needle in the haystack of modern web design.
- **Dynamic content:** Strategies for pinpointing elements that are loaded after the initial page render, often using AJAX technology.
- **Working with forms and user input fields:** Techniques for locating text boxes, dropdowns, buttons, and more.
- **Selenium WebDriver integration:** Seamlessly combine your locator expertise with the powerful Selenium WebDriver Framework.
- **Troubleshooting and optimization:** How to debug issues and write selectors that are both efficient and reliable.

Become an Element Location Master

By the end of this book, your ability to wield XPath and CSS Selectors for element location will have dramatically transformed. You'll possess the skills to:

- Read HTML structure and identify elements with ease.
- Strategically choose the most appropriate selector type for any situation.
- Effortlessly locate even the most elusive elements.
- Write optimized, resilient, and accurate selectors for your automation scripts.

Let's embark on this exciting journey of discovery and become an expert in conquering the world of web element location!

Section 1:
Element Discovery Fundamentals

Understanding HTML Structure

Outline

1. What is HTML and its Importance
2. Basic HTML Document Structure
3. Common HTML Elements and Tags
4. Hierarchical Structure of HTML
5. Understanding DOM (Document Object Model)
6. Tools for Inspecting HTML Structure
7. Chapter Summary

What is HTML and its Importance

HTML, or HyperText Markup Language, is the standard language used to create and structure content on the World Wide Web. It serves as the backbone of all web pages, providing the essential framework for organizing text, images, links, forms, and other multimedia content. Here's a deeper dive into what HTML is and why it is so crucial:

What is HTML?

- **Definition**: HTML is a markup language, which means it uses tags to structure content. The term "HyperText" refers to the capability to link different pieces of content together, enabling navigation through hyperlinks.
- **Core Purpose**: HTML's primary role is to define the structure and layout of a web page. It sets up the basic elements that are then styled and enhanced with CSS and JavaScript.

Components of HTML

- **Elements and Tags**: HTML consists of elements, each represented by a tag or a pair of tags. For example, the <p> tag is used for paragraphs, and the <a> tag is for hyperlinks. Most HTML elements contain content within opening and closing tags.
- **Attributes**: Elements can have attributes that provide additional information. Common attributes include id, class, src, href, and alt. These attributes are crucial for styling and automation.

Importance of HTML in Web Development

- **Foundation of Websites**: Every website begins with HTML. It sets the structure for all other web technologies like CSS (for styling) and JavaScript (for interactivity).
- **Compatibility and Standards**: HTML is a standardized language, ensuring compatibility across different browsers and devices. This standardization is essential for consistent user experiences.
- **Ease of Learning and Use**: HTML is relatively easy to learn and use, allowing even beginners to create simple web pages quickly.

Importance of HTML in Web Automation and Testing

- **Locator Strategy**: In web automation tools like Selenium WebDriver, HTML is crucial because it's the basis for locating and interacting with web elements. Test scripts use XPath, CSS Selectors, and other strategies to identify elements within the HTML structure.
- **Understanding Web Page Structure**: Knowledge of HTML is essential for anyone involved in web automation, as it allows testers and developers to understand how a web page is constructed, enabling more effective testing and debugging.
- **Dynamic Content**: Understanding HTML helps in dealing with dynamic content. Websites often use JavaScript and AJAX to change the HTML structure on the fly, making it essential to comprehend how elements are added, removed, or modified.

In summary, HTML is the cornerstone of web development and automation. Its simplicity and flexibility make it a fundamental tool for building web content and a critical skill for those involved in web automation, like Selenium testers. Understanding HTML allows developers and testers to work effectively with web pages, ensuring accurate and efficient automation processes.

Basic HTML Document Structure

HTML (HyperText Markup Language) is the fundamental language used to create web pages. Understanding the basic structure of an HTML document is essential for both web developers and those involved in web automation. Here's a breakdown of the essential components and their roles:

1. The HTML Document Outline

An HTML document typically follows a specific outline, comprising several key sections:

- **Doctype Declaration**: The <!DOCTYPE> declaration at the top of the document specifies the version of HTML in use. It ensures that the browser interprets the HTML correctly.
- **HTML Tag**: The <html> tag wraps the entire content of the web page, indicating the start and end of the HTML document.
- **Head Section**: The <head> section contains metadata about the document, like its title, character set, stylesheets, scripts, and more.
- **Body Section**: The <body> section contains the actual content displayed on the web page, such as text, images, forms, links, and other elements.

2. Doctype Declaration

- **Purpose**: The <!DOCTYPE> declaration is not technically an HTML tag, but it informs the browser which version of HTML is being used. It helps ensure consistent rendering across different browsers.
- **Common Doctypes**: In modern HTML, the most common doctype is <!DOCTYPE html>, which indicates HTML5. This declaration should be the first line in the document.

3. The HTML Tag

- **Structure**: The <html> tag encompasses all other elements. It often has attributes like lang, indicating the document's language (e.g., <html lang="en">).

4. The Head Section

- **Content**: The <head> section contains metadata and other information not directly visible on the web page. It includes elements like:
  - **Title**: The <title> tag sets the page's title, visible in the browser's title bar or tab.
  - **Meta**: The <meta> tag provides metadata such as character set (<meta charset="UTF-8">), viewport settings, and other information.

- ○ **Link**: The `<link>` tag is used for external resources, like stylesheets (e.g., `<link rel="stylesheet" href="styles.css">`).
- ○ **Script**: The `<script>` tag allows you to include or link to JavaScript code.

5. The Body Section

- **Content**: The `<body>` section holds the actual content of the web page. This is where elements like paragraphs, headings, images, links, forms, tables, and others are placed.
- **Common Elements**: Within the body, you can find a variety of tags, including:
  - ○ **Text-based**: `<p>`, `<h1>` - `<h6>`, `<span>`, etc.
  - ○ **Interactive**: `<button>`, `<a>`, `<form>`, etc.
  - ○ **Media**: `<img>`, `<video>`, `<audio>`, etc.
  - ○ **Containers**: `<div>`, `<section>`, `<article>`, etc.

6. Closing the HTML Document

- **End of Body**: The `</body>` tag indicates the end of the body content.
- **End of HTML**: The `</html>` tag closes the HTML document.

7. Example

```
<!DOCTYPE html>
<html lang="en">
<head>
    <meta charset="UTF-8">
    <title>My First Web Page</title>
</head>
<body>
    <h1>Welcome to My Website</h1>
    <p>This is a simple example of an HTML page.</p>
 </body>
</html>
```

In summary, the basic structure of an HTML document consists of a doctype declaration, an enclosing HTML tag, a head section with metadata, and a body section with the actual content. Understanding this structure is crucial for web development and automation, providing a foundation for creating and interacting with web pages.

Common HTML Elements and Tags

HTML (HyperText Markup Language) uses a variety of elements and tags to structure and define content on web pages. Understanding these common elements is key for both web development and automation tasks. Here's a detailed overview of the most commonly used HTML elements and their purposes:

1. Text-Based Elements

- **Headings**: HTML has six levels of headings, from `<h1>` to `<h6>`, with `<h1>` being the most prominent. They are used to structure content and indicate the hierarchy of information.
- **Paragraphs**: The `<p>` tag represents a paragraph of text.
- **Line Breaks**: The `<br>` tag creates a single line break. It's a self-closing tag.
- **Text Formatting**: Tags like `<strong>`, `<em>`, `<b>`, `<i>`, and `<u>` are used to apply bold, italic, and underline styles to text.

2. Hyperlinks and Navigation

- **Links**: The <a> (anchor) tag is used to create hyperlinks. It typically has an href attribute indicating the destination URL.
- **Lists**: HTML has ordered lists (<ol>) and unordered lists (<ul>), with list items (<li>). Ordered lists are numbered, while unordered lists use bullet points.
- **Navigation**: The <nav> tag indicates a section of the page intended for navigation links.

3. Media and Multimedia

- **Images**: The <img> tag is used to display images. It has attributes like src (source of the image) and alt (alternative text for accessibility).
- **Audio and Video**: The <audio> and <video> tags are used to embed audio and video content, respectively. They can have source elements to specify file types.
- **Embedding Content**: The <iframe> tag allows you to embed other content, such as videos or entire web pages, within an HTML page.

4. Forms and User Input

- **Forms**: The <form> tag defines a form for user input. It can contain various input elements and attributes like action (where to send the form data) and method (GET or POST).
- **Input Fields**: The <input> tag is used for user input. It has different type attributes, such as text, password, checkbox, radio, email, number, date, etc.
- **Labels and Buttons**: The <label> tag is used to label input fields, providing accessibility and context. The <button> tag represents a clickable button.

5. Tables and Tabular Data

- **Tables**: The <table> tag is used to create tables. It typically contains <tr> (table rows), <th> (table headers), and <td> (table data cells).
- **Table Attributes**: Tables can have attributes to define styles, alignments, and other properties.

6. Document Structure and Layout

- **Sections and Containers**: The <div> tag is a general-purpose container used to group elements. Other container tags include <section>, <article>, <header>, and <footer>.
- **Meta Information**: The <meta> tag in the head section provides metadata about the document, such as character set, viewport settings, and other information.
- **Scripts and Styles**: The <script> tag is used to include JavaScript, and the <style> tag can contain inline CSS.

7. Attributes in HTML

- **ID and Class**: The id and class attributes are used to uniquely identify elements or group them for styling and scripting purposes.
- **Global Attributes**: Attributes like title, style, data-*, and lang can be applied to most HTML elements, providing additional information and flexibility.

In summary, these are some of the most common HTML elements and tags, each serving a specific purpose in structuring and presenting web content. Understanding these elements is crucial for web developers and those involved in automation, like Selenium testers, as they form the basis for creating and interacting with web pages.

Hierarchical Structure of HTML

The hierarchical structure of HTML is crucial for understanding how elements are related to each other on a web page. This structure determines the way content is organized, styled, and rendered by web browsers. In a hierarchical structure, elements are nested within other elements, creating a tree-like layout known as the Document Object Model (DOM). Here's a detailed exploration of this concept:

1. The Document Object Model (DOM)

- **Definition**: The DOM represents the logical structure of an HTML document as a tree, where each node is an element, attribute, or text.
- **Hierarchy**: In the DOM, each element can have parent and child nodes. This nesting creates a hierarchy that defines the relationships among different elements on a page.
- **Navigation**: Understanding the DOM is essential for web automation and manipulation, as it determines how elements can be accessed and modified.

2. Parent-Child Relationships

- **Parent and Child**: In HTML, a parent element contains one or more child elements. For example, a <div> containing a <p> and an <a> tag has a parent-child relationship.
- **Common Parent-Child Examples**: Lists (<ul> and <li>), tables (<table>, <tr>, <td>), forms (<form>, <input>), and sections (<section>, <article>, <header>, <footer>).

3. Siblings and Ancestor-Descendant Relationships

- **Siblings**: Elements that share the same parent are siblings. Sibling relationships are crucial for locating elements in complex structures.
- **Ancestor-Descendant**: An ancestor element contains other elements as descendants. For example, a <div> can have multiple nested elements, making it an ancestor of all its nested descendants.

4. Nested Structures and Grouping

- **Nesting**: HTML allows elements to be nested within other elements to create complex structures. For example, a <div> can contain multiple <p> and <a> tags.
- **Grouping and Containers**: The <div> tag is a common container used to group related elements. Other containers include <section>, <article>, and <nav>.
- **Deep Nesting**: In complex web pages, elements may be deeply nested, requiring precise understanding of the hierarchy for effective navigation and automation.

5. Implications for CSS and XPath

- **CSS Selectors**: The hierarchical structure is key to writing effective CSS selectors. You can use descendant selectors (div p), child selectors (div > p), sibling selectors (div + p, div ~ p), and others to target elements.
- **XPath**: XPath relies heavily on the hierarchical structure to locate elements. You can use parent-child relationships (/div/p), descendant relationships (//div//p), and other XPath expressions to navigate the DOM.

6. Practical Examples of HTML Hierarchy

- **Web Page Layout**: A typical web page has a hierarchical structure with a <header>, <main>, <footer>, and possibly multiple sections and articles within the <main>.

- **Forms and Tables**: Forms have a parent `<form>` element with child input fields and other interactive elements. Tables consist of a parent `<table>` with nested rows (`<tr>`) and data cells (`<td>`).
- **Navigation Menus**: Navigation menus often consist of a parent `<nav>` element with nested lists (`<ul>`, `<li>`, `<a>`), representing the hierarchical structure of the menu.

In summary, the hierarchical structure of HTML is foundational to understanding how web pages are built and interact with CSS and XPath. Recognizing parent-child, sibling, and ancestor-descendant relationships helps developers and testers navigate the DOM, select elements accurately, and create robust automation scripts.

Understanding DOM (Document Object Model)

The Document Object Model (DOM) is a crucial concept in web development and automation, providing a structured representation of an HTML document. It defines the logical structure of documents and the way elements are accessed, modified, or interacted with. Here's an in-depth look at the DOM and its importance in web technologies:

1. What is the DOM?

- **Definition**: The DOM is a platform- and language-independent interface that represents the structure of an HTML or XML document as a tree of objects. It enables programming languages like JavaScript to interact with web page content.
- **Tree Structure**: The DOM is often depicted as a tree, where each node represents an element, attribute, or text content within the document.
- **Standardization**: The DOM is standardized by the World Wide Web Consortium (W3C), ensuring consistent behavior across different browsers and platforms.

2. Key Components of the DOM

- **Document Node**: The root node representing the entire document. It is typically the `<html>` element.
- **Element Nodes**: Nodes that represent HTML elements like `<div>`, `<p>`, `<a>`, etc. These nodes can have attributes and child nodes.
- **Text Nodes**: Nodes containing text content within elements. For example, the text inside a `<p>` tag is a text node.
- **Attribute Nodes**: Nodes representing attributes of elements, such as `id`, `class`, `href`, etc.
- **Other Nodes**: Nodes representing comments, processing instructions, and other specialized content.

3. The DOM and Web Browsers

- **Rendering Web Pages**: Web browsers use the DOM to render and display web pages. They parse the HTML document and construct the DOM tree, which is then rendered visually.
- **Dynamic Content**: The DOM allows web pages to be dynamic and interactive. JavaScript and other scripting languages can manipulate the DOM, enabling content to change without reloading the page.

4. Navigating the DOM

- **Parent-Child Relationships**: In the DOM tree, each element can have parent and child relationships. Understanding these relationships is crucial for navigating the DOM.
- **Siblings and Ancestors**: Sibling nodes share the same parent, while ancestor nodes represent the lineage of a given node.

- **Traversal Methods**: JavaScript and other programming languages provide methods to traverse the DOM, such as `document.getElementById`, `document.querySelector`, and `document.querySelectorAll`.

5. The DOM in Web Automation

- **Locating Elements**: Web automation tools like Selenium WebDriver use the DOM to locate elements for interaction. XPath and CSS selectors are common methods for selecting nodes in the DOM tree.
- **Dynamic Elements**: As web pages become more dynamic with AJAX and JavaScript, the DOM changes, making it crucial to understand how elements are added, removed, or modified.
- **Interacting with the DOM**: Automation scripts can interact with the DOM to simulate user actions, such as clicking buttons, entering text, or retrieving content.

6. Modifying the DOM

- **JavaScript and the DOM**: JavaScript allows direct manipulation of the DOM, enabling developers to create interactive web experiences. Methods like `appendChild`, `removeChild`, and `setAttribute` are used to modify the DOM.
- **DOM Events**: The DOM also handles events like clicks, keypresses, and mouse movements, allowing developers to create event-driven interactions.

7. Best Practices with the DOM

- **Performance Considerations**: Direct manipulation of the DOM can impact performance. Batch operations and minimizing reflows are common best practices.
- **Accessibility**: Proper structure and use of attributes like `aria-*` are important for accessibility and compliance with web standards.
- **Testing and Debugging**: Understanding the DOM is essential for debugging and testing web applications. Tools like browser developer tools can help inspect and manipulate the DOM for troubleshooting.

In summary, the Document Object Model (DOM) is a fundamental concept in web development and automation. It provides a structured representation of HTML documents, allowing interaction, navigation, and modification. Understanding the DOM is crucial for creating dynamic web applications and building robust web automation scripts.

Tools for Inspecting HTML Structure

Inspecting HTML structure is a crucial skill for web developers and testers. It allows you to understand how a web page is constructed, identify elements for manipulation or automation, and troubleshoot issues. Various tools can help with these tasks, offering features to inspect, edit, and interact with HTML and related technologies like CSS and JavaScript. Here's an overview of the most common tools for inspecting HTML structure:

1. Browser Developer Tools

Most modern web browsers come with built-in developer tools designed for inspecting and debugging web pages. These tools are among the most widely used for inspecting HTML structure.

- **Chrome DevTools**: Google Chrome's developer tools offer a comprehensive set of features for inspecting HTML, CSS, and JavaScript. You can access it by right-clicking on a web page and selecting "Inspect" or using the keyboard shortcut `Ctrl + Shift + I`.
  - **Elements Panel**: This panel shows the HTML structure of the web page. You can expand and collapse elements, view attributes, and see how the browser renders the DOM.

- Styles Panel: Allows you to view and modify CSS associated with HTML elements. You can add, remove, or change styles in real time.
- Console Panel: This panel provides a JavaScript console for interacting with the DOM and executing scripts.
- **Firefox Developer Tools**: Similar to Chrome DevTools, Firefox offers a set of developer tools for inspecting and debugging.
  - Inspector: Equivalent to Chrome's Elements panel, allowing you to explore and interact with the HTML structure.
  - CSS and Layout Tools: Provides detailed information about CSS styles and layout properties.
- **Edge Developer Tools**: Microsoft Edge has its developer tools, resembling Chrome's due to their common Chromium-based engine.
- **Safari Web Inspector**: Safari offers a comprehensive set of developer tools for inspecting and debugging on macOS and iOS devices.

2. Third-Party Tools

In addition to browser-based developer tools, several third-party tools can help inspect HTML structure.

- **SelectorsHub**: A powerful tool for generating and validating XPath and CSS selectors. It integrates with browser developer tools and offers features to simplify XPath/CSS selector creation.
- **Firebug**: Although discontinued, Firebug was once a popular Firefox extension for inspecting and debugging HTML and JavaScript. Its features are now integrated into Firefox Developer Tools.
- **Web Developer Extension**: A browser extension available for Chrome and Firefox, providing additional tools for inspecting and manipulating web pages. It includes features for inspecting forms, images, and other elements.

3. Features to Look For

When using tools for inspecting HTML structure, certain features are particularly useful:

- **Element Inspection**: The ability to inspect individual elements, view their attributes, and understand their position in the DOM hierarchy.
- **Real-Time Editing**: Tools that allow you to edit HTML or CSS in real time to test changes or troubleshoot issues.
- **Selector Generation**: Tools that help generate XPath or CSS selectors for automation or testing purposes.
- **Performance Analysis**: Features to analyze performance, such as network activity, JavaScript execution, and rendering times.
- **Accessibility Checks**: Tools that provide information on accessibility compliance, such as ARIA attributes and semantic HTML.

In summary, tools for inspecting HTML structure are essential for understanding how web pages are built, debugging issues, and building automation scripts. Browser developer tools are the most common, offering comprehensive features for inspecting, modifying, and interacting with HTML, CSS, and JavaScript. Third-party tools can supplement these features, providing additional functionality for XPath/CSS selector generation, performance analysis, and more.

Chapter Summary

This chapter provided a comprehensive overview of HTML structure, its key components, and related concepts. Here's a summary of the major topics covered in the chapter:

What is HTML and its Importance

- HTML (HyperText Markup Language) is the foundational language for creating web pages.
- It provides the structure and organization for content on the internet, forming the basis for all websites.
- Understanding HTML is critical for web development and automation, as it allows you to create, locate, and interact with web elements.

Basic HTML Document Structure

- An HTML document typically starts with a `<!DOCTYPE>` declaration, followed by the `<html>`, `<head>`, and `<body>` sections.
- The `<head>` section contains metadata, styles, and scripts, while the `<body>` section holds the visible content.
- A proper understanding of this structure is essential for building and interacting with web pages.

Common HTML Elements and Tags

- HTML uses various elements and tags to represent different types of content, such as headings, paragraphs, links, forms, and media.
- Important attributes like `id`, `class`, and `href` play a key role in identifying and selecting elements.
- Knowing common elements and tags helps in both web development and automation tasks.

Hierarchical Structure of HTML

- HTML has a hierarchical structure, with parent-child relationships, sibling nodes, and ancestor-descendant relationships.
- The Document Object Model (DOM) represents this structure as a tree, allowing navigation and manipulation of elements.
- Understanding the hierarchical structure is crucial for building complex web pages and writing effective automation scripts.

Understanding the Document Object Model (DOM)

- The DOM is a platform- and language-independent representation of an HTML document.
- It allows you to interact with and manipulate web elements programmatically, enabling dynamic content and interactivity.
- Navigating the DOM is key for web automation tools like Selenium, which rely on XPath and CSS selectors to locate elements.

Tools for Inspecting HTML Structure

- Various tools help inspect and analyze HTML structure, with browser developer tools being the most commonly used.
- Chrome DevTools, Firefox Developer Tools, and similar tools in other browsers offer features for inspecting, modifying, and interacting with the HTML structure.
- Third-party tools like SelectorsHub provide additional functionality, especially for generating XPath and CSS selectors.

Conclusion

This chapter laid the foundation for understanding HTML structure and its importance in web development and automation. By covering key components, hierarchical relationships, and tools for inspection, it set the stage for more advanced topics in XPath, CSS selectors, and web automation with Selenium.

Inspecting Web Elements in Browsers

Outline

1. Understanding the Role of Web Inspectors
2. Navigating Browser Developer Tools
3. Identifying Key Elements in a Web Page
4. Techniques for Inspecting Elements
5. Extracting Information for Automation
6. Chapter Summary

Understanding the Role of Web Inspectors

Web inspectors play a pivotal role in web development and automated testing. They offer a range of functionalities that allow you to delve into the structure and behavior of a web page. This section will introduce the concept of web inspectors, their importance in Selenium WebDriver-based automation, and how they can be used to streamline the process of locating web elements.

What Are Web Inspectors?

Web inspectors, also known as developer tools or dev tools, are built-in utilities in web browsers designed for developers and testers. They provide a comprehensive interface to explore, analyze, and manipulate the elements and resources on a web page. With web inspectors, you can:

- **Inspect the Document Object Model (DOM)**: View the entire HTML structure, including nested elements, attributes, and relationships.
- **Analyze CSS**: Examine styles applied to each element, including inherited styles and specific rules.
- **Debug JavaScript**: Set breakpoints, step through code, and inspect variable values during script execution.
- **Monitor Network Activity**: Track HTTP requests and responses, including AJAX calls.
- **Interact with Elements**: Modify the DOM and CSS in real time to test changes and troubleshoot issues.

Why Web Inspectors Are Important for Selenium WebDriver

Selenium WebDriver is a popular tool for automating web applications, and web inspectors are indispensable for creating reliable test scripts. Here's why they are crucial:

- **Element Location**: Web inspectors help you identify unique attributes for elements, which is essential for building robust XPath and CSS selectors.
- **Debugging**: When automation scripts fail, web inspectors allow you to examine the state of the web page and identify the root cause of the problem.
- **Understanding Dynamic Content**: Many web applications rely on dynamic content, which can be challenging to test. Web inspectors help you understand how elements change and how to adapt your automation scripts accordingly.
- **Cross-Browser Compatibility**: By using web inspectors in multiple browsers, you can ensure that your test scripts are compatible with different environments.

How Web Inspectors Streamline Automation

Web inspectors offer a range of features that make the process of automating web tests more efficient:

- **Quick Element Identification**: You can quickly locate elements by using the "Inspect" function, hover-over techniques, or dedicated search features.
- **On-the-Fly Testing**: Modify the DOM or CSS directly in the inspector to test hypotheses without modifying the actual codebase.
- **Detailed Error Reporting**: Inspectors provide detailed error messages, helping you diagnose issues with scripts, element location, or JavaScript execution.
- **Performance Insights**: By monitoring network activity and JavaScript performance, you can identify bottlenecks and optimize your automation scripts.

Understanding the role of web inspectors is foundational for anyone working with Selenium WebDriver. By leveraging their capabilities, you can build more reliable automation scripts, troubleshoot issues efficiently, and gain a deeper understanding of the web applications you're testing. In the following sections, we'll dive deeper into the specific functionalities of web inspectors and how to use them to inspect web elements effectively.

Navigating Browser Developer Tools

Browser developer tools are powerful resources for anyone working with web pages, offering insights into the HTML structure, CSS styles, JavaScript functionality, and more. This chapter focuses on exploring these tools and understanding how to use them effectively to inspect web elements for Selenium WebDriver automation.

Introduction to Browser Developer Tools

Modern browsers like Google Chrome, Mozilla Firefox, Microsoft Edge, and Safari come with built-in developer tools. These tools are designed to assist developers and testers in inspecting, debugging, and analyzing web pages. The core functionality across these browsers is similar, although there may be slight differences in interface and additional features.

What You Can Do with Developer Tools

- **Inspect HTML Structure**: Explore the Document Object Model (DOM) to understand the page's hierarchy.
- **View and Edit CSS Styles**: See applied CSS rules and experiment with changes in real-time.
- **Debug JavaScript**: Set breakpoints, monitor script execution, and evaluate variables.
- **Analyze Network Activity**: Examine HTTP requests and responses, track AJAX calls, and assess performance.
- **Profile Performance**: Investigate performance bottlenecks and identify resource-intensive operations.

Accessing Developer Tools

Accessing developer tools is straightforward in most browsers. The following are the common methods to open these tools:

Using Keyboard Shortcuts

- **Google Chrome**: Press `Ctrl + Shift + I` (Windows/Linux) or `Cmd + Opt + I` (Mac).
- **Mozilla Firefox**: Press `Ctrl + Shift + I` (Windows/Linux) or `Cmd + Opt + I` (Mac).
- **Microsoft Edge**: Press F12 or `Ctrl + Shift + I`.
- **Safari**: Enable "Show Develop menu in menu bar" in Preferences > Advanced, then press `Cmd + Opt + C`.

Accessing Through the Browser Menu

Most browsers offer a menu option to open developer tools:

- In Chrome, Firefox, and Edge, click the menu icon (three dots or lines) in the upper-right corner, then select "More Tools" > "Developer Tools."
- In Safari, after enabling the Develop menu, select "Develop" > "Show Web Inspector."

Right-Click and Inspect

A quick method to inspect a specific element is to right-click on it and select "Inspect" or "Inspect Element." This opens developer tools and highlights the chosen element in the DOM.

Key Sections of Developer Tools

Developer tools contain various panels with specialized functions. Here's a brief overview of the most commonly used panels:

Elements/Inspector Panel

This panel allows you to explore the HTML structure of the web page. You can expand and collapse nodes, view attributes, and see the applied CSS styles. It is also possible to edit the DOM directly to test changes.

Console Panel

The console displays JavaScript output, errors, and other messages. It is also an interactive space where you can execute JavaScript code to interact with the page.

Network Panel

This panel shows all network activity, including HTTP requests, AJAX calls, and asset loading. It is useful for debugging network-related issues and understanding the sequence of network events.

Sources/Debugger Panel

Here, you can view the page's source code, set breakpoints, and step through JavaScript execution. It is valuable for debugging complex scripts and understanding the logic behind web interactions.

Performance Panel

The performance panel provides insights into the web page's resource usage and speed. You can record sessions to identify performance bottlenecks and optimize scripts.

Practical Use Cases for Automation

Developer tools are invaluable for Selenium WebDriver automation. Here are some common scenarios where they are especially useful:

- **Finding Unique Element Identifiers**: Use the Elements panel to locate elements with unique attributes for building XPath and CSS selectors.
- **Debugging Automation Failures**: When a Selenium script fails, use developer tools to inspect the page and diagnose the issue.
- **Monitoring AJAX-Based Interactions**: The Network panel helps you understand the behavior of AJAX-based elements, which is critical for creating reliable automation scripts.

Navigating browser developer tools is an essential skill for anyone involved in web automation. By understanding the key functionalities and how to access them, you'll be able to inspect, analyze, and troubleshoot web pages effectively. This foundation will enable you to create robust Selenium WebDriver scripts and optimize your automation processes.

Identifying Key Elements in a Web Page

Understanding how to identify key elements on a web page is crucial for Selenium WebDriver automation. It allows you to interact with the correct elements, automate tasks, and build robust test scripts. This section discusses techniques for identifying key web elements, focusing on commonly used HTML elements and effective ways to locate them.

Importance of Identifying Key Elements

Key elements on a web page typically include buttons, links, input fields, form elements, and other interactive components. Proper identification of these elements helps ensure that your Selenium scripts interact with the intended elements, reducing the risk of errors and unexpected behavior.

Typical Key Elements on a Web Page

- **Headers**: <h1>, <h2>, <h3>, etc. are commonly used to represent titles and sections.
- **Buttons**: <button>, <input type="button">, or <a> tags used as buttons.
- **Links**: <a> tags with href attributes.
- **Input Fields**: <input>, <textarea>, and other form elements.
- **Images**: <img> tags, which may also act as links.
- **Interactive Elements**: Elements that trigger JavaScript events, like dropdowns and pop-ups.

Techniques for Identifying Elements

Here are several techniques for identifying key elements on a web page, using both basic and advanced methods.

Right-Click and Inspect

The simplest way to identify an element is to right-click on it and select "Inspect" or "Inspect Element." This action opens the developer tools and highlights the selected element in the DOM, allowing you to see its attributes, styles, and position in the HTML structure.

Using Search Features in Developer Tools

Developer tools often include a search function to find elements by text, tag name, class, or attribute. This feature is helpful when you know some characteristic of the element but cannot easily locate it visually.

Exploring the DOM Tree

The "Elements" panel in developer tools displays the entire DOM tree. By expanding and collapsing nodes, you can explore the web page's structure and find key elements. This approach is useful for understanding parent-child relationships and locating elements within nested structures.

Identifying Unique Attributes

Attributes like id, name, and class are commonly used to identify elements. Look for unique or descriptive attributes that can serve as reliable identifiers in Selenium WebDriver scripts. For example, an element with a unique id can be quickly located using XPath or CSS selectors.

Using Hover-Over Techniques

When inspecting elements in the developer tools, hovering over nodes in the DOM highlights the corresponding elements on the web page. This technique helps visualize the relationships between elements and can guide you to the correct components.

Dealing with Frames and Iframes

Frames and iframes create separate contexts on a web page. To identify elements within frames, you need to switch to the correct context in the developer tools. This can be done by locating the frame or iframe in the DOM, right-clicking, and selecting "Switch to Frame."

Tips for Identifying Key Elements

Here are some additional tips to help you identify key elements on a web page:

- **Use Descriptive Labels**: Look for elements with descriptive `alt`, `title`, or `data-*` attributes, which can provide clues about their function.
- **Analyze CSS Classes**: CSS classes often indicate the role of an element (e.g., "button," "header," "input-field").
- **Check for Event Listeners**: Use the "Event Listeners" tab in developer tools to find elements with attached JavaScript events, indicating interactive components.
- **Document Your Findings**: Keep notes on unique attributes, relationships, and other information that will help you build Selenium WebDriver selectors.

Identifying key elements on a web page is a fundamental skill for web automation. By using a combination of techniques, including right-click and inspect, search features, DOM exploration, and hover-over methods, you can locate important elements and gather the necessary information for Selenium WebDriver automation scripts.

Techniques for Inspecting Elements

Inspecting web elements is essential for understanding a web page's structure, behavior, and functionality, especially when using Selenium WebDriver for automation. The ability to effectively inspect elements allows you to create robust automation scripts, identify unique identifiers, and troubleshoot issues. This section explores various techniques for inspecting elements on a web page, including common practices and advanced strategies.

Overview of Inspection Techniques

To inspect web elements, you typically use browser developer tools, sometimes called "DevTools." These tools provide a comprehensive interface for exploring the Document Object Model (DOM), analyzing CSS styles, debugging JavaScript, and examining network activity. Here's a breakdown of key techniques for inspecting elements:

Using Right-Click and Inspect

The most straightforward method to inspect an element is to right-click on it in the browser and select "Inspect" or "Inspect Element." This action opens the developer tools and highlights the corresponding element in the DOM, allowing you to view its attributes, structure, and applied styles.

Navigating the DOM

Once in the developer tools, you can navigate the DOM to explore the page's structure. Expand or collapse nodes to examine parent-child relationships and understand the hierarchy of elements.

Hovering Over Elements

In the "Elements" or "Inspector" panel, hovering over a DOM node will typically highlight the corresponding element on the web page. This visual feedback helps you identify which elements are related and where they are located on the page.

Searching for Elements

Developer tools often include search functionality that allows you to find elements by tag name, attribute, class, or inner text. This technique is particularly useful when you know certain details about the element but can't locate it visually.

Advanced Inspection Techniques

While the basic techniques cover most inspection scenarios, advanced methods are sometimes necessary for complex or dynamic web pages. Let's explore these advanced techniques in more detail:

Handling Hidden Elements

Hidden elements are common in modern web design, often due to CSS properties or JavaScript logic. To inspect hidden elements, consider the following approaches:

- **Toggle Visibility**: Modify the CSS properties in the developer tools to change the `display` or `visibility` property and make hidden elements visible.
- **Inspect Computed Styles**: Use the "Computed" tab in the developer tools to understand the applied CSS rules and identify why an element is hidden.
- **Check JavaScript**: Examine the JavaScript logic in the "Sources" or "Console" panel to see if scripts are manipulating element visibility.

Inspecting Dynamic Content

Dynamic content, such as content loaded via AJAX or elements that change based on user interactions, can be challenging to inspect. These techniques help with dynamic content:

- **Monitor Network Activity**: Use the "Network" panel to track AJAX requests and understand when content is loaded. This can help you identify the point at which certain elements become available.
- **Reload and Observe**: Refresh the page and watch for changes in the DOM as content loads. This approach can help identify elements that are added or removed dynamically.
- **Use JavaScript Breakpoints**: Set breakpoints in JavaScript code to pause execution and inspect the DOM at various stages, providing insights into dynamic changes.

Dealing with Frames and Iframes

Frames and iframes create separate document contexts on a web page, making element inspection more complex. Here's how to work with frames:

- **Switching Context**: In the developer tools, locate the frame or iframe, then right-click and select "Switch to Frame" to change the inspection context. This action allows you to explore the DOM within the frame.
- **Identify Frame Relationships**: Understand the parent-child relationships between frames and the main document to ensure you're inspecting the correct context.

Inspecting web elements is a critical skill for web automation. By mastering a combination of basic and advanced techniques, you can efficiently navigate browser developer tools, understand the web page's structure, and build robust automation scripts with Selenium WebDriver.

Extracting Information for Automation

Extracting relevant information from a web page is crucial for building effective automation scripts with Selenium WebDriver. This section focuses on various techniques to gather information from browser developer tools and convert it into useful data for automation. You'll learn how to identify unique attributes, build robust selectors, and understand the context in which elements exist to ensure your automation scripts are reliable and efficient.

Why Information Extraction Is Important

When creating automation scripts with Selenium WebDriver, you need accurate information about web elements. This information allows you to:

- **Locate Elements**: Use unique attributes to create XPath and CSS selectors.
- **Understand Element Relationships**: Determine parent-child relationships, siblings, and other structural connections.
- **Deal with Dynamic Content**: Identify how elements change in response to user interactions or asynchronous data loading.
- **Optimize Scripts**: Use information on resource usage and network activity to create efficient automation workflows.

Extracting Unique Attributes

Unique attributes are vital for creating reliable element locators. Here's how to find them:

Identifying Unique IDs

An id attribute is one of the most reliable identifiers, as it should be unique within a web page. In developer tools, inspect elements to check for unique id attributes. If an element has a unique id, you can build simple and robust XPath or CSS selectors to locate it.

Working with Class Names

While class names are not necessarily unique, they can help identify elements that share common characteristics. Look for distinctive class names that describe the element's role, such as "header," "button," or "input-field." When using class names to build selectors, consider the potential for changes or conflicts with other elements.

Exploring Other Attributes

Attributes like name, data-*, alt, and title can also be used to identify elements. The "Attributes" section in developer tools shows all attributes for a selected element. Look for unique or descriptive attributes that can be used to create XPath and CSS selectors.

Building Robust Selectors

Once you have extracted unique attributes, the next step is to build selectors for Selenium WebDriver. Here are some guidelines for building robust selectors:

XPath Selectors

XPath provides a powerful way to navigate the DOM and locate elements. To build reliable XPath selectors, consider the following:

- **Use Unique Attributes**: If an element has a unique id, create an XPath selector using the @id attribute (e.g., //element[@id='unique-id']).
- **Leverage Element Relationships**: Use parent-child, sibling, or ancestor-descendant relationships to build context-based XPath selectors.
- **Include Conditions**: Add conditions to XPath selectors to refine them based on attributes, text content, or other characteristics.

CSS Selectors

CSS selectors are another common way to locate elements. When building CSS selectors, consider these tips:

- **Use Simple Selectors**: Start with simple selectors based on `id` or class names (e.g., `#unique-id` or `.button-class`).
- **Combine Multiple Attributes**: For more complex selectors, combine multiple attributes or class names to create specificity.
- **Utilize Pseudo-Classes**: Use pseudo-classes like `nth-child`, `nth-of-type`, or `first-child` to target specific elements within a parent.

Understanding Context and Relationships

Understanding the context in which elements exist is key to building robust automation scripts. When extracting information for automation, consider the following:

Parent-Child Relationships

Examine the parent-child relationships in the DOM to understand the element's structure and position. This understanding can help you create XPath selectors based on the element's context.

Sibling Relationships

Identify sibling elements to determine if the target element has a specific position among its siblings. CSS selectors with `nth-child` or `nth-of-type` are useful for this purpose.

Handling Dynamic Content

For dynamic web pages, monitor the DOM for changes and understand how elements are added, removed, or modified. This information is crucial for creating reliable automation scripts that can adapt to changing content.

Extracting information for automation involves identifying unique attributes, building robust selectors, and understanding the context of web elements. By mastering these techniques, you can create reliable Selenium WebDriver automation scripts that are less likely to break due to changes in the web page structure.

Chapter Summary

In this chapter, we explored the tools and techniques for inspecting web elements in modern browsers, which is a crucial skill for web automation with Selenium WebDriver. Here's a summary of the key concepts and techniques discussed in the chapter.

Understanding Browser Developer Tools

Browser developer tools (DevTools) are built-in utilities that allow you to inspect, analyze, and manipulate web pages. These tools provide a detailed view of the page's Document Object Model (DOM), CSS styles, JavaScript code, and network activity. Key components of developer tools include the "Elements" or "Inspector" panel for DOM inspection, the "Console" for JavaScript debugging, and the "Network" panel for tracking HTTP requests.

Techniques for Inspecting Elements

Several methods are available for inspecting elements on a web page. The most common technique is right-clicking on an element and selecting "Inspect" or "Inspect Element." This opens the developer tools and focuses on the selected element in the DOM, allowing you to view its attributes, styles, and parent-child relationships.

Other useful techniques include hovering over elements in the DOM to highlight them on the page, using search functions to locate elements by text or attribute, and exploring the DOM structure to understand the page's hierarchy.

Advanced Techniques for Complex Scenarios

For more complex web pages, advanced techniques may be required. These include:

- **Handling Hidden Elements**: To inspect elements hidden by CSS or JavaScript, you can toggle their visibility by modifying CSS properties or examine the JavaScript code that controls their visibility.
- **Inspecting Dynamic Content**: Dynamic content often loads asynchronously or changes based on user interactions. Techniques such as monitoring network activity and setting JavaScript breakpoints help understand these changes.
- **Working with Frames and Iframes**: When inspecting elements within frames or iframes, it's necessary to switch context to the appropriate frame in the developer tools.

Extracting Information for Automation

Extracting information for automation involves identifying unique attributes, understanding element relationships, and building reliable selectors. This chapter discussed techniques for finding unique identifiers, such as id, name, and specific CSS classes. Additionally, we covered building XPath and CSS selectors based on these unique attributes and other element characteristics.

Conclusion

Inspecting web elements in browsers is a fundamental skill for web automation. By mastering the use of developer tools and the various techniques for inspecting elements, you can build more reliable Selenium WebDriver scripts, diagnose issues effectively, and understand the complex structure of modern web pages. This foundational knowledge paves the way for creating robust automation frameworks and integrating XPath and CSS selectors into your Selenium scripts.

Locating Elements with ID and Link Text

Outline

Introduction to ID and Link Text

When developing automated tests with Selenium WebDriver, one of the most crucial tasks is to reliably locate web elements on a page. Two fundamental and highly effective methods for this purpose are using the HTML "ID" attribute and identifying hyperlinks by their text (often called "Link Text").

In this section, we will discuss the basics of these approaches and demonstrate why they're essential for efficient Selenium test automation. You'll learn:

- What makes the ID attribute a unique and reliable locator.
- How Link Text can be used to find specific hyperlinks.
- When these locators might not be suitable and what to do about it.

First, let's examine why these two methods are among the simplest yet most effective for finding elements on a web page. We'll explore how you can implement them in your test scripts and discuss best practices for each approach.

Overall, this chapter aims to equip you with foundational knowledge for successful automation, laying the groundwork for more advanced element-locating techniques in later sections. Let's get started!

Benefits of Using ID for Element Location

The "ID" attribute in HTML is one of the most reliable and efficient methods for locating elements in Selenium WebDriver. Here's why using ID-based locators is a key practice for test automation:

1. Uniqueness The ID attribute is meant to be unique within a single HTML document. This property makes it highly effective for pinpointing a specific element without ambiguity. If an element has a unique ID, there's no confusion or risk of selecting the wrong item.

2. Speed Locating elements by ID is typically faster than other methods. Since the ID is unique, browsers and Selenium WebDriver can quickly locate the corresponding element, reducing the overhead in your automated tests.

3. Readability Using IDs to locate elements can make your test scripts more readable and understandable. When reviewing or debugging code, it's clear which elements are being referenced. This clarity also aids in maintaining and updating test scripts.

4. Stability Since IDs are meant to be stable and unique, tests that rely on ID-based locators tend to be more robust and less prone to breaking due to minor changes in the web page structure. This stability contributes to more reliable test automation.

5. Universal Support All major browsers and Selenium WebDriver versions support ID-based element location. This universal support ensures that tests using ID locators will work consistently across different environments and setups.

However, it's essential to be aware of certain caveats when using ID locators:

- **Avoiding Duplicate IDs**: Although IDs are meant to be unique, some developers might inadvertently use the same ID for multiple elements. This issue can lead to confusion and unreliable test outcomes.
- **Dynamic IDs**: Some frameworks or tools might generate dynamic IDs, which can change with each page load. In these cases, relying solely on ID locators might not be suitable.

In summary, using ID-based locators offers several significant benefits for Selenium test automation, including uniqueness, speed, readability, stability, and universal support. By leveraging these advantages, you can create robust and efficient automated tests.

Locating Elements by ID

The ID attribute in HTML provides one of the most straightforward and efficient methods for locating elements in Selenium WebDriver. Because IDs are unique within an HTML document, you can pinpoint specific elements quickly and reliably. Let's explore how to use ID-based locators in Selenium WebDriver and discuss their benefits and common scenarios.

Finding Elements with `By.id()`

To locate an element by its ID, Selenium WebDriver offers the `By.id()` method. This method retrieves the element with the specified ID, allowing you to interact with it in various ways. Here's an example in Java for locating a button with the ID "submitButton":

```
WebElement submitButton = driver.findElement(By.id("submitButton"));
```

Once you've located the element, you can perform various actions, like clicking, sending text input, or extracting information.

Advantages of ID-based Locators

Using IDs to locate elements provides several benefits:

- **Uniqueness**: IDs are typically unique within an HTML document, ensuring that you're interacting with the intended element.
- **Speed**: Because IDs are unique, locating elements by ID is generally faster than other methods, as there's less ambiguity.
- **Readability**: Scripts that use ID-based locators are easier to understand and maintain, since it's clear which elements are being referenced.

Common Use Cases for ID Locators

IDs are useful in a wide range of scenarios. Here are some common examples:

- **Buttons and Forms**: IDs are often used for buttons, input fields, and form elements, providing a reliable way to locate these interactive components.
- **Navigation and Layout**: Elements that play a key role in the page's structure, such as navigation bars or specific sections, often have unique IDs.
- **User Interaction**: Elements that trigger user actions, like links, toggles, or menu items, frequently use IDs for identification.

Handling Edge Cases with IDs

While using IDs is generally straightforward, there are a few edge cases to be aware of:

- **Duplicate IDs**: In rare cases, developers may accidentally use the same ID for multiple elements. This can lead to unexpected results and requires careful handling, usually by using additional locators to distinguish between elements.
- **Dynamic IDs**: Some web frameworks generate dynamic IDs that change with each session or page load. In these cases, relying solely on ID might not be sufficient, and you might need additional strategies to locate elements.

Best Practices for ID-based Locators

To ensure success when using ID locators, consider the following best practices:

- **Work with Developers**: If possible, work with developers to ensure that IDs are unique and consistent across the application.
- **Fallback Locators**: In cases where IDs are not reliable, consider using additional locators (like class names or XPath) to support your test scripts.
- **Testing for Uniqueness**: If you encounter issues with ID-based locators, check for duplicate IDs on the page and address them with developers if needed.

Locating elements by ID is a core technique for Selenium WebDriver automation, providing unique and efficient element identification. By understanding how to use this method and applying best practices, you can create robust and reliable automated tests.

Locating Elements by Link Text

Link Text is a method in Selenium WebDriver used to locate hyperlinks on a web page. This approach is straightforward and effective for identifying elements with specific text content, particularly for navigation or interactivity. In this section, you'll learn how to use Link Text in Selenium WebDriver and when to choose this method for locating elements.

Finding Elements with `By.linkText()`

To locate elements by Link Text, Selenium WebDriver provides the `By.linkText()` method. This approach retrieves hyperlinks that exactly match the specified text. Here's an example in Java for finding a hyperlink with the text "Contact Us":

```java
WebElement contactLink = driver.findElement(By.linkText("Contact Us"));
```

Once you've located the link, you can perform actions like clicking or retrieving its attributes (such as the URL it's pointing to).

Finding Elements with `By.partialLinkText()`

In addition to exact matches, Selenium WebDriver also offers a method to find links with partial text matches. This is useful when the full text is dynamic or contains varying characters. Here's an example for finding a link with partial text:

```java
WebElement aboutLink = driver.findElement(By.partialLinkText("About"));
```

This command finds any link containing the specified partial text, allowing for more flexible element location.

Use Cases for Link Text Locators

Link Text locators are best used in scenarios where you need to find specific hyperlinks or buttons with text labels. Common use cases include:

- **Navigation Links**: Locating elements like "Home," "Contact Us," "About Us," etc.
- **Button-like Links**: Some buttons on a web page are implemented as hyperlinks with text, making Link Text a convenient locator.
- **Dynamic Links**: Using partial Link Text helps locate elements with varying content.

Handling Edge Cases with Link Text

While Link Text locators are useful, there are a few considerations to keep in mind:

- **Exact Matches**: The By.linkText() method requires an exact match with the link text. If there's extra whitespace or a different case, it might not work as expected.
- **Special Characters**: If the link text contains special characters or symbols, ensure you're matching them correctly.
- **Multiple Matches**: If more than one link has the same text, the locator may return the first match, which might not be the intended one.

Best Practices for Link Text Locators

To make the best use of Link Text locators, consider these best practices:

- **Consistent Text**: Work with developers to ensure that link text is consistent and unlikely to change frequently.
- **Fallback Locators**: If there's uncertainty with Link Text, consider using other locators like XPath or CSS Selectors as a fallback.
- **Exact or Partial**: Use By.linkText() for exact matches and By.partialLinkText() for flexibility with partial matches.

Locating elements by Link Text is a straightforward and effective method, particularly for finding hyperlinks and text-based buttons. By understanding the scenarios where this approach is most useful and applying best practices, you can use Link Text locators effectively in your Selenium WebDriver test scripts.

Handling Variations and Edge Cases

While ID and Link Text are reliable methods for locating web elements, there are situations where these approaches can lead to challenges due to variations and edge cases. In this section, you'll learn how to handle these situations and ensure your Selenium WebDriver scripts remain robust and flexible.

Variations with ID Locators

ID locators are generally reliable, but you might encounter situations where they become less effective. Here are some common variations and strategies to address them:

1. Duplicate IDs Although IDs should be unique within a single HTML document, there may be cases where the same ID is mistakenly used for multiple elements. This can create ambiguity and lead to unreliable test results. To handle this issue:

- **Identify the Source of the Problem**: Check the HTML structure for duplicate IDs. If possible, communicate with the development team to ensure IDs are unique.
- **Use Alternative Locators**: If duplicate IDs can't be resolved, consider using additional locators such as class names, XPath, or CSS Selectors to distinguish between elements.

2. Dynamic IDs Some frameworks or applications generate IDs dynamically, which means the ID changes with each session or page load. This variation can make ID-based locators unreliable. To address this:

- **Use Stable Attributes**: If IDs are dynamic, consider using other stable attributes, such as class names or data attributes, to locate elements.
- **Employ Relative Locators**: Use relative locators (e.g., locating elements based on their position relative to another element) when dynamic IDs are an issue.

Variations with Link Text Locators

Link Text locators can also face challenges due to variations in text content. Here are some common scenarios and approaches to handle them:

1. Inconsistent Link Text If link text contains typos, changes frequently, or varies due to localization or other factors, it can make locating elements challenging. To manage this:

- **Use By.partialLinkText()**: This method allows for partial matching, providing flexibility when full text varies.
- **Fallback Locators**: Use XPath or CSS Selectors as a backup strategy if Link Text is unreliable.

2. Special Characters and Spaces Links containing special characters, extra spaces, or unconventional formatting can lead to mismatches. To handle this:

- **Trim Spaces**: Ensure the link text is trimmed to avoid issues with leading or trailing spaces.
- **Escaping Special Characters**: Properly escape special characters if they are part of the link text.

3. Multiple Links with the Same Text If multiple links share the same text, the locator might retrieve the wrong element. Here's what you can do:

- **Use Context**: If possible, use additional locators or context-based approaches (such as parent elements) to distinguish between links with similar text.
- **Combine Locators**: Combine Link Text with other locators like XPath or CSS Selectors for greater specificity.

Handling variations and edge cases with ID and Link Text locators is crucial for maintaining robust Selenium WebDriver test scripts. By understanding these challenges and applying best practices, you can ensure your scripts remain reliable, even in complex scenarios. Use fallback locators, relative locators, and combined approaches to adapt to variations and maintain effective element location.

Best Practices for ID and Link Text

Locating web elements using ID and Link Text is a fundamental part of Selenium WebDriver automation. While these methods are generally straightforward, following best practices ensures robust and reliable scripts. In this section, let's discuss best practices for using ID and Link Text to locate elements in your Selenium tests.

Best Practices for ID Locators

1. Ensure Uniqueness of IDs IDs should be unique within an HTML document. This uniqueness is crucial for avoiding confusion and ensuring reliable test outcomes. Work with your development team to ensure IDs are unique and consistently applied.

2. Handle Duplicate IDs Despite best intentions, duplicate IDs can sometimes occur. If your script encounters duplicate IDs, consider:

- **Using Additional Locators**: Combine the ID locator with other attributes like class names or element hierarchy to isolate the correct element.
- **Raising Awareness**: Communicate with developers about the impact of duplicate IDs on test automation, advocating for unique IDs.

3. Manage Dynamic IDs Dynamic IDs can complicate test automation, as they change with each session or page load. To address this challenge:

- **Use Alternative Locators**: If IDs are dynamic, rely on stable attributes like class names, data attributes, or text-based locators.
- **Relative Positioning**: Use relative locators or XPath expressions that navigate based on element hierarchy, rather than absolute IDs.

4. Combine ID with Other Locators To enhance reliability, consider combining ID with other locators when necessary. This approach provides a fallback mechanism and helps in cases where ID-based locators might fail.

Best Practices for Link Text Locators

1. Use Exact Matches for Consistency When using By.linkText(), ensure the text matches exactly, including spaces and special characters. This consistency minimizes the risk of unexpected results.

2. Consider Partial Link Text If link text might vary slightly, consider using By.partialLinkText() to allow for partial matches. This flexibility is useful when dealing with dynamic or localized content.

3. Address Multiple Matches If more than one element has the same link text, you might get unexpected results. To address this:

- **Use Context**: Employ locators that consider the surrounding context, like parent elements or specific sections of the page.
- **Combine Locators**: Combine Link Text with other locators like XPath or CSS Selectors to narrow down the search.

4. Handle Special Characters and Spaces Ensure that Link Text is trimmed and special characters are properly escaped to avoid misinterpretation. This step is crucial when dealing with complex text content.

General Best Practices for ID and Link Text

1. Test with Different Scenarios To ensure robustness, test your scripts with various scenarios, including edge cases where IDs might not be unique or Link Text might vary.

2. Use Fallback Strategies Have backup plans in place, such as alternative locators or relative locators, in case ID or Link Text-based locators fail.

3. Document Locator Strategies Document your locator strategies for each script or test case. This documentation helps in debugging and understanding the rationale behind certain locator choices.

Following these best practices for ID and Link Text locators will help you create reliable and robust Selenium WebDriver scripts. By ensuring ID uniqueness, handling dynamic elements, and considering variations in Link Text, you can build test scripts that withstand changes and remain effective over time.

Chapter Summary

In this chapter, we explored the key methods for locating web elements in Selenium WebDriver using ID and Link Text. These fundamental approaches are simple yet effective, offering unique benefits for Selenium automation.

Main Points Covered

1. **Introduction to ID and Link Text**:
   - We discussed why ID and Link Text are crucial for element location in Selenium, highlighting their simplicity and effectiveness.
2. **Benefits of Using ID for Element Location**:
   - ID is unique within an HTML document, making it fast, reliable, and easy to use. Additionally, it enhances readability and stability in test scripts.
3. **Locating Elements by ID**:
   - We demonstrated how to use the `By.id()` method to locate elements by their ID, with code examples and practical use cases.
   - We also discussed how to handle edge cases, such as duplicate or dynamic IDs.
4. **Locating Elements by Link Text**:
   - This section outlined the use of `By.linkText()` and `By.partialLinkText()` to locate hyperlinks or buttons with text labels.
   - We covered variations and common use cases, as well as edge cases like inconsistent or dynamic link text.
5. **Handling Variations and Edge Cases**:
   - We addressed common challenges with ID and Link Text, providing solutions for duplicate IDs, dynamic IDs, inconsistent link text, and special characters.
   - Strategies such as using alternative locators, combining locators, and using relative positioning were discussed.
6. **Best Practices for ID and Link Text**:
   - This section offered best practices for ensuring robust and reliable element location. We highlighted the importance of ensuring unique IDs, using fallback strategies, and combining locators when needed.
   - Best practices for Link Text included using exact matches, addressing multiple matches, and handling special characters.

Key Takeaways

- ID-based locators are unique, fast, and efficient, but can be impacted by duplicate or dynamic IDs.
- Link Text locators are useful for hyperlinks, with flexibility provided by `By.partialLinkText()`, but can face challenges with multiple matches and special characters.
- To handle variations and edge cases, it's important to consider fallback locators, relative positioning, and effective communication with developers.
- Following best practices helps ensure reliable and robust Selenium test scripts, even in changing environments.

In summary, this chapter covered the basics of locating elements with ID and Link Text, providing examples and best practices.

Using Name and Class to Find Elements

Outline

1. What are "name" and "class" attributes in HTML?
2. Finding elements using the "name" attribute
3. Locating elements by class
4. Handling multiple elements with the same class
5. Using compound class names
6. Practical examples with Selenium WebDriver
7. Chapter Summary

What are "name" and "class" attributes in HTML?

In HTML, attributes provide additional information about elements, serving various purposes such as identification, styling, or behavior customization. Two common attributes often used in web development are "name" and "class."

"Name" Attribute

- **Purpose**: The "name" attribute is primarily used to identify form elements in HTML, such as `<input>`, `<textarea>`, `<select>`, `<button>`, etc. It's especially useful in backend processing when forms are submitted, as it specifies the key under which the data will be sent.
- **Usage**: You'll typically find the "name" attribute in forms, allowing web servers to map submitted data back to specific fields. For example, in a login form, you might have:

```
<input type="text" name="username" />
<input type="password" name="password" />
```

When the form is submitted, the server can easily identify which data corresponds to each field.

"Class" Attribute

- **Purpose**: The "class" attribute is used to apply CSS styling and group elements for layout or behavior purposes. It's commonly used for identifying elements by category or functionality, allowing for consistent styling and easier DOM selection.
- **Usage**: Elements can have one or multiple class names, which can be used to apply specific styles or behaviors. For example:

```
<div class="container main-content"></div>
<button class="btn btn-primary"></button>
```

In this example, the `<div>` has two class names, while the `<button>` has two different ones, potentially corresponding to specific styles or scripts.

Differences Between "Name" and "Class"

- **Scope**: The "name" attribute is mainly used in form-related contexts to facilitate data identification during form submissions. The "class" attribute has a broader scope, often used for styling and element categorization.
- **Multiplicity**: An element can only have one "name" attribute but can have multiple "class" attributes.

- **Usage in Automation**: In web automation frameworks like Selenium, both attributes can be used to locate elements. The "name" attribute is typically used for locating form fields, while the "class" attribute is commonly used to select elements by category or style.

In summary, the "name" attribute is key for identifying form elements, aiding in backend data processing, while the "class" attribute is crucial for styling and element categorization, playing a vital role in frontend development and web automation.

Finding elements using the "name" attribute

The "name" attribute in HTML is commonly used to identify form-related elements like `<input>`, `<textarea>`, `<select>`, etc. It's especially useful in backend processing and form submissions. When automating interactions with web pages, Selenium WebDriver can use the "name" attribute to locate elements for further actions like clicking, typing, or retrieving text.

How to Find Elements Using the "name" Attribute

To locate elements using the "name" attribute with Selenium, you can use the `By.name()` method. This method retrieves the first element it finds with a matching "name" attribute. Here's a step-by-step guide to finding elements using the "name" attribute:

Step 1: Identify the Element with the "name" Attribute

To use the "name" attribute to locate elements, you must first identify which elements have a "name" attribute in your HTML structure. This is typically found in form-related elements. Here's an example of a login form with "name" attributes:

```html
<form>
  <input type="text" name="username" />
  <input type="password" name="password" />
  <button type="submit" name="login">Login</button>
</form>
```

Step 2: Use Selenium to Find the Element

In Selenium WebDriver, use the `findElement(By.name("name_value"))` method to locate an element with a specific "name" attribute. Here's how to find the "username" input field in the example above:

```java
WebElement usernameField = driver.findElement(By.name("username"));
```

Similarly, to find the "password" field, you would use:

```java
WebElement passwordField = driver.findElement(By.name("password"));
```

Step 3: Interact with the Located Element

Once you've located the desired element, you can interact with it using Selenium WebDriver commands. For instance, you can enter text, click buttons, or retrieve text. To enter text into the "username" field, you can use the sendKeys method:

```java
usernameField.sendKeys("myUsername");
```

Similarly, you can click the "Login" button using its "name" attribute:

```java
WebElement loginButton = driver.findElement(By.name("login"));
```

```
loginButton.click();
```

Handling Edge Cases

- **Multiple Elements with the Same "name" Attribute**: If there are multiple elements with the same "name" attribute, Selenium's `findElement` method will return the first matching element. To handle multiple elements, consider using `findElements` to get a list of all elements with a specific "name" attribute:

```
List<WebElement> fields = driver.findElements(By.name("username"));
```

- **Error Handling**: If no element is found with the specified "name" attribute, Selenium throws a `NoSuchElementException`. Ensure you handle this exception to avoid test failures or crashes:

```
try {
  WebElement element = driver.findElement(By.name("username"));
} catch (NoSuchElementException e) {
  System.out.println("Element not found!");
}
```

By following these steps, you can effectively find and interact with elements using the "name" attribute in Selenium WebDriver, enabling smooth automation of web-based tasks and tests.

Locating elements by class

Locating elements by the "class" attribute in HTML is a common approach in web automation, as the "class" attribute is widely used to group and style elements on a webpage. Selenium WebDriver provides methods to find elements based on their class names, allowing you to interact with them programmatically.

How to Find Elements by Class

To locate elements using the "class" attribute in Selenium, you can use the `By.className()` method. This method retrieves the first element with a matching class name. Here's a guide on how to locate elements by class and some best practices to consider.

Step 1: Identify the Element with the "class" Attribute

Examine the HTML structure to identify which elements have the desired class name. The "class" attribute is commonly used for styling, categorization, and scripting purposes. Here's an example with several elements having class attributes:

```
<div class="container">
  <button class="btn btn-primary">Click Me</button>
  <button class="btn btn-secondary">Don't Click Me</button>
  <input class="form-control" type="text" />
</div>
```

Step 2: Use Selenium to Find the Element

To find an element by its class name, use the `findElement(By.className("class_name"))` method. If there are multiple classes, ensure you use the correct class name. Here's how to locate the first button with the "btn" class:

```
WebElement firstButton = driver.findElement(By.className("btn"));
```

Step 3: Interact with the Located Element

Once you've found the element, you can interact with it using Selenium WebDriver. For example, to click the first button with the "btn" class, you can use the click() method:

```
firstButton.click();
```

Similarly, you can find the input field with the "form-control" class and send keys to it:

```
WebElement inputField = driver.findElement(By.className("form-control"));
inputField.sendKeys("Hello World");
```

Handling Edge Cases and Troubleshooting

- **Multiple Class Names**: If an element has multiple class names, By.className() can only find it using one of those class names. Ensure you use the correct class name.
- **Errors and Exception Handling**: If no element is found with the specified class name, Selenium throws a NoSuchElementException. It's good practice to handle this exception to prevent test failures or crashes:

```
try {
  WebElement element =
driver.findElement(By.className("nonexistent-class"));
} catch (NoSuchElementException e) {
  System.out.println("Element not found!");
}
```

Locating elements by the "class" attribute in Selenium is a common and effective method, especially when you know the expected structure and organization of the webpage. By following these steps, you can reliably find elements by class and interact with them as needed for automation tasks and web testing.

Handling multiple elements with the same class

Handling multiple elements with the same class is a common scenario in web automation and testing. The "class" attribute in HTML is frequently used for styling, grouping, and categorization, leading to multiple elements sharing the same class name. In Selenium, you can locate and interact with multiple elements having the same class using the findElements(By.className("...")) method.

Here's a guide on handling multiple elements with the same class in Selenium WebDriver.

Finding Multiple Elements with the Same Class

The findElements(By.className("class_name")) method returns a list of all elements matching the specified class name. You can then interact with individual elements from the list or loop through all of them to perform a common action.

Example: Finding All Buttons with the Same Class

Consider a scenario where you have multiple buttons on a webpage with the same class name:

```
<div class="button-container">
  <button class="btn">First Button</button>
  <button class="btn">Second Button</button>
  <button class="btn">Third Button</button>
</div>
```

To find all buttons with the class "btn," you can use the `findElements` method:

```
List<WebElement> buttons = driver.findElements(By.className("btn"));
```

Interacting with Multiple Elements

After obtaining the list of elements, you can interact with them individually or loop through the list to apply actions to all of them.

Example: Clicking the First Button

To interact with the first button in the list, you can use indexing:

```
buttons.get(0).click();  // Clicks the first button
```

Example: Clicking All Buttons

If you want to perform an action on all elements with the same class, you can use a loop to iterate through the list:

```
for (WebElement button : buttons) {
    button.click();  // Click each button
}
```

Handling Variations in Element Structure

Sometimes, elements with the same class may have different structures or attributes. You might need additional checks to ensure you're interacting with the correct element.

Example: Finding a Specific Button Based on Text

To find a button with a specific text value, you can loop through the list and check the text of each element:

```
for (WebElement button : buttons) {
    if (button.getText().equals("Second Button")) {
        button.click();  // Click the button with the specified text
        break;  // Exit loop after finding the desired button
    }
}
```

Dealing with Uncertain Element Counts

If the number of elements with a given class is unpredictable, ensure you handle cases where no elements or too many elements are found.

Handling No Elements Found

If `findElements` returns an empty list, handle it gracefully to avoid errors:

```
if (buttons.isEmpty()) {
    System.out.println("No buttons with class 'btn' found.");
} else {
    // Continue with interactions
}
```

Handling More Elements Than Expected

If you expect a specific number of elements but find more, consider refining your search criteria or adding additional checks to ensure you're interacting with the correct elements.

Handling multiple elements with the same class in Selenium requires flexibility and proper error handling. By using `findElements`, you can interact with a group of elements sharing the same class name, whether it's clicking specific elements, processing lists, or performing additional checks to ensure correct interactions.

Using compound class names

In HTML, elements can have multiple class names to support complex styling and functionality. These are called compound class names, and they're separated by spaces within the `class` attribute. This feature is helpful for applying multiple styles and scripts to elements. However, it can complicate locating elements in web automation frameworks like Selenium WebDriver.

Here's an explanation of compound class names and a guide on how to work with them in Selenium.

What are Compound Class Names?

Compound class names occur when an element has more than one class name. This is common in modern web development, where elements often need different styling or functionality based on multiple categories.

For example, consider the following HTML snippet:

```
<div class="container main-content"></div>
<button class="btn btn-primary"></button>
<button class="btn btn-secondary"></button>
```

The `<div>` element has two class names, "container" and "main-content," while the buttons have multiple class names indicating button styles.

Locating Elements with Compound Class Names in Selenium

Selenium WebDriver allows you to locate elements based on their class names using the `By.className()` method. However, this method finds elements based on a single class name, not a combination of class names. This can lead to unintended results when working with compound class names.

Finding Elements with a Single Class Name

To locate elements with a single class name, you can use `findElement(By.className("..."))` or `findElements(By.className("..."))`. This approach works well when you need to find elements with a specific class:

```
WebElement primaryButton = driver.findElement(By.className("btn-primary"));
```

In this example, you locate the first button with the "btn-primary" class.

Finding Elements with Multiple Class Names

If you need to find elements with a specific combination of class names, using `By.className()` won't work directly, as it treats the class name as a single token. Instead, you can use `By.cssSelector()` to create more complex queries that consider multiple class names.

Here's an example of finding elements with both "btn" and "btn-primary" class names:

```
WebElement primaryButton =
driver.findElement(By.cssSelector(".btn.btn-primary"));
```

This approach ensures that you're selecting elements that contain all specified class names, reducing the risk of misidentifying elements.

Handling Errors and Edge Cases

- **Handling No Elements Found**: If findElement doesn't find an element with the specified class name, it throws a NoSuchElementException. It's good practice to handle this exception gracefully:

```
try {
  WebElement element =
driver.findElement(By.cssSelector(".btn.btn-primary"));
} catch (NoSuchElementException e) {
  System.out.println("Element with specified class names not found.");
}
```

- **Avoiding Ambiguity**: Ensure that your class name selections are specific enough to avoid unintended results. When using compound class names, make sure the CSS selector accurately represents the intended combination.

Using compound class names in Selenium WebDriver requires a clear understanding of HTML structure and the ability to create precise CSS selectors. The By.cssSelector() method allows you to select elements with multiple class names, giving you the flexibility to interact with more complex elements. By handling exceptions and ensuring accurate queries, you can effectively work with compound class names in Selenium automation tasks.

Practical Examples with Selenium WebDriver

Using Selenium WebDriver to locate web elements is crucial for automating web-based tasks like form submissions, data scraping, or automated testing. In this section, we will explore practical examples of using "name" and "class" selectors in Selenium to interact with different types of web elements. This guide will cover various examples demonstrating common interactions with elements identified by "name" and "class."

Setup and Initialization

Before delving into examples, ensure Selenium WebDriver is properly set up and that you've configured the necessary browser drivers (like ChromeDriver, GeckoDriver for Firefox, etc.).

```
import org.openqa.selenium.WebDriver;
import org.openqa.selenium.chrome.ChromeDriver;

public class SeleniumSetup {
    public static void main(String[] args) {
        System.setProperty("webdriver.chrome.driver",
"/path/to/chromedriver");

        WebDriver driver = new ChromeDriver();

        // Navigate to a webpage
        driver.get("https://www.example.com");
```

```
        // Don't forget to close the WebDriver at the end of your script
        driver.quit();
    }
}
```

Practical Example 1: Locating and Interacting with Elements by "Name"

The "name" attribute is commonly used in form elements like `<input>`, `<textarea>`, `<button>`, and `<select>`. Here's an example showing how to locate an element by its "name" attribute and interact with it.

Example: Filling Out a Login Form

```java
import org.openqa.selenium.By;
import org.openqa.selenium.WebDriver;
import org.openqa.selenium.WebElement;

public class FillLoginForm {
    public static void main(String[] args) {
        WebDriver driver = new ChromeDriver();

        // Navigate to a login page
        driver.get("https://www.example.com/login");

        // Find the username input field by its "name" attribute and enter a
value
        WebElement usernameField = driver.findElement(By.name("username"));
        usernameField.sendKeys("myUserName");

        // Find the password input field by its "name" attribute and enter a
value
        WebElement passwordField = driver.findElement(By.name("password"));
        passwordField.sendKeys("myPassword");

        // Find and click the login button by its "name" attribute
        WebElement loginButton = driver.findElement(By.name("login"));
        loginButton.click();

        driver.quit();
    }
}
```

Practical Example 2: Locating and Interacting with Elements by "Class"

The "class" attribute is used for styling and grouping similar elements. Here's an example of locating elements by class and interacting with them.

Example: Clicking Buttons with Specific Class Names

```java
import org.openqa.selenium.By;
import org.openqa.selenium.WebDriver;
import org.openqa.selenium.WebElement;
import org.openqa.selenium.chrome.ChromeDriver;
```

```
public class ClickButtons {
    public static void main(String's args) {
        WebDriver driver = new ChromeDriver();

        // Navigate to a page with buttons
        driver.get("https://www.example.com/buttons");

        // Find and click a button with a specific class name
        WebElement firstButton =
driver.findElement(By.className("btn-primary"));
        firstButton.click();

        // Find all buttons with a common class and click each
        List<WebElement> allButtons =
driver.findElements(By.className("btn"));
        for (WebElement button : allButtons) {
            button.click();  // Clicks each button with the "btn" class
        }

        driver.quit();
    }
}
```

Handling Edge Cases and Troubleshooting

While working with Selenium, you might encounter situations where elements are missing, or you have multiple elements with the same "name" or "class." Here are some common issues and solutions:

- **NoSuchElementException**: If an element with a specified "name" or "class" isn't found, Selenium throws a NoSuchElementException. Handle this exception to avoid test failures or crashes:

```
try {
  WebElement element = driver.findElement(By.name("nonexistent-name"));
} catch (NoSuchElementException e) {
  System.out.println("Element not found!");
}
```

- **Multiple Elements with the Same Class**: If there are multiple elements with the same class, use findElements(By.className("...")) to get a list of all matching elements, then interact with the desired one based on its position or other characteristics:

```
List<WebElement> elements =
driver.findElements(By.className("common-class"));
if (!elements.isEmpty()) {
    elements.get(0).click();  // Click the first element with the class
}
```

These practical examples should give you a solid foundation for using Selenium WebDriver with "name" and "class" selectors to automate web interactions and tests.

Chapter Summary

In this chapter, we explored how to locate web elements using the "name" and "class" attributes in HTML. These are fundamental techniques in web automation and Selenium WebDriver, offering a reliable way to interact with web pages for tasks like form submissions, button clicks, and data extraction. Here's a summary of the key points and best practices covered in this chapter.

The "Name" Attribute

- **Purpose**: The "name" attribute is commonly used to identify form elements such as input fields, buttons, and text areas. It's crucial in backend processing for form submissions.
- **Locating Elements by Name**: To find elements with a specific "name" attribute, Selenium WebDriver provides the By.name() method. This approach is useful for interacting with form fields or buttons during automation.
- **Practical Applications**: You learned how to use the "name" attribute to find elements like username and password fields in a login form, allowing you to simulate user input and form submission.
- **Error Handling**: If an element with the specified "name" attribute is not found, Selenium throws a NoSuchElementException. Implementing proper error handling ensures robustness in your automation scripts.

The "Class" Attribute

- **Purpose**: The "class" attribute is used for styling and grouping similar elements. It's one of the most common attributes in HTML for identifying and categorizing elements.
- **Locating Elements by Class**: Selenium WebDriver's By.className() method allows you to find elements based on their class name. This technique is handy for finding groups of similar elements, like buttons or div containers.
- **Dealing with Compound Class Names**: If an element has multiple class names, using By.cssSelector() is often more effective than By.className(), allowing you to specify combinations of class names.
- **Practical Applications**: Examples demonstrated how to find elements by class, such as clicking buttons with a specific class name or interacting with input fields with a common class. You also learned how to handle multiple elements with the same class and how to interact with each accordingly.
- **Handling Edge Cases**: Proper error handling is crucial when using class-based selectors, as the presence of multiple elements with the same class or compound class names can lead to ambiguity.

Conclusion and Best Practices

- **Element Discovery Fundamentals**: This chapter highlighted the importance of understanding HTML structure and how "name" and "class" attributes can be leveraged to find elements.
- **Combining Locating Strategies**: In real-world scenarios, combining "name" and "class" selectors with other locating strategies, such as XPath and CSS Selectors, can improve reliability and flexibility.
- **Error Handling and Troubleshooting**: Ensure you implement robust error handling to manage exceptions like NoSuchElementException or when there are multiple elements with the same class.

By the end of this chapter, you should have a solid understanding of how to find and interact with web elements using "name" and "class" attributes. These techniques are foundational for creating effective Selenium WebDriver automation scripts and will help you confidently navigate various web automation scenarios.

Section 2:
Introduction to XPath

Exploring SelectorsHub for XPath

Outline

1. What is SelectorsHub?
2. Installing and Setting Up SelectorsHub
3. Key Features of SelectorsHub
4. Navigating the SelectorsHub Interface
5. Using SelectorsHub for XPath Development
6. Common Use Cases for SelectorsHub
7. Tips for Efficient XPath Creation with SelectorsHub
8. Chapter Summary

What is SelectorsHub?

SelectorsHub is a browser extension designed to assist in creating, validating, and testing XPath and CSS selectors for web development and automation tasks. It offers a user-friendly interface for building and refining selectors, helping users identify and interact with web elements more effectively. Here's a breakdown of what SelectorsHub provides:

- **XPath and CSS Selector Generation**: Automatically generates XPath and CSS selectors for selected web elements, saving time and effort in crafting these selectors manually.
- **Customization and Refinement**: Users can customize generated selectors or create their own from scratch, using SelectorsHub's tools to fine-tune their expressions.
- **Validation and Testing**: SelectorsHub allows users to test XPath and CSS selectors in real-time, highlighting matching elements on a web page to ensure accuracy.
- **Debugging Support**: The extension can help identify common issues with selectors, such as locating dynamic elements or handling complex HTML structures.
- **Cross-Browser Compatibility**: Available for multiple browsers like Chrome, Firefox, Edge, and others, making it versatile for a range of development environments.

SelectorsHub is especially useful for developers and testers working with automation tools like Selenium WebDriver, enabling them to create robust and reliable selectors to interact with web elements for automated testing and other tasks. It serves as an essential resource for those looking to streamline and improve their web element location workflows.

Installing and Setting Up SelectorsHub

To install and set up SelectorsHub, you need to follow a few simple steps. Here is a detailed guide to get you started with this helpful tool.

Step 1: Choose Your Browser

SelectorsHub is available as a browser extension for multiple browsers, including Chrome, Firefox, Edge, and others. Select the browser you commonly use for development or testing.

Step 2: Find SelectorsHub in Your Browser's Extension Store

1. **For Chrome**: Open the Chrome Web Store, and search for "SelectorsHub." You can find it at [Chrome Web Store] (https://chrome.google.com/webstore/).
2. **For Firefox**: Go to the Firefox Add-ons site, and search for "SelectorsHub." It can be found at [Firefox Add-ons] (https://addons.mozilla.org/).
3. **For Edge**: Visit the Microsoft Edge Add-ons site, and search for "SelectorsHub." The link to the add-on store is [Edge Add-ons] (https://microsoftedge.microsoft.com/addons/).

Step 3: Install SelectorsHub

1. **In Chrome**: Click the "Add to Chrome" button, then confirm by clicking "Add Extension." After installation, you will see the SelectorsHub icon in your extension toolbar.
2. **In Firefox**: Click "Add to Firefox," then confirm with "Add." The SelectorsHub icon will appear in the extension area after installation.
3. **In Edge**: Click "Get," then "Add Extension." The SelectorsHub icon will appear in your browser's toolbar after installation.

Step 4: Launch SelectorsHub

Click the SelectorsHub icon in your browser's extension toolbar to launch it. You will typically find it near the address bar.

Step 5: Access a Web Page to Use SelectorsHub

Open a web page where you'd like to use SelectorsHub for XPath or CSS selector testing. Click on the SelectorsHub icon to open its interface within your browser's developer tools panel.

Step 6: Customize the SelectorsHub Interface

SelectorsHub allows you to customize its settings to suit your workflow. You can:

- **Choose Default Selector**: Select whether you want XPath or CSS to be the default selector.
- **Toggle Features**: Adjust visibility and interaction options within the SelectorsHub interface.
- **Choose Color Themes**: Change the color theme for a more comfortable viewing experience.

Step 7: Start Using SelectorsHub

Once SelectorsHub is set up, you can start using it to generate, test, and refine XPath and CSS selectors. To use it:

1. **Select a Web Element**: Click on the desired element on the web page to see the automatically generated XPath and CSS selectors.
2. **Modify and Validate Selectors**: You can edit the generated selectors or create your own. SelectorsHub highlights matching elements to help validate your changes.

That's it! You're now ready to use SelectorsHub to improve your XPath and CSS selector creation process. Use this tool to streamline your web element location tasks and increase your efficiency.

Key Features of SelectorsHub

SelectorsHub is a versatile tool designed to streamline the creation, validation, and testing of XPath and CSS selectors for various purposes, such as web development and automated testing. Here's a comprehensive overview of the key features that make SelectorsHub valuable:

1. Automated XPath and CSS Selector Generation

SelectorsHub can automatically generate XPath and CSS selectors for any web element you select, saving you time and reducing the likelihood of human error. This feature is useful for quickly obtaining a basic selector for an element.

2. Customizable Selector Options

SelectorsHub allows users to customize the generated selectors to suit their specific needs. You can choose different attributes, use index-based selectors, and even create relative XPath paths. This flexibility enables you to tailor selectors to fit complex or dynamic web elements.

3. Real-Time Selector Validation

With SelectorsHub, you can test and validate XPath and CSS selectors in real-time. The tool highlights matching elements on the web page, allowing you to verify that your selector is accurate and effective. This immediate feedback helps you refine your selectors efficiently.

4. XPath and CSS Selector Comparison

SelectorsHub provides an option to generate and compare multiple XPath and CSS selectors for the same element. This feature is useful for exploring different approaches to locating elements and determining the most reliable selector for your use case.

5. Robust XPath and CSS Selector Strategies

The tool supports advanced XPath and CSS strategies, such as parent-child relationships, ancestor-descendant paths, and attribute-based selections. SelectorsHub helps you explore these advanced techniques, which can be beneficial when dealing with complex HTML structures.

6. Integration with Browser Developer Tools

SelectorsHub integrates seamlessly with browser developer tools, allowing you to use it alongside other common web development utilities. This integration ensures a smooth workflow for inspecting, creating, and validating selectors.

7. Support for Multiple Browsers

SelectorsHub is available as a browser extension for popular browsers like Chrome, Firefox, Edge, and others. This cross-browser support ensures you can use it in your preferred environment without limitations.

8. Contextual Suggestions and Tips

SelectorsHub provides helpful suggestions and tips to guide you in creating optimal selectors. It can suggest different XPath or CSS patterns, helping you develop a deeper understanding of these concepts.

9. Debugging and Troubleshooting Tools

If you encounter issues with your selectors, SelectorsHub can assist in diagnosing common problems. The tool offers debugging capabilities, allowing you to pinpoint and correct errors in your XPath or CSS selectors.

10. Community and Developer Support

SelectorsHub has a strong community of users and developers who contribute to its ongoing development. You can find resources, tutorials, and support to help you make the most of the tool.

Overall, SelectorsHub's features are designed to make XPath and CSS selector creation more accessible, efficient, and accurate, benefiting both newcomers and experienced developers alike.

Navigating the SelectorsHub Interface

Navigating the SelectorsHub interface effectively is crucial for making the most out of this powerful tool. Here's a detailed guide on how to use and understand the various components of SelectorsHub:

Launching SelectorsHub

Once you've installed SelectorsHub in your browser, you can open it by clicking on its icon in the browser's extension toolbar. This action typically opens the SelectorsHub panel within your browser's developer tools. If not, you can manually access it through your browser's developer tools menu.

The SelectorsHub Interface Components

SelectorsHub has a user-friendly interface designed to simplify XPath and CSS selector creation. Here's a breakdown of the key sections:

1. **Element Inspector**
   - This section allows you to inspect a web element on the page. Click the "Select" button (usually represented by a cursor icon), then hover over the element you want to select. Once you've selected an element, it will be highlighted, and SelectorsHub will generate potential XPath and CSS selectors for that element.
2. **Selector Display Area**
   - This area displays the automatically generated XPath and CSS selectors for the selected element. You'll typically see the XPath expression in one tab and the CSS selector in another.
   - You can customize the selector by modifying the attributes used in its construction. Click on the attributes (such as id, class, or name) to include or exclude them from the selector.
3. **XPath and CSS Selector Options**
   - These options allow you to choose specific methods for generating selectors. For example, you can toggle whether to use relative or absolute XPath, include or exclude attribute values, or choose different types of selectors (like contains, starts-with, or ends-with).
   - This flexibility is helpful when dealing with dynamic or complex web elements where you need customized selectors.
4. **Selector Validation and Highlighting**
   - As you create or modify selectors, SelectorsHub automatically highlights matching elements on the web page, providing immediate feedback on the accuracy of your selectors.
   - This feature is useful for validating your XPath or CSS expressions, ensuring they correctly identify the intended elements.
5. **Additional Tools and Features**
   - SelectorsHub offers additional tools like a "Copy" button to copy the generated XPath or CSS selector to your clipboard, making it easy to paste into your automation scripts or development environment.
   - You can also find tools for advanced XPath techniques, like ancestor/descendant relationships or following/preceding nodes.
6. **Settings and Preferences**

- SelectorsHub allows you to customize various settings to fit your workflow. You can adjust themes, toggle features, and choose default selector types.
- You can also access additional resources, such as tutorials, documentation, and community support, through links in the settings menu.

Tips for Navigating SelectorsHub

- **Experiment with Selector Variants**: Try different XPath and CSS selector strategies to see which one works best for your specific use case.
- **Use Real-Time Validation**: Keep an eye on the highlighted elements to ensure your selectors are accurate.
- **Customize Your Workflow**: Adjust the settings to create a comfortable and efficient working environment.

By mastering the SelectorsHub interface, you'll gain a powerful tool to help with XPath and CSS selector creation, allowing you to locate web elements with ease and confidence.

Using SelectorsHub for XPath Development

SelectorsHub is a handy browser extension designed to facilitate the development of XPath expressions. This guide will help you understand how to use SelectorsHub for efficient XPath development, from basic operations to advanced features.

1. Selecting a Web Element

To start using SelectorsHub, you need to select a web element. Open the developer tools in your browser and launch SelectorsHub. Click on the "Select" icon (usually represented by a cursor or target symbol) and hover over the web element you want to inspect. Click to select it, and it will be highlighted, with corresponding XPath and CSS selectors appearing in the SelectorsHub interface.

2. Understanding Auto-Generated XPath

SelectorsHub automatically generates an XPath expression for the selected element. The default XPath typically uses common attributes like `id`, `class`, `name`, etc. Examine this XPath to understand how it targets the web element. The generated XPath might be simple or complex, depending on the HTML structure and attributes.

3. Customizing XPath Expressions

SelectorsHub allows you to customize XPath expressions in several ways:

- **Attribute Selection**: Click on different attributes to include or exclude them from the XPath. You can use `id`, `class`, `name`, `text()`, and others.
- **XPath Functions**: Apply XPath functions like `contains`, `starts-with`, or `ends-with` to refine the selector. This is useful when dealing with dynamic content or partial matches.
- **Hierarchy and Relationships**: Modify the XPath to represent parent-child or ancestor-descendant relationships. You can also add indexing for elements with multiple siblings.

4. Validating XPath with Real-Time Feedback

SelectorsHub provides real-time feedback by highlighting elements that match your XPath expression. As you make changes, the highlighted elements will update accordingly. This validation process helps ensure that your XPath is accurate and targets the correct element(s).

5. Working with Relative and Absolute XPath

SelectorsHub can generate both relative and absolute XPath. Absolute XPath describes the complete path from the root of the HTML document, while relative XPath starts from a specific point, making it more flexible and less likely to break with minor changes in the HTML structure. Experiment with both to determine which best suits your needs.

6. Leveraging Advanced XPath Techniques

SelectorsHub supports advanced XPath features, allowing you to create more sophisticated selectors:

- **Parent-Child Relationships**: Use `//` for descendant relationships and `/` for direct child relationships.
- **Attribute Conditions**: Create complex conditions using multiple attributes and logical operators like `and` or `or`.
- **Navigating Through the DOM**: Use preceding/following nodes, sibling relationships, and other advanced XPath navigation methods to target specific elements.

7. Copying and Using XPath Expressions

Once you've created the desired XPath expression, use the "Copy" button in SelectorsHub to copy it to your clipboard. You can then paste it into your Selenium WebDriver scripts or other automation tools. This feature streamlines the development process by allowing you to quickly integrate the XPath into your test cases or automation tasks.

8. Troubleshooting and Best Practices

If your XPath expression doesn't work as expected, consider the following:

- **Check for Typos**: Ensure the XPath syntax is correct, with proper brackets, slashes, and attribute names.
- **Simplify the XPath**: Start with a basic expression and gradually add complexity to identify the point of failure.
- **Use SelectorsHub Features**: Leverage the real-time validation and XPath functions to refine and troubleshoot your expressions.

By following these steps, you can effectively use SelectorsHub for XPath development, creating robust and reliable XPath expressions for a variety of web automation and testing scenarios.

Common Use Cases for SelectorsHub

SelectorsHub is a versatile tool designed to assist in creating, validating, and testing XPath and CSS selectors. Its flexibility makes it useful for various use cases in web development, automated testing, and debugging. Here's a breakdown of common scenarios where SelectorsHub can be invaluable:

1. Creating XPath and CSS Selectors for Automation Frameworks

SelectorsHub is frequently used by QA engineers and test automation developers to create reliable XPath and CSS selectors for frameworks like Selenium WebDriver, Cypress, and others. It helps generate precise selectors for automated test scripts, enabling robust test automation.

2. Handling Dynamic Web Elements

SelectorsHub allows you to create XPath and CSS selectors that adapt to dynamic content. This is useful when dealing with web pages that frequently change, such as those with JavaScript-driven content or AJAX-based elements. The ability to use functions like `contains`, `starts-with`, or `ends-with` helps locate elements even when their attributes change.

3. Inspecting Complex HTML Structures

For complex web pages with nested elements, SelectorsHub simplifies the process of locating specific components. It helps you navigate through parent-child, ancestor-descendant, and sibling relationships to create XPath expressions that accurately target the desired elements.

4. Validating XPath and CSS Selectors

SelectorsHub's real-time validation and highlighting features are excellent for testing XPath and CSS selectors. This functionality allows you to validate selectors during development, ensuring they correctly identify the intended elements. It's particularly useful for debugging when a selector isn't behaving as expected.

5. Generating Selectors for Web Scraping

Web scraping often involves extracting specific data from web pages. SelectorsHub can generate XPath and CSS selectors to identify data points for scraping. Its ability to customize selectors makes it a valuable tool for web scraping projects, where precision is crucial.

6. Working with Forms and User Inputs

SelectorsHub is helpful when dealing with forms and user input fields. You can create XPath and CSS selectors to locate form elements like input boxes, buttons, and dropdowns. This use case is beneficial for automated form testing, filling, or scraping.

7. Comparing XPath and CSS Selectors

SelectorsHub allows you to generate and compare multiple XPath and CSS selectors for the same element. This feature is useful when exploring different approaches to locate an element, helping you choose the most robust and maintainable option.

8. Debugging and Troubleshooting Selector Issues

If an XPath or CSS selector isn't working, SelectorsHub's debugging tools can help identify the problem. You can test selectors in real-time and use the tool's feedback to pinpoint the source of the issue, whether it's a syntax error, incorrect attribute, or wrong relationship.

9. Optimizing Selector Performance

SelectorsHub offers features that help optimize the performance of XPath and CSS selectors. By analyzing the generated selectors, you can identify potential performance bottlenecks and make adjustments to improve efficiency. This use case is beneficial for large-scale automated testing projects where performance is critical.

10. Educational and Learning Tool

SelectorsHub is an excellent resource for learning XPath and CSS selectors. Its interactive interface and real-time validation make it a great educational tool for developers, testers, and anyone interested in understanding how to create effective selectors.

Overall, SelectorsHub's wide range of features and flexibility makes it a versatile tool for various use cases in web development, automated testing, web scraping, and debugging. By understanding these common scenarios, you can leverage SelectorsHub to improve your workflows and enhance your XPath and CSS selector skills.

Tips for Efficient XPath Creation with SelectorsHub

XPath creation can be a challenging task, especially when dealing with complex or dynamic web elements. SelectorsHub is designed to make this process easier, offering tools and features that streamline XPath development. Here are some tips for creating efficient XPath expressions using SelectorsHub:

1. Start Simple, Then Build Complexity

Begin with basic XPath expressions and gradually add complexity. This approach helps ensure that each component of the XPath works as intended, reducing the risk of errors. Use relative XPath as much as possible, as it's more flexible and less prone to breakage.

2. Use Distinct Attributes

When creating XPath, choose unique and stable attributes, such as id, name, or class, to identify web elements. If possible, avoid attributes that are subject to frequent change, like inline styles or dynamic data attributes.

3. Leverage XPath Functions

SelectorsHub allows you to use XPath functions like contains, starts-with, and ends-with. These functions are helpful for creating flexible XPath expressions that can handle varying attribute values or text content.

4. Incorporate Relationships

Utilize parent-child, ancestor-descendant, and sibling relationships in your XPath expressions. This approach can help you navigate complex HTML structures and ensure your XPath targets the correct elements.

5. Use Indexing Wisely

When elements are part of a larger collection, like a list or table, use indexing to specify which element to target. Be cautious with indexing, as it can become unstable if the web page structure changes. Ensure your XPath is adaptable by choosing stable indices or combining indexing with unique attributes.

6. Validate Selectors in Real-Time

SelectorsHub provides real-time feedback by highlighting matching elements on the web page. As you create or modify XPath expressions, use this feature to ensure your XPath targets the correct elements. This immediate validation helps you catch errors early and refine your XPath efficiently.

7. Use Context-Based Selectors

Create XPath expressions based on context rather than relying solely on absolute paths. This approach makes your XPath more resilient to changes in the HTML structure. SelectorsHub allows you to create relative XPath, which is preferable to absolute XPath for this reason.

8. Explore Multiple XPath Variants

SelectorsHub can generate multiple XPath expressions for the same element. Explore these variants to find the most robust and efficient one. You might discover new techniques or approaches that work better for your specific use case.

9. Organize and Document Your XPath

Keep track of your XPath expressions by documenting them. Use descriptive names and comments in your automation scripts to explain the purpose and structure of each XPath. This practice helps with maintenance and debugging.

10. Troubleshoot and Debug Effectively

If an XPath expression doesn't work as expected, use SelectorsHub's debugging tools to identify the issue. Check for syntax errors, incorrect attributes, or misaligned relationships. By isolating the problem, you can correct the XPath and create a more robust solution.

By following these tips, you can create efficient, reliable, and adaptable XPath expressions with SelectorsHub. These best practices will help you navigate the complexities of XPath development, enabling you to build robust selectors for web automation, testing, and other tasks.

Chapter Summary

In this chapter, we explored SelectorsHub, a powerful tool for creating and validating XPath expressions. Here's a summary of the key points covered:

1. **Introduction to SelectorsHub**: SelectorsHub is a browser extension that streamlines XPath and CSS selector creation, offering features like auto-generation, customization, real-time validation, and debugging.
2. **Installing and Setting Up SelectorsHub**: We provided step-by-step instructions for installing SelectorsHub on popular browsers like Chrome, Firefox, and Edge. Once installed, the extension integrates with the browser's developer tools, allowing you to access its features conveniently.
3. **Navigating the SelectorsHub Interface**: We examined the key components of SelectorsHub's interface, including the Element Inspector, Selector Display Area, XPath and CSS Selector Options, and additional tools like real-time validation and customization settings.
4. **Using SelectorsHub for XPath Development**: This section focused on how to use SelectorsHub to create and refine XPath expressions. We discussed selecting web elements, customizing XPath, validating in real-time, and leveraging advanced XPath techniques like parent-child relationships and indexing.
5. **Common Use Cases for SelectorsHub**: SelectorsHub is useful in various scenarios, including creating XPath for automation frameworks like Selenium, handling dynamic web elements, inspecting complex HTML structures, generating selectors for web scraping, and validating XPath expressions.
6. **Tips for Efficient XPath Creation with SelectorsHub**: We shared practical tips for creating efficient XPath expressions, emphasizing the importance of starting simple, leveraging XPath functions, using context-based selectors, and validating in real-time.

SelectorsHub is a versatile and powerful tool for XPath development, offering a user-friendly interface and robust features to aid web developers and testers. By following the advice and techniques discussed in this chapter, you can create efficient and reliable XPath expressions for various use cases, from web automation to testing and debugging.

Building XPath with Attributes

Outline

1. What Are XPath Attributes?
2. Identifying Key Attributes for XPath
3. Basic XPath with Attributes
4. Using XPath Functions with Attributes
5. XPath with Multiple Attributes
6. Attribute-Based XPath for Dynamic Content
7. Best Practices for Attribute-Based XPath
8. Chapter Summary

What Are XPath Attributes?

XPath attributes are a fundamental component of XPath, a language used to navigate and query XML or HTML documents. Attributes in XPath refer to the properties or characteristics that define HTML or XML elements, allowing users to create XPath expressions that can precisely locate elements based on these attributes. Here's a comprehensive explanation of what XPath attributes are and why they are crucial in building effective XPath expressions:

Understanding Attributes in HTML and XML

In HTML and XML, attributes are additional pieces of information associated with elements. They are key-value pairs that provide further context or define specific properties of an element. Common attributes in HTML include `id`, `class`, `name`, `href`, and `src`, among others. Attributes can be used to identify, categorize, or define behavior for HTML elements.

XPath and Attributes

XPath uses a variety of syntaxes and operators to navigate through XML or HTML documents. Attributes play a significant role in XPath because they offer a means to create unique and specific expressions to locate elements. Here's how attributes are used in XPath:

- **Attribute Syntax**: In XPath, attributes are accessed using the @ symbol. For example, `@id` refers to the `id` attribute of an element, while `@class` refers to the `class` attribute. An XPath expression that targets an element by its attribute might look like `//div[@id='example']`.
- **Locating Elements with Attributes**: Attributes can be used to pinpoint specific elements in a document. For instance, if you know that a `button` element has a unique `id` attribute, you can use XPath to locate it with `//button[@id='submit']`.
- **XPath Functions with Attributes**: XPath provides functions like `contains`, `starts-with`, and `ends-with`, allowing you to create expressions based on partial matches of attribute values. For example, you might use `contains(@class, 'active')` to locate an element with a class name that includes 'active'.

Why XPath Attributes Are Important

Attributes are critical in XPath because they provide a flexible and reliable way to create expressions that can adapt to varying structures or dynamic content. Here are some reasons why XPath attributes are crucial:

- **Uniqueness**: Attributes like id or name can uniquely identify elements, making them a reliable basis for XPath expressions.
- **Stability**: Attributes are generally stable and less likely to change than other element properties, providing robustness to XPath expressions.
- **Flexibility**: Using XPath functions with attributes allows for flexible matching, which is essential when dealing with dynamic content or complex structures.
- **Optimization**: Attribute-based XPath can be more efficient, especially when targeting unique or infrequently changing elements, contributing to better performance in automation tasks.

In summary, XPath attributes are the backbone of many XPath expressions, providing a means to locate, navigate, and interact with elements in XML or HTML documents. They offer a balance between specificity and flexibility, allowing XPath expressions to be both robust and adaptable. Understanding how to work with attributes in XPath is a foundational skill for anyone working with web automation, testing, or data extraction.

Identifying Key Attributes for XPath

When creating XPath expressions, identifying the key attributes to target is crucial for locating the desired elements accurately and efficiently. The right attributes can make XPath expressions more robust, flexible, and easier to maintain. This section focuses on the key attributes that are commonly used in XPath and provides insights on how to choose the best ones for your use case.

Commonly Used Attributes

In HTML documents, some attributes are frequently used to create XPath expressions due to their uniqueness and stability. Here are some of the most common ones:

- **id**: The id attribute is designed to be unique within an HTML document, making it a reliable attribute for XPath expressions. If an element has a unique id, it can be directly targeted using XPath, like //*[@id='element_id'].
- **class**: The class attribute groups elements with similar styles or functions. XPath can use the class attribute to locate elements, either individually or as part of a group. You can also use functions like contains to target elements with a specific class, such as //*[contains(@class, 'active')].
- **name**: The name attribute is commonly used in form fields and other interactive elements. It is often unique within a form or a specific context, making it a useful attribute for XPath, e.g., //input[@name='username'].
- **href**: This attribute is found in anchor (<a>) tags and typically contains a URL or link destination. XPath can use href to locate specific links, like //a[@href='/home'].
- **src**: Often used in media elements like images or iframes, the src attribute points to the source location of a file. XPath expressions can target elements based on their source, like //img[@src='image.png'].

Choosing the Best Attributes for XPath

While the common attributes mentioned above are widely used, the best attribute to target depends on the specific context and requirements. Here are some tips to help you choose the best attributes for XPath:

- **Uniqueness**: Prioritize attributes that are unique within the scope of the XPath expression. A unique id is often the best choice, as it directly targets the intended element without ambiguity.
- **Stability**: Choose attributes that are less likely to change over time. Attributes related to styling, such as inline styles or dynamic attributes, might change frequently, making them less reliable.

- **Context**: Consider the context of the HTML document. If you are working within a form, the name attribute might be more useful. If targeting navigation links, href is more appropriate.
- **Combining Attributes**: In some cases, using a combination of attributes provides greater specificity and robustness. This is particularly helpful when dealing with elements that share common attributes but differ in others.

Special Considerations

In addition to common attributes, other attributes may be useful depending on the scenario:

- **Dynamic Attributes**: When dealing with dynamic content, you might need to use attributes that reflect changing states, such as data-* attributes or aria-* attributes. These attributes can provide additional context for XPath expressions.
- **Text Content**: While not an attribute, XPath can target elements based on text content using the text() function. This can be useful when attributes are insufficient, such as targeting buttons by their label, like //button[text()='Submit'].

Identifying key attributes for XPath is a critical step in creating effective and robust XPath expressions. By focusing on attributes that are unique, stable, and appropriate for the context, you can build XPath expressions that are both efficient and reliable. Use this knowledge to streamline your XPath development and enhance your web automation, testing, and data extraction workflows.

Basic XPath with Attributes

XPath (XML Path Language) is a flexible language used to navigate XML and HTML documents. One of the core features of XPath is its ability to locate elements based on attributes. Attributes are key-value pairs associated with elements that can be used to create specific and reliable XPath expressions. In this section, we will discuss the basics of XPath with attributes, including simple expressions and common practices for creating effective XPath.

The Basic Structure of XPath with Attributes

XPath allows you to create expressions that point to specific elements in an XML or HTML document. When using attributes, the typical syntax is //element[@attribute='value']. This syntax identifies elements with a specific attribute and value.

For example, to locate a <div> element with an id of "content", you would use the following XPath expression:

//div[@id='content']

Commonly Used Attributes

The following are common attributes used to create XPath expressions:

- **id**: This attribute is often unique within an HTML document. Using id can be the most reliable way to create XPath. Example:

  //input[@id='username']

- **class**: This attribute groups elements by style or functionality. You can target elements by class, either precisely or using functions like contains. Example:

  //div[@class='alert']

- **name**: Commonly used for form fields, the name attribute is useful in locating elements. Example:

  //input[@name='email']

- **href**: This attribute is often used in anchor tags, pointing to URLs. You can locate links using href. Example:

  //a[@href='/home']

- **src**: This attribute is typically used in media elements like images and iframes, indicating the source location. Example:

  //img[@src='logo.png']

Building Simple XPath Expressions

To create basic XPath expressions with attributes, follow these steps:

1. **Identify the Element**: Use a browser's developer tools to inspect the HTML structure and find the target element.
2. **Choose an Attribute**: Look for unique or stable attributes like id, name, or class. Avoid attributes that are dynamic or subject to frequent change.
3. **Construct the XPath Expression**: Use the attribute to build the XPath expression. Start with a basic expression, such as //element[@attribute='value'].
4. **Validate the XPath**: Test the XPath expression to ensure it selects the correct element(s). You can use tools like SelectorsHub or XPath testers in browser developer tools for validation.

Basic XPath with attributes is a foundational skill for web automation, testing, and data extraction. By understanding common attributes and learning how to use XPath functions, you can create reliable XPath expressions that accurately locate elements. Use these principles to build robust XPath expressions, leading to more effective automation scripts and testing scenarios.

Using XPath Functions with Attributes

XPath functions offer powerful tools for working with attributes, allowing you to create flexible, dynamic, and robust XPath expressions. These functions can help you locate elements based on partial matches, specific patterns, or relationships within the HTML structure. In this section, we'll explore how to use XPath functions with attributes and provide examples to illustrate their application.

Common XPath Functions for Attributes

Here are some of the most commonly used XPath functions when working with attributes:

- **contains()**: This function checks whether an attribute contains a specific substring. It's useful when the exact value of an attribute might vary or when dealing with class names that represent multiple styles or states.
- **starts-with()**: This function checks if an attribute starts with a specific substring. It's handy for identifying elements with attributes that follow a predictable pattern.
- **ends-with()**: Although not a built-in XPath function, you can create an XPath expression that mimics "ends-with" behavior by using substring or substring-after.
- **not()**: This function negates a condition, allowing you to create expressions that exclude elements with specific attributes or attribute values.

Using `contains()` with Attributes

The `contains()` function is one of the most flexible tools for creating XPath expressions based on attributes. It allows you to search for elements where an attribute contains a specific value or substring. This is especially useful for attributes like `class`, which might contain multiple class names.

Example: Finding all `<div>` elements with a class that includes "active":

```
//div[contains(@class, 'active')]
```

Example: Locating `<a>` elements with `href` attributes containing "product":

```
//a[contains(@href, 'product')]
```

Using `starts-with()` with Attributes

The `starts-with()` function helps you find elements where an attribute begins with a specific substring. This function is valuable when attributes follow a naming convention or pattern.

Example: Finding all `<input>` elements where the name attribute starts with "user":

```
//input[starts-with(@name, 'user')]
```

Example: Locating `<div>` elements where the `id` starts with "section":

```
//div[starts-with(@id, 'section')]
```

Using `substring` to Mimic `ends-with()`

While XPath does not have a built-in `ends-with()` function, you can achieve similar results by using the `substring` function in combination with other XPath operations.

Example: Finding all `<a>` elements where the `href` ends with ".pdf":

```
//a[substring(@href, string-length(@href) - 3) = '.pdf']
```

Using `not()` with Attributes

The `not()` function allows you to negate a condition, enabling you to exclude elements based on attribute values or characteristics.

Example: Finding all `<div>` elements that do not have the class "hidden":

```
//div[not(contains(@class, 'hidden'))]
```

Example: Locating `<input>` elements where the `type` is not "password":

```
//input[not(@type = 'password')]
```

Combining Functions with Attributes

XPath functions can be combined to create more complex expressions. This flexibility allows you to create robust XPath expressions that handle various scenarios.

Example: Finding all `<div>` elements with a class containing "active" but not containing "inactive":

```
//div[contains(@class, 'active') and not(contains(@class, 'inactive'))]
```

XPath functions with attributes are powerful tools for creating dynamic and flexible XPath expressions. By using functions like `contains()`, `starts-with()`, `substring`, and `not()`, you can create expressions that adapt to changing conditions and target specific elements effectively. These functions, when used in combination with other XPath techniques, can help you build robust XPath expressions for a variety of use cases, from web automation to data extraction and beyond.

XPath with Multiple Attributes

XPath expressions can be constructed to target elements with multiple attributes, providing a more specific way to locate elements in complex or dynamic HTML structures. This approach can be useful when you need to narrow down the results to find unique or specific elements. In this section, we'll explore how to create XPath expressions using multiple attributes and discuss strategies for constructing robust and reliable XPath expressions.

Combining Multiple Attributes

Combining multiple attributes in an XPath expression is a common technique for achieving greater specificity. The general syntax for an XPath expression with multiple attributes is:

```
//element[@attribute1='value1' and @attribute2='value2']
```

This expression targets elements that meet both attribute conditions. You can also use logical operators like `or` to create more flexible expressions. Here are some scenarios where using multiple attributes is beneficial:

1. Locating Unique Elements

When a single attribute isn't enough to uniquely identify an element, combining multiple attributes can help. This is often useful when elements share common attributes but differ in others.

Example: Finding a `<div>` element with `class='content'` and `data-role='main'`:

```
//div[@class='content' and @data-role='main']
```

2. Handling Ambiguity

Sometimes, an attribute like `class` can be shared across multiple elements. By combining it with another attribute, you can reduce ambiguity and target the correct element.

Example: Locating a `<button>` with `class='btn'` and `type='submit'`:

```
//button[@class='btn' and @type='submit']
```

3. Creating Flexible Conditions

Using logical operators like `and` and `or`, you can create flexible conditions in your XPath expressions. This approach allows you to include multiple potential attributes to target elements with more variability.

Example: Finding all `<input>` elements with either `name='email'` or `name='user_email'`:

```
//input[@name='email' or @name='user_email']
```

4. Working with Dynamic Content

When dealing with dynamic content, attributes might change depending on user interaction or other factors. Combining multiple attributes can create XPath expressions that handle these variations.

Example: Locating a <div> with a dynamic id and a stable class:

```
//div[starts-with(@id, 'dynamic-') and @class='content']
```

Tips for Using Multiple Attributes in XPath

Here are some best practices for working with XPath expressions that use multiple attributes:

- **Prioritize Unique and Stable Attributes**: When combining attributes, choose those that are unique and stable. This approach helps ensure your XPath expression remains robust over time.
- **Avoid Over-Specification**: While using multiple attributes can improve specificity, avoid over-specification, which can make the XPath expression fragile. Strive for a balance between specificity and flexibility.
- **Test and Validate Your XPath**: After creating an XPath expression with multiple attributes, validate it to ensure it selects the correct elements. Use tools like SelectorsHub or browser developer tools to test your expressions.
- **Use Logical Operators Appropriately**: Understand the difference between and and or when combining attributes. Use and when both conditions must be met, and or when either condition is acceptable.

XPath with multiple attributes is a powerful technique for creating specific and robust XPath expressions. By combining attributes, you can target unique elements, reduce ambiguity, and create flexible conditions for handling dynamic content. Following best practices and testing your XPath expressions will help ensure they work reliably in various scenarios, supporting your automation, testing, and web development efforts.

Attribute-Based XPath for Dynamic Content

Dynamic content on web pages can be challenging for XPath, as the structure or attributes of elements may change due to user interactions, JavaScript, or other factors. Attribute-based XPath provides a flexible approach to creating robust XPath expressions that can adapt to these changes. In this section, we'll explore how to create attribute-based XPath expressions for dynamic content and provide strategies for maintaining XPath robustness in dynamic environments.

Understanding Dynamic Content

Dynamic content refers to web elements that change over time or based on user actions. This could involve adding or removing elements, modifying attributes, or changing content. Common examples of dynamic content include:

- **AJAX Requests**: Content updated through AJAX without reloading the page.
- **JavaScript-Driven Changes**: Elements that change attributes or structure based on JavaScript events.
- **User Interactions**: Changes triggered by user actions like clicks, inputs, or form submissions.

Using Attribute-Based XPath for Dynamic Content

Attribute-based XPath focuses on attributes that are more likely to remain stable, even in dynamic contexts. Here are some key techniques for building XPath expressions to handle dynamic content:

1. Using Stable Attributes

Identify attributes that remain stable despite dynamic changes. For example, `id`, `name`, and `class` are often more stable than others. Prioritize these attributes to create your XPath expressions.

Example: Locating an element with a unique `id` that doesn't change:

```
//div[@id='static-element']
```

2. Utilizing Functions for Flexibility

XPath functions like `contains()`, `starts-with()`, or `substring()` allow for flexible attribute matching, which is beneficial for dynamic content. These functions can create XPath expressions that adapt to changing conditions.

Example: Finding a `<div>` where the `class` contains a common substring:

```
//div[contains(@class, 'content')]
```

Example: Locating a `<button>` with a dynamic `id` pattern using `starts-with()`:

```
//button[starts-with(@id, 'dynamic-')]
```

3. Combining Attributes for Robustness

Combining multiple attributes can create a more robust XPath expression. This approach is useful when you need to ensure an element meets several conditions, providing more specificity in dynamic contexts.

Example: Finding a `<div>` with a stable `class` and a dynamic `id`:

```
//div[contains(@class, 'section') and starts-with(@id, 'dynamic-')]
```

4. Handling Dynamic Collections

When working with dynamic collections, such as lists or tables, XPath expressions can use attributes and indexing to locate specific elements. Index-based XPath can help target elements within collections that may change.

Example: Locating the first item in a dynamic list by index:

```
//ul[@class='dynamic-list']/li[1]
```

Best Practices for Attribute-Based XPath in Dynamic Content

To ensure your XPath expressions remain robust in dynamic content, consider the following best practices:

- **Prioritize Relative XPath**: Use relative XPath instead of absolute XPath, as it is more flexible and less prone to breakage when elements are added or removed.
- **Focus on Uniqueness**: Ensure that the attributes used in your XPath expression are unique enough to avoid ambiguity.
- **Avoid Over-Specification**: While specificity is important, avoid over-specification, as it can lead to brittle XPath expressions.
- **Use Real-Time Validation**: Tools like SelectorsHub can help validate XPath expressions in real-time, ensuring they work as expected in dynamic environments.
- **Regularly Update and Test XPath**: As web pages evolve, regularly update and test your XPath expressions to ensure they remain accurate and reliable.

Attribute-based XPath provides a robust and flexible approach for dealing with dynamic content. By focusing on stable attributes, using functions for flexibility, and combining attributes for robustness, you can create XPath expressions that adapt to changing conditions. By following best practices and using real-time validation tools, you can ensure your XPath expressions remain effective in dynamic web environments.

Best Practices for Attribute-Based XPath

Creating reliable XPath expressions based on attributes requires a combination of knowledge, experience, and best practices. Attribute-based XPath is a powerful technique, but it can lead to brittle or inefficient expressions if not used correctly. This section outlines the best practices for attribute-based XPath, providing guidance on creating robust and maintainable XPath expressions.

1. Prioritize Unique and Stable Attributes

Select attributes that are unique and stable to ensure your XPath expressions are specific and reliable. The `id` attribute is often the best choice because it is designed to be unique within an HTML document. However, if the `id` is absent or not unique, consider using other attributes like `name`, `class`, or `data-*` attributes.

2. Use Relative XPath

Relative XPath starts from a specific context rather than from the root of the document. It is generally more robust and flexible than absolute XPath, which can break if the document structure changes. Relative XPath with attributes helps you create expressions that are less likely to become outdated.

3. Avoid Over-Specification

While it's important to create specific XPath expressions, over-specification can lead to brittle expressions. Avoid including unnecessary attributes or creating overly complex expressions. Aim for a balance between specificity and flexibility to ensure your XPath expressions are robust in various scenarios.

4. Utilize XPath Functions

XPath functions like `contains()`, `starts-with()`, and `not()` allow for more flexible attribute-based XPath expressions. These functions can handle dynamic content, partial matches, and complex conditions. Use them to create expressions that adapt to changing environments.

Example: Using `contains()` to locate elements with a specific substring in their attribute:

```
//div[contains(@class, 'active')]
```

5. Combine Multiple Attributes

In some cases, you may need to use multiple attributes to achieve greater specificity. Combining attributes with logical operators like `and` and `or` can create more robust XPath expressions.

Example: Combining two attributes to locate an element with a specific `class` and `data-role`:

```
//div[@class='content' and @data-role='main']
```

6. Test and Validate XPath Expressions

Regularly test and validate your XPath expressions to ensure they work as expected. Use tools like SelectorsHub or browser developer tools to validate your expressions in real-time. This practice helps you catch errors early and ensures your XPath expressions are accurate.

7. Consider the Context

When creating attribute-based XPath, consider the context in which the expression will be used. For example, if you're working within a specific section of a web page, use context-based XPath to ensure your expression targets the correct elements.

Example: Finding an element within a specific section:

```
//div[@id='section1']//button[@class='submit']
```

8. Use Indexing with Caution

Indexing can be useful when working with collections or lists of elements. However, over-reliance on indexing can lead to fragile XPath expressions. Use indexing sparingly and only when necessary to avoid potential issues if the document structure changes.

9. Document Your XPath Expressions

Document your XPath expressions in your codebase or test scripts to explain their purpose and structure. This practice helps with maintainability and debugging, especially when working with complex XPath expressions.

10. Stay Updated with Web Changes

Web pages evolve over time, with changes to structure, attributes, or content. Regularly update your XPath expressions to account for these changes. Staying updated with the latest practices and tools in XPath development will help ensure your expressions remain effective and reliable.

By following these best practices for attribute-based XPath, you can create robust and maintainable XPath expressions. These practices ensure that your XPath expressions are specific enough to locate the desired elements while remaining flexible enough to adapt to changing conditions. Test and validate your XPath expressions regularly to maintain accuracy, and document them for easier maintenance and debugging. With these best practices, you can build reliable XPath expressions that support your automation, testing, and web development efforts.

Chapter Summary

In this chapter, we explored the process of building XPath expressions with attributes, providing key insights and techniques to create robust and reliable XPath expressions. Here's a summary of the main points covered in the chapter:

What Are XPath Attributes?

- XPath attributes are key-value pairs associated with HTML elements that can be used to create XPath expressions for web automation, testing, and data extraction. The most common attributes used in XPath include id, class, name, href, and src.

Identifying Key Attributes for XPath

- Choosing the right attributes is crucial for building effective XPath expressions. This section explained how to identify and select attributes that are unique, stable, and suitable for specific contexts. We discussed common attributes like `id`, `class`, and `name` and provided tips for selecting the best attributes.

Basic XPath with Attributes

- The basics of building XPath expressions with attributes were covered in this section. We discussed the general structure of XPath expressions, how to target elements using attributes, and how to use simple functions like `contains()` and `starts-with()`. This section also provided examples of common XPath expressions using various attributes.

Using XPath Functions with Attributes

- XPath functions allow for more flexibility and dynamic behavior. We explored common XPath functions like `contains()`, `starts-with()`, and `not()` that can be used with attributes to create complex XPath expressions. We provided examples of how these functions can be applied to create robust XPath expressions.

XPath with Multiple Attributes

- Combining multiple attributes can lead to more specific and reliable XPath expressions. This section discussed the benefits of using multiple attributes and provided strategies for creating XPath expressions that target elements based on multiple conditions. We explained how to use logical operators like `and` and `or` to create complex conditions.

Attribute-Based XPath for Dynamic Content

- Dynamic content requires flexible XPath expressions that can adapt to changes. We discussed how to create attribute-based XPath expressions that work with dynamic content, focusing on stable attributes and using functions for flexibility. This section also covered best practices for handling dynamic collections and creating robust XPath expressions in dynamic environments.

Best Practices for Attribute-Based XPath

- This section provided a comprehensive list of best practices for building attribute-based XPath expressions. It included tips for choosing unique and stable attributes, avoiding over-specification, using relative XPath, and combining attributes for robustness. The section also emphasized the importance of regular testing and validation to ensure XPath expressions remain effective.

Conclusion

In conclusion, this chapter provided a detailed exploration of building XPath expressions with attributes, covering everything from basic techniques to advanced strategies for dynamic content. By understanding and applying the best practices and functions discussed in this chapter, readers can create robust, flexible, and reliable XPath expressions for their automation, testing, and web development projects.

XPath for Locating Text-based Elements

Outline

1. Understanding Text in XPath
2. Using `text()` in XPath Expressions
3. Locating Elements with Exact Text
4. Using Functions to Locate Partial Text
5. Combining Text with Attributes
6. Handling Dynamic Text in XPath
7. Best Practices for Locating Text-based Elements
8. Chapter Summary

Understanding Text in XPath

Text content plays a significant role in XPath expressions, especially when you need to locate elements based on their textual content rather than their structure or attributes. This section will delve into how text is represented in XPath, the various ways to extract it, and the common use cases for text-based XPath expressions.

What Is Text in XPath?

In XML and HTML, text is the readable content within elements. It might be the visible text on a web page, such as paragraph text, headings, button labels, or even alt text for images. In XPath, text nodes represent this textual content, allowing you to extract and manipulate it to create XPath expressions.

XPath's `text()` Function

XPath provides the `text()` function to work with text nodes. It allows you to create XPath expressions that target elements based on their text content. When you use `text()`, you're referring to the inner text of an element, rather than its attributes or other elements it might contain.

Example: Selecting a paragraph (<p>) element containing specific text:

```
//p[text()='Hello, world!']
```

When to Use Text-Based XPath

Text-based XPath expressions are useful in various scenarios, including:

- **Locating Elements by Label**: When elements are identified by their visible text, such as buttons or links.
- **Verifying Text Content**: In automated testing, to check that a web page contains the expected text.
- **Navigating Structures with Limited Attributes**: When elements don't have unique attributes, but their text content is consistent and reliable.

Limitations of Text-Based XPath

Text-based XPath expressions can be powerful, but they also have some limitations:

- **Ambiguity**: If multiple elements contain the same text, text-based XPath can be ambiguous, leading to unintended results.

- **Dynamic Content**: If the text content changes frequently, text-based XPath can become brittle or unreliable.
- **Whitespace and Formatting**: Text nodes in HTML may include whitespace, line breaks, or other formatting artifacts that can affect XPath expressions.

Using Text-Based XPath in Combination with Other Techniques

To overcome some limitations, text-based XPath is often combined with other XPath techniques, like attribute-based XPath or index-based XPath. This combination can provide more specificity and robustness.

Example: Selecting a specific <button> with a particular text and class:

```
//button[text()='Submit' and @class='primary']
```

Understanding text in XPath is crucial for creating effective and robust XPath expressions. The text() function allows you to extract and work with text content, but it's important to consider the limitations and potential ambiguities. By combining text-based XPath with other techniques, you can build XPath expressions that are both flexible and reliable, supporting a variety of use cases in web automation, testing, and web scraping.

Using text() in XPath Expressions

The text() function in XPath is used to reference the textual content within an XML or HTML element. This function is crucial for creating XPath expressions that identify elements based on their text, making it a common tool in web automation, testing, and data extraction. In this section, we'll explore how to use text() in XPath expressions, discuss common use cases, and highlight important considerations when working with text-based XPath.

Understanding the text() Function

The text() function in XPath retrieves the text content within an element. When used in an XPath expression, it can target elements based on the exact or partial match of their text. Here's a basic example demonstrating how to use text() to select elements based on their text content:

Example: Selecting a paragraph (<p>) with the exact text "Hello, world!":

```
//p[text()='Hello, world!']
```

Using text() to Locate Elements with Exact Text

One of the most straightforward applications of text() is to locate elements with exact text matches. This approach is useful when you need to identify elements with specific labels or content.

Example: Locating a <button> with the text "Submit":

```
//button[text()='Submit']
```

Example: Finding an <h1> with the text "Welcome":

```
//h1[text()='Welcome']
```

Using Functions with text() for Partial Matches

XPath functions like contains(), starts-with(), and substring() can be used with text() to create expressions for partial text matches. This flexibility allows you to target elements based on text patterns, even if the text isn't an exact match.

Example: Finding a <div> with text containing "error":

```
//div[contains(text(), 'error')]
```

Example: Locating a <h2> where the text starts with "Chapter":

```
//h2[starts-with(text(), 'Chapter')]
```

Using text() in Complex XPath Expressions

In more complex XPath expressions, text() can be combined with other elements, attributes, or functions to create specific and robust expressions. This approach can help you navigate complicated HTML structures or handle dynamic content.

Example: Finding a specific <button> within a <div> with a known id:

```
//div[@id='button-container']//button[text()='Confirm']
```

Example: Locating an <a> with a specific text and href value:

```
//a[text()='Click here' and @href='/next-page']
```

Important Considerations for text() in XPath

While text() is a powerful tool, there are some considerations to keep in mind:

- **Whitespace and Formatting**: Text content in HTML might include extra whitespace or line breaks, which can affect XPath expressions. Be aware of how whitespace is handled in your XPath expressions.
- **Ambiguity**: If multiple elements contain the same text, XPath might return more than one result. Use additional attributes or functions to reduce ambiguity.
- **Dynamic Content**: If text changes frequently, consider using partial matches or combining text-based XPath with attribute-based XPath to increase robustness.

Using text() in XPath expressions is an effective way to target elements based on their text content. By leveraging exact matches, partial matches, and complex XPath expressions, you can create robust XPath expressions for various use cases. However, it's important to consider potential issues with whitespace, ambiguity, and dynamic content. With careful design and validation, you can build reliable XPath expressions that meet your automation, testing, and web scraping needs.

Locating Elements with Exact Text

Locating elements with exact text in XPath is a common technique for targeting specific HTML elements based on their textual content. This approach is often used in web automation and testing to ensure that the correct elements are identified and interacted with. In this section, we'll explore how to locate elements with exact text, discuss common use cases, and highlight best practices for creating reliable XPath expressions.

Using text() to Find Elements with Exact Text

XPath's `text()` function allows you to select elements based on their exact text content. When an element's text content matches the specified text, it is selected by the XPath expression.

Example: Locating a paragraph (<p>) with the exact text "Hello, world!":

```
//p[text()='Hello, world!']
```

Example: Finding a heading (<h1>) with the exact text "Welcome":

```
//h1[text()='Welcome']
```

Common Use Cases for Exact Text XPath

Locating elements with exact text is useful in a variety of scenarios, including:

- **Web Automation**: In Selenium and other automation frameworks, you may need to find buttons, links, or other elements based on their exact text to simulate user interactions.
- **Automated Testing**: Exact text XPath expressions can be used to verify that a web page displays the correct text, ensuring that elements are rendered properly.
- **Web Scraping**: If you need to extract specific text from a web page, exact text XPath expressions can target the desired elements.

Handling Variability in Text

When creating XPath expressions for exact text, consider the following:

- **Whitespace and Formatting**: Exact text matching is sensitive to whitespace and line breaks. Ensure your expected text matches the actual text, including any hidden or extra whitespace.
- **Case Sensitivity**: XPath expressions are case-sensitive. Ensure the text case matches exactly, or consider converting it to a consistent case using XPath functions like `translate()`.
- **Ambiguity**: If multiple elements contain the same exact text, XPath might return multiple results. Consider additional attributes or context to reduce ambiguity.

Best Practices for Locating Elements with Exact Text

To create robust XPath expressions for exact text, follow these best practices:

- **Use Relative XPath**: Relative XPath is more flexible and less prone to breakage than absolute XPath. This approach helps ensure your XPath expressions remain robust as web page structures change.
- **Combine with Attributes**: To reduce ambiguity and increase specificity, consider combining text-based XPath with attribute-based XPath. This approach can help you locate elements with exact text and unique attributes.
- **Test and Validate XPath**: Always validate your XPath expressions to ensure they work as expected. Tools like SelectorsHub or browser developer tools can help you test XPath expressions in real-time.
- **Account for Dynamic Content**: If the web page has dynamic content that might affect text, consider alternative approaches, such as using partial text matches or attribute-based XPath.

Locating elements with exact text in XPath is a valuable technique for web automation, testing, and web scraping. By using the `text()` function and following best practices, you can create robust and reliable XPath expressions that precisely target elements with specific text. Be mindful of potential issues with whitespace, case sensitivity, and ambiguity, and test your XPath expressions to ensure they work in various scenarios. With these strategies, you can create effective XPath expressions for a range of use cases.

Using Functions to Locate Partial Text

XPath functions provide powerful tools to create flexible expressions for locating elements based on partial text. These functions are particularly useful when exact text matches are too rigid or when dealing with dynamic content that might vary. This section explores various XPath functions to locate partial text, discusses common use cases, and provides examples to illustrate their application.

XPath Functions for Partial Text

XPath offers several functions that allow you to locate elements based on partial text. The most commonly used functions for this purpose are `contains()`, `starts-with()`, and `substring()`. These functions give you flexibility in creating XPath expressions that match text patterns, even when the full text is uncertain or varies.

Using `contains()` for Partial Text

The `contains()` function checks whether a given string contains a specific substring. This function is useful when you need to locate elements with text that includes a specific word or pattern.

Example: Locating a `<div>` where the text contains "error":

```
//div[contains(text(), 'error')]
```

Example: Finding a `<span>` with text containing "Welcome":

```
//span[contains(text(), 'Welcome')]
```

Using `starts-with()` for Partial Text

The `starts-with()` function checks whether a string starts with a specified substring. This function is useful when elements follow a consistent pattern at the beginning of their text content.

Example: Finding a `<h1>` where the text starts with "Chapter":

```
//h1[starts-with(text(), 'Chapter')]
```

Example: Locating a `<p>` where the text starts with "Hello":

```
//p[starts-with(text(), 'Hello')]
```

Using `substring()` for Partial Text

The `substring()` function extracts a part of a string, allowing you to locate elements based on specific portions of their text. Although less common than `contains()` or `starts-with()`, `substring()` can be useful for more complex partial text matching.

Example: Locating an element where the text's first three characters are "Day":

```
//div[substring(text(), 1, 3) = 'Day']
```

Common Use Cases for Partial Text XPath

Partial text matching is useful in a variety of scenarios, including:

- **Dynamic Content**: When text varies but follows a common pattern, partial text functions can help create robust XPath expressions.

- **Web Automation**: In automated tests, you might need to interact with elements based on partial text, such as buttons or links with variable text.
- **Web Scraping**: Partial text matching can be useful for extracting data from web pages where exact text may not be known in advance.

Best Practices for Locating Partial Text

When creating XPath expressions for partial text, follow these best practices:

- **Combine with Attributes**: To increase specificity and reduce ambiguity, consider combining partial text matching with attribute-based XPath.
- **Use Context**: Use relative XPath to add context to your XPath expressions, which can help improve robustness and avoid unintended matches.
- **Test and Validate**: Always test your XPath expressions to ensure they work as expected. Tools like SelectorsHub or browser developer tools can help you validate your XPath in real-time.

Using functions to locate partial text in XPath provides flexibility and adaptability, making it easier to create robust XPath expressions in dynamic environments. By leveraging functions like `contains()`, `starts-with()`, and `substring()`, you can create XPath expressions that handle varying or uncertain text. However, always validate your XPath expressions and consider combining them with attribute-based XPath for greater reliability. These techniques will help you build effective XPath expressions for a variety of use cases, from web automation to data extraction and testing.

Combining Text with Attributes

Combining text-based XPath with attribute-based XPath can create robust and flexible expressions that improve the accuracy of element location in automation and web development scenarios. By combining these two approaches, you can achieve a balance between specificity and adaptability. This section explores how to combine text with attributes in XPath, provides common use cases, and discusses best practices for creating effective XPath expressions.

Why Combine Text with Attributes?

Combining text-based and attribute-based XPath can offer several benefits:

- **Reduced Ambiguity**: If multiple elements contain the same text, adding attribute conditions can help distinguish between them.
- **Increased Robustness**: Combining text and attributes creates more robust XPath expressions, especially in dynamic environments.
- **Enhanced Specificity**: The combination allows for more precise targeting, reducing the likelihood of incorrect element selection.

Examples of Combining Text with Attributes

Let's explore some examples of how to combine text and attributes in XPath expressions:

Example 1: Locating a Button with Specific Text and a Class

This XPath expression locates a `<button>` with the text "Submit" and a `class` attribute indicating it's a primary action:

```
//button[text()='Submit' and @class='primary']
```

Example 2: Finding a Link with Specific Text and a URL

Here, the XPath expression finds an <a> element with the text "Home" and a specific href attribute:

```
//a[text()='Home' and @href='/home']
```

Example 3: Selecting an Element with Text and Additional Attributes

This XPath expression targets a <div> with specific text and a data-role attribute, commonly used in web applications to indicate an element's role or purpose:

```
//div[text()='Dashboard' and @data-role='main']
```

When to Use Text and Attributes in Combination

Combining text with attributes is useful in various situations, including:

- **Identifying Unique Elements**: When you need to ensure that an XPath expression uniquely identifies a specific element.
- **Handling Dynamic Content**: If the text might vary or change, attributes can provide additional stability.
- **Reducing Ambiguity**: When elements share the same text, adding attribute conditions can clarify which element to target.

Best Practices for Combining Text with Attributes

To create effective XPath expressions that combine text and attributes, consider these best practices:

- **Choose Unique Attributes**: Select attributes that are unique or stable to avoid ambiguity.
- **Use Relative XPath**: Relative XPath expressions are more flexible and less prone to breakage than absolute XPath.
- **Validate XPath Expressions**: Test your XPath expressions to ensure they work as expected. Tools like SelectorsHub or browser developer tools can help validate your XPath in real-time.
- **Account for Dynamic Content**: If the web page structure or content changes frequently, be cautious with exact text matches and consider using functions like contains() for flexibility.
- **Document Your XPath**: Keep a record of your XPath expressions and their intended purposes, making it easier to maintain and troubleshoot.

Combining text with attributes in XPath expressions creates a powerful and flexible approach to locating elements. By following best practices and ensuring your XPath expressions are robust and validated, you can improve the accuracy of your web automation and testing scenarios. The combination of text and attributes allows you to create specific XPath expressions while maintaining flexibility, ensuring your XPath expressions remain effective over time and across different use cases.

Handling Dynamic Text in XPath

XPath expressions can be challenged by dynamic text, where content changes due to user interactions, JavaScript events, or AJAX updates. Handling dynamic text in XPath requires strategies that allow expressions to adapt to varying content while maintaining reliability. This section discusses methods for dealing with dynamic text in XPath, provides examples, and offers best practices for creating robust XPath expressions.

Understanding Dynamic Text

Dynamic text refers to text content that can change during the lifecycle of a web page. Common reasons for text changes include:

- **User Interaction**: Clicking a button, filling out a form, or other user-driven events.

- **JavaScript Events**: JavaScript code that modifies text content.
- **AJAX Updates**: Content updated without reloading the entire page.

Strategies for Handling Dynamic Text in XPath

To create XPath expressions that handle dynamic text, you need to use flexible techniques that can adapt to changing conditions. Here are some common strategies:

1. Using Partial Text Matching

XPath functions like `contains()` and `starts-with()` are useful for dynamic text because they allow for partial text matching. This flexibility helps create XPath expressions that can locate elements even when the full text changes.

Example: Finding a `<div>` where the text contains "error":

```
//div[contains(text(), 'error')]
```

Example: Locating a `<span>` where the text starts with "Chapter":

```
//span[starts-with(text(), 'Chapter')]
```

2. Combining Text with Attributes

Combining text-based XPath with attribute-based XPath can increase robustness when dealing with dynamic text. This approach provides additional context and specificity to the XPath expression, reducing ambiguity.

Example: Finding a `<button>` with text containing "Submit" and a `class` of "primary":

```
//button[contains(text(), 'Submit') and @class='primary']
```

3. Using Relative XPath for Context

Relative XPath starts from a specific context rather than from the root of the document. This approach allows you to create XPath expressions that are less likely to break if the structure changes. Adding context through relative XPath can help handle dynamic text.

Example: Locating a button within a specific section with text containing "Confirm":

```
//div[@id='section1']//button[contains(text(), 'Confirm')]
```

Best Practices for Handling Dynamic Text in XPath

To create robust XPath expressions for dynamic text, consider these best practices:

- **Use Flexible XPath Functions**: Functions like `contains()`, `starts-with()`, and `substring()` allow for more adaptable XPath expressions, enabling you to handle varying text content.
- **Combine Text and Attributes**: To increase specificity and reduce ambiguity, consider combining text-based XPath with attribute-based XPath.
- **Test and Validate XPath**: Always test your XPath expressions to ensure they work as expected. Tools like SelectorsHub or browser developer tools can help validate your XPath in real-time.
- **Account for Dynamic Changes**: If the web page content changes frequently, consider alternative approaches, such as using partial text matches or focusing on stable attributes.

- **Document Your XPath Expressions**: Keep a record of your XPath expressions and their intended purposes, making it easier to maintain and troubleshoot.

Handling dynamic text in XPath requires flexible strategies and a solid understanding of XPath functions. By using partial text matching, combining text with attributes, and employing relative XPath for context, you can create robust XPath expressions that adapt to changing content. By following best practices and validating your XPath expressions regularly, you can ensure they remain effective in dynamic environments, supporting your automation, testing, and web development needs.

Best Practices for Locating Text-based Elements

Locating text-based elements with XPath requires precision and flexibility. To create robust XPath expressions, you need to consider various factors, such as the stability of text content, potential ambiguity, and changes in web page structure. In this section, we'll discuss best practices for locating text-based elements, providing tips to create effective XPath expressions for web automation, testing, and scraping.

1. Use Relative XPath

Relative XPath expressions are more adaptable and less prone to breakage when the web page structure changes. Instead of specifying an exact path from the root, relative XPath starts from a given context, providing flexibility.

Example: Locating a button within a specific section with text "Submit":

```
//div[@id='section1']//button[text()='Submit']
```

2. Employ XPath Functions for Flexibility

XPath functions like `contains()`, `starts-with()`, and `substring()` allow you to create expressions that can handle varying or dynamic text content. These functions are useful for locating text-based elements when exact matches might be too restrictive.

Example: Finding a `<div>` with text containing "error":

```
//div[contains(text(), 'error')]
```

3. Combine Text with Attributes

Combining text-based XPath with attribute-based XPath creates more specific and robust expressions. This approach helps reduce ambiguity and allows for more precise targeting.

Example: Finding a button with the text "Submit" and `class='primary'`:

```
//button[text()='Submit' and @class='primary']
```

4. Test and Validate XPath

Regularly test and validate your XPath expressions to ensure they work as expected. Tools like SelectorsHub or browser developer tools can help you validate XPath in real-time. Testing is crucial, especially when dealing with text-based elements that might change or vary.

5. Consider Whitespace and Case Sensitivity

Text-based XPath expressions can be affected by whitespace and case sensitivity. Be aware that extra spaces, line breaks, or mixed casing can impact the reliability of XPath expressions. Ensure your expected text matches the actual text, including any hidden or extra whitespace.

6. Account for Dynamic Content

If the web page contains dynamic content, ensure your XPath expressions can handle changes. Consider using partial text matching or focusing on stable attributes to increase robustness. Avoid over-reliance on exact text matches when dealing with dynamic content.

7. Document Your XPath Expressions

Document your XPath expressions, explaining their purpose and structure. This practice makes it easier to maintain and troubleshoot XPath expressions, especially in complex automation frameworks or large-scale testing scenarios.

Locating text-based elements with XPath requires a combination of precision and flexibility. By following best practices like using relative XPath, employing XPath functions for flexibility, combining text with attributes, and validating XPath expressions, you can create robust and reliable XPath expressions for various use cases. Keep in mind the potential issues with whitespace and dynamic content, and document your XPath expressions for easier maintenance and troubleshooting. By adopting these best practices, you can build effective XPath expressions that meet the demands of web automation, testing, and data extraction.

Chapter Summary

This chapter explored various techniques for locating elements based on their text content using XPath. We discussed the importance of text-based XPath, common functions for text manipulation, and strategies to create robust expressions. Here's a summary of the key points covered:

Understanding Text in XPath

- Text in XPath refers to the readable content within HTML elements. The `text()` function is used to extract and work with text nodes, allowing XPath expressions to locate elements based on their textual content.

Using `text()` in XPath Expressions

- The `text()` function is central to text-based XPath. It can be used to create XPath expressions that identify elements with specific text. We explored the use of `text()` for exact text matches and provided examples demonstrating how to locate elements like buttons or headings by their text.

Locating Elements with Exact Text

- Exact text matching is a common use case for XPath, useful for scenarios like web automation and automated testing. We discussed how to create XPath expressions that locate elements based on exact text content and highlighted the importance of accounting for whitespace and case sensitivity.

Using Functions to Locate Partial Text

- XPath functions like `contains()`, `starts-with()`, and `substring()` offer flexibility when locating elements with partial text. We explored how to use these functions to create XPath expressions that adapt to varying or dynamic text content. Examples included finding elements where text contains a specific word or starts with a specific prefix.

Combining Text with Attributes

- Combining text-based XPath with attribute-based XPath can create more robust and specific expressions. This approach helps reduce ambiguity and provides additional context. We provided examples of how to combine text with attributes for improved accuracy and reliability.

Handling Dynamic Text in XPath

- Dynamic text can present challenges in XPath, but using flexible strategies can help. We discussed methods for handling dynamic text, including using partial text matching, combining text with attributes, and employing relative XPath for context. This section also highlighted the importance of considering dynamic content when creating XPath expressions.

Best Practices for Locating Text-based Elements

- This section outlined best practices for creating robust XPath expressions for text-based elements. We emphasized the importance of relative XPath, using XPath functions for flexibility, combining text with attributes, and validating XPath expressions. Additional tips included accounting for dynamic content and documenting XPath expressions for easier maintenance and troubleshooting.

Conclusion

Overall, this chapter provided a comprehensive guide to locating text-based elements with XPath. By understanding the role of text in XPath expressions, using functions to manipulate text, and following best practices, readers can create robust XPath expressions for a variety of use cases. The chapter concluded by encouraging readers to continue exploring advanced XPath techniques in the following sections, ensuring they are equipped with the skills needed for web automation, testing, and data extraction.

Handling Dynamic Elements with XPath

Outline

1. Understanding Dynamic Elements
2. Identifying Common Challenges with Dynamic Elements
3. Strategies for Handling Dynamic Elements
4. Using XPath Functions to Adapt to Dynamic Content
5. Dealing with AJAX-based Changes
6. Best Practices for XPath with Dynamic Elements
7. Chapter Summary

Understanding Dynamic Elements

Dynamic elements are a common challenge in web automation and testing. Unlike static elements, which remain constant after a page loads, dynamic elements can change due to user interactions, AJAX updates, or JavaScript-based modifications. Understanding what makes elements dynamic and why this poses challenges for XPath expressions is crucial for creating robust and reliable automation scripts.

What Are Dynamic Elements?

Dynamic elements are HTML elements that can change after the initial page load. These changes can occur for various reasons, including:

- **User Interactions**: Clicking a button, entering text, or selecting an option may trigger dynamic changes in the DOM.
- **AJAX Updates**: AJAX (Asynchronous JavaScript and XML) allows web pages to update content without a full page reload. This can lead to elements appearing, disappearing, or being modified dynamically.
- **JavaScript-Driven Changes**: JavaScript can change attributes, text content, or even the structure of the DOM in response to events or conditions.

Why Are Dynamic Elements Challenging?

Dynamic elements can make XPath-based automation and testing more complex for several reasons:

- **Changing Attributes**: Attributes like id, class, or name can change dynamically, affecting the reliability of XPath expressions that rely on them.
- **Variable Text Content**: Elements whose text content changes based on user input or other factors can be hard to locate consistently.
- **Element Addition/Removal**: Dynamic elements might be added or removed from the DOM, disrupting XPath expressions that depend on a specific structure.

Common Scenarios Involving Dynamic Elements

Understanding common scenarios where dynamic elements are encountered can help develop effective strategies for handling them:

- **Form Interactions**: Filling out forms can trigger dynamic changes, such as validation messages or updating elements based on input.
- **Navigation and Tabs**: Navigating through different tabs or sections on a page can lead to elements being dynamically loaded or changed.

- **AJAX-Powered Content**: Web applications that rely on AJAX often have dynamic elements that update without reloading the entire page.

How to Identify Dynamic Elements

Identifying dynamic elements requires careful observation and analysis. Here are some methods to help identify dynamic elements:

- **Inspecting the DOM**: Use browser developer tools to inspect the DOM and look for signs of dynamic behavior, such as JavaScript event listeners, AJAX requests, or changes in attributes.
- **Monitoring Changes**: Observe the page while interacting with it to see which elements change or are affected by user actions.
- **Testing Timing and Delays**: If elements appear or disappear after a delay, it may indicate dynamic behavior related to AJAX or JavaScript events.

Understanding dynamic elements is critical for creating robust XPath expressions and effective automation scripts. These elements introduce challenges that require flexible and adaptable XPath strategies. By identifying dynamic elements and recognizing their common scenarios, you can develop techniques to handle them effectively. In the following sections, we'll explore strategies for dealing with dynamic elements using XPath, offering tips and best practices to ensure your XPath expressions remain reliable in dynamic environments.

Identifying Common Challenges with Dynamic Elements

Dynamic elements in web applications can present significant challenges for automation and testing. Because these elements change based on user interactions, AJAX updates, or JavaScript events, XPath expressions that work in static contexts might become unreliable when dealing with dynamic content. Understanding these challenges is key to building robust XPath expressions. Here, we'll discuss common issues associated with dynamic elements and why they require special attention in automation frameworks like Selenium WebDriver.

1. Changing Attributes

One of the primary challenges with dynamic elements is that their attributes can change after the initial page load. This can happen for several reasons, such as:

- **JavaScript Modifications**: JavaScript code can dynamically update attributes like id, class, name, etc.
- **Dynamic Styling**: Attributes related to styling or visibility, like style, class, or hidden, can change to indicate a state change.
- **Variable IDs**: Elements with dynamic IDs may have different values based on session, user, or other conditions, leading to inconsistencies in XPath expressions.

2. Dynamic Text Content

Dynamic elements might have text content that changes, presenting another common challenge for XPath-based automation. This can occur when:

- **Text Changes with Interactions**: User actions like clicking, typing, or selecting options can alter text content.
- **AJAX Updates**: Text might change as part of AJAX-based content updates, causing elements to have varying or unpredictable text.
- **Conditional Text Changes**: Text might change based on conditions, like error messages that appear upon validation failure.

3. Element Addition and Removal

Dynamic elements can be added to or removed from the DOM, complicating XPath-based automation. This can occur when:

- **AJAX Loads New Content**: Elements are dynamically inserted into the DOM when new content is loaded via AJAX.
- **JavaScript Events Add or Remove Elements**: User interactions or events might trigger JavaScript functions that insert or remove elements from the DOM.
- **Modal Windows or Pop-ups**: These elements often involve adding or removing content based on user actions.

4. Timing Issues

Dynamic elements can introduce timing issues, leading to potential race conditions or synchronization problems. This challenge occurs when:

- **Elements Appear with Delays**: Some elements may take time to appear due to animations or AJAX requests.
- **Implicit and Explicit Waits**: Automation scripts might need to wait for elements to become visible or interactable before proceeding.
- **Changing Structures**: If the DOM structure changes over time, XPath expressions might need to adapt to different contexts.

5. Ambiguity and Multiple Matches

Dynamic elements can lead to ambiguity in XPath expressions, especially when:

- **Multiple Elements with Similar Attributes**: Dynamic behavior might cause multiple elements to share similar or identical attributes, leading to ambiguity in XPath expressions.
- **Unstable Structure**: When the structure changes, XPath expressions might match unintended elements, causing incorrect behavior in automation scripts.

Identifying common challenges with dynamic elements is crucial for creating robust XPath expressions in automation and testing. Understanding issues like changing attributes, dynamic text content, element addition/removal, timing, and ambiguity can help you develop effective strategies to handle them. In the following sections, we'll explore techniques for handling dynamic elements with XPath, offering best practices to ensure your XPath expressions remain adaptable and reliable in dynamic web environments.

Strategies for Handling Dynamic Elements

Dynamic elements can pose significant challenges for automation frameworks like Selenium WebDriver due to their changing nature. Strategies for handling dynamic elements with XPath focus on creating flexible, robust, and adaptable expressions. In this section, we'll explore effective techniques to address the challenges posed by dynamic elements and discuss best practices to create resilient XPath expressions.

1. Use Relative XPath

Relative XPath is more flexible than absolute XPath, allowing you to create expressions that are less prone to breakage as the page structure changes. By starting from a known context or landmark, you can navigate dynamic structures without relying on a rigid path from the document root.

Example: Finding a button within a specific section based on its position:

```
//div[@id='container']//button[text()='Submit']
```

2. Leverage XPath Functions for Flexibility

XPath functions like `contains()`, `starts-with()`, and `substring()` are useful for handling dynamic elements because they allow for partial matches and adaptability. These functions enable you to create expressions that can adjust to changes in text or attributes.

Example: Finding a `<div>` where the class contains "dynamic":

```
//div[contains(@class, 'dynamic')]
```

Example: Locating an element where the ID starts with a common prefix:

```
//div[starts-with(@id, 'dynamic-')]
```

3. Combine Multiple Attributes

Combining multiple attributes in an XPath expression can increase specificity and robustness. This approach can help reduce ambiguity and improve reliability when dealing with dynamic elements.

Example: Finding a button with a specific class and text:

```
//button[contains(@class, 'action') and text()='Confirm']
```

4. Use Index-Based XPath with Caution

Index-based XPath can be helpful when working with dynamic collections, but it should be used cautiously to avoid brittleness. If the structure changes, indexing might lead to incorrect elements being selected.

Example: Locating the first item in a dynamic list:

```
//ul[@id='list']/li[1]
```

5. Employ Explicit Waits for Synchronization

Dynamic elements often require synchronization to ensure they are present and interactable before automation scripts proceed. Explicit waits allow you to wait for specific conditions, reducing the risk of race conditions.

Example: Using Selenium WebDriver to wait for a button to become clickable:

```python
from selenium.webdriver.support.ui import WebDriverWait
from selenium.webdriver.support import expected_conditions as EC
from selenium.webdriver.common.by import By

WebDriverWait(driver, 10).until(EC.element_to_be_clickable((By.XPATH,
"//button[text()='Confirm']")))
```

6. Monitor DOM Changes

Monitoring changes to the DOM can help identify when dynamic elements are added or removed. This knowledge can guide the creation of XPath expressions that adapt to these changes.

Example: Observing changes to a specific section of the DOM in browser developer tools to identify dynamic behavior.

7. Test and Validate XPath

Regularly test and validate your XPath expressions to ensure they work as expected, especially when dealing with dynamic elements. Tools like SelectorsHub or browser developer tools can assist in validating XPath in real-time.

Strategies for handling dynamic elements with XPath focus on flexibility, adaptability, and robustness. By using relative XPath, leveraging XPath functions, combining multiple attributes, and employing explicit waits, you can create resilient XPath expressions that handle dynamic content effectively. Regular testing and validation are crucial to ensure your XPath expressions remain reliable as the web page structure changes. Following these strategies and best practices will help you create robust automation scripts and maintain effective test frameworks.

Using XPath Functions to Adapt to Dynamic Content

XPath functions are versatile tools that allow you to create flexible and adaptable XPath expressions. When dealing with dynamic content, these functions can help manage changes in text, attributes, or structure, enabling your XPath expressions to remain robust. This section explores various XPath functions that can be used to adapt to dynamic content, with examples demonstrating their practical application.

1. `contains()`

The `contains()` function checks whether a given string contains a specific substring. This function is useful for adapting to dynamic content because it allows for partial matches, making XPath expressions more flexible.

Example: Finding a `<div>` where the class contains "dynamic":

```
//div[contains(@class, 'dynamic')]
```

Example: Locating a `<button>` where the text contains "Submit":

```
//button[contains(text(), 'Submit')]
```

2. `starts-with()`

The `starts-with()` function checks whether a string starts with a specific substring. This function is useful when elements have variable text or attributes that follow a common pattern.

Example: Finding a `<div>` where the ID starts with "section":

```
//div[starts-with(@id, 'section')]
```

Example: Locating a `<span>` where the text starts with "Error":

```
//span[starts-with(text(), 'Error')]
```

3. `substring()`

The `substring()` function extracts a portion of a string based on specified positions. Although less commonly used than `contains()` or `starts-with()`, `substring()` can be helpful for creating XPath expressions that target specific segments of text or attribute values.

Example: Finding a `<div>` where the last three characters of the ID are "123":

```
//div[substring(@id, string-length(@id) - 2) = '123']
```

4. `normalize-space()`

The `normalize-space()` function removes leading and trailing whitespace, and replaces sequences of spaces with a single space. This function is useful for dealing with dynamic content that may contain irregular spacing.

Example: Finding a `<div>` where the normalized text is "Welcome User":

```
//div[normalize-space(text()) = 'Welcome User']
```

5. `not()`

The `not()` function negates a condition, allowing you to create XPath expressions that exclude elements based on specific criteria. This can be useful when adapting to dynamic content where certain elements need to be avoided.

Example: Finding a `<div>` that does not have the class "hidden":

```
//div[not(contains(@class, 'hidden'))]
```

Combining Functions for Dynamic Content

XPath functions can be combined to create more complex and adaptable expressions. This flexibility is valuable when dealing with dynamic content, allowing you to handle multiple conditions.

Example: Finding a `<div>` where the class contains "dynamic" and the text contains "Content":

```
//div[contains(@class, 'dynamic') and contains(text(), 'Content')]
```

Best Practices for Using XPath Functions

To effectively use XPath functions to adapt to dynamic content, consider these best practices:

- **Use Functions for Flexibility**: Functions like `contains()`, `starts-with()`, and `substring()` allow for adaptable XPath expressions.
- **Combine Multiple Functions**: Combining functions can create complex XPath expressions that adapt to various conditions.
- **Test and Validate XPath**: Regularly test your XPath expressions to ensure they work with dynamic content. Tools like SelectorsHub can help validate XPath in real-time.
- **Use Relative XPath**: Relative XPath is more flexible and less prone to breakage, making it ideal for dynamic content.
- **Combine with Attributes**: Adding attribute-based conditions can increase specificity and robustness.

Using XPath functions to adapt to dynamic content is a powerful approach for creating robust XPath expressions. Functions like `contains()`, `starts-with()`, and `normalize-space()` offer flexibility and adaptability, allowing you to handle changes in text, attributes, and structure. By following best practices and regularly testing your XPath expressions, you can create reliable and robust XPath-based automation scripts that effectively manage dynamic content.

Dealing with AJAX-based Changes

AJAX (Asynchronous JavaScript and XML) allows web pages to update content without reloading the entire page. While this technology enables dynamic and interactive user experiences, it presents challenges for XPath-based automation and testing. Handling AJAX-based changes requires strategies that ensure XPath expressions are robust and adaptable. This section explores effective methods for dealing with AJAX-based changes, providing tips and best practices to create reliable XPath expressions.

Understanding AJAX-based Changes

AJAX enables asynchronous updates, allowing web pages to modify content, add or remove elements, or change attributes without a full page reload. Common AJAX-based changes include:

- **Loading New Content**: Sections of a page may update dynamically as new data is fetched from the server.
- **Form Submission**: AJAX-based forms can submit data and update the page with validation results or additional content.
- **Interactive Elements**: User interactions with elements like buttons or dropdowns might trigger AJAX updates, leading to dynamic changes in the DOM.

Strategies for Handling AJAX-based Changes

To effectively deal with AJAX-based changes, you need to create flexible XPath expressions and use synchronization techniques to ensure reliable automation and testing. Here are some key strategies:

1. Use Relative XPath for Flexibility

Relative XPath is more adaptable to changing DOM structures, allowing you to navigate the page without relying on a fixed path from the document root. This flexibility is crucial for handling AJAX-based changes.

Example: Finding a button within a dynamically loaded section:

```
//div[@id='dynamic-content']//button[text()='Submit']
```

2. Employ Explicit Waits for Synchronization

Explicit waits are essential when dealing with AJAX-based changes. These waits allow you to pause automation scripts until specific conditions are met, ensuring elements are present and interactable.

Example: Using Selenium WebDriver to wait for an element to be clickable after an AJAX update:

```python
from selenium.webdriver.support.ui import WebDriverWait
from selenium.webdriver.support import expected_conditions as EC
from selenium.webdriver.common.by import By

WebDriverWait(driver, 10).until(EC.element_to_be_clickable((By.XPATH,
"//button[text()='Confirm']")))
```

3. Leverage XPath Functions for Adaptability

XPath functions like `contains()`, `starts-with()`, and `normalize-space()` allow you to create flexible XPath expressions that can adapt to dynamic content. These functions are helpful when dealing with changing text or attributes due to AJAX-based changes.

Example: Finding a `<div>` where the class contains "dynamic":

```
//div[contains(@class, 'dynamic')]
```

4. Combine Text with Attributes

Combining text-based XPath with attribute-based XPath increases specificity and robustness. This approach helps reduce ambiguity and improve reliability in dynamic environments.

Example: Finding a `<button>` with specific text and a unique class:

```
//button[text()='Submit' and @class='primary']
```

Best Practices for Dealing with AJAX-based Changes

To ensure robust XPath expressions for AJAX-based changes, consider these best practices:

- **Use Explicit Waits**: Explicit waits are crucial for ensuring elements are present before interacting with them.
- **Combine Text and Attributes**: This combination creates robust XPath expressions that can handle dynamic changes.
- **Use Flexible XPath Functions**: Functions like `contains()` and `starts-with()` allow for adaptable XPath expressions.
- **Test and Validate XPath**: Regular testing is essential to ensure XPath expressions work with AJAX-based changes. Tools like SelectorsHub can help validate XPath in real-time.
- **Document Your XPath**: Keeping a record of your XPath expressions helps with maintenance and troubleshooting.

Dealing with AJAX-based changes in XPath requires a flexible and adaptable approach. By using relative XPath, explicit waits, flexible XPath functions, and combining text with attributes, you can create robust XPath expressions that manage dynamic changes effectively. Following best practices and regular testing will help ensure your XPath expressions remain reliable in dynamic web environments, supporting robust automation and testing.

Best Practices for XPath with Dynamic Elements

Working with dynamic elements in XPath-based automation and testing presents unique challenges. These elements can change due to user interactions, AJAX updates, or JavaScript-driven events, affecting the stability of XPath expressions. To ensure reliable and robust automation, you must adopt best practices for handling dynamic elements with XPath. In this section, we'll outline key strategies and best practices to help you navigate these challenges effectively.

1. Use Relative XPath for Flexibility

Relative XPath allows you to navigate the DOM without relying on a rigid structure, making it more adaptable to changes. This approach reduces the risk of breakage when elements are added or removed.

Example: Finding a button within a specific section:

```
//div[@id='container']//button[text()='Confirm']
```

2. Employ Explicit Waits for Synchronization

Dynamic elements often require synchronization to ensure they are present and interactable before automation scripts proceed. Explicit waits allow you to wait for specific conditions, reducing the risk of race conditions.

Example: Using Selenium WebDriver to wait for a button to become clickable:

```python
from selenium.webdriver.support.ui import WebDriverWait
from selenium.webdriver.support import expected_conditions as EC
from selenium.webdriver.common.by import By
```

```
WebDriverWait(driver, 10).until(EC.element_to_be_clickable((By.XPATH,
"//button[text()='Confirm']")))
```

3. Use Flexible XPath Functions

XPath functions like `contains()`, `starts-with()`, and `substring()` provide flexibility, allowing you to create XPath expressions that adapt to dynamic content. These functions help manage variable text and changing attributes.

Example: Finding a `<div>` where the class contains "dynamic":

```
//div[contains(@class, 'dynamic')]
```

4. Combine Text and Attributes

Combining text-based XPath with attribute-based XPath creates more robust expressions. This approach can help reduce ambiguity and improve reliability in dynamic environments.

Example: Finding a `<button>` with specific text and a unique class:

```
//button[text()='Submit' and @class='primary']
```

5. Monitor DOM Changes

Monitoring changes in the DOM can help identify when dynamic elements are added or removed. Observing the DOM while interacting with a web page provides insights into dynamic behavior and informs XPath strategies.

Example: Using browser developer tools to inspect the DOM and observe dynamic changes.

6. Account for Timing Issues

Dynamic elements can introduce timing issues, leading to synchronization challenges. Ensure that your automation scripts account for these delays and use explicit waits to avoid race conditions.

7. Test and Validate XPath

Regular testing and validation are crucial to ensure XPath expressions work with dynamic elements. Tools like SelectorsHub or browser developer tools can help validate XPath in real-time.

8. Document Your XPath Expressions

Documenting your XPath expressions and their intended purposes helps with maintenance and troubleshooting, especially in complex automation frameworks or large-scale testing scenarios.

Dealing with dynamic elements in XPath-based automation requires a combination of flexibility, adaptability, and careful synchronization. By using relative XPath, explicit waits, flexible XPath functions, and combining text with attributes, you can create robust XPath expressions that manage dynamic changes effectively. Regular testing and validation are crucial to ensure your XPath expressions remain reliable. Following these best practices will help you create robust automation scripts and ensure successful testing in dynamic web environments.

Chapter Summary

This chapter focused on the unique challenges posed by dynamic elements in web automation and testing and provided strategies for addressing them with XPath. Dynamic elements, which can change due to user interactions, AJAX updates, or JavaScript events, require flexible and robust XPath expressions. Here is a summary of the key topics covered:

Understanding Dynamic Elements

- **Definition**: Dynamic elements are those that change after a web page has loaded, often due to AJAX updates, JavaScript events, or user interactions.
- **Challenges**: Identifying and handling dynamic elements can be complex, especially when attributes or text content change, or when elements are added or removed from the DOM.

Identifying Common Challenges with Dynamic Elements

- **Changing Attributes**: Attributes like `id`, `class`, and `name` might change dynamically, making XPath expressions unstable.
- **Dynamic Text Content**: Text within elements can change due to user interactions or AJAX updates, complicating XPath-based targeting.
- **Element Addition and Removal**: Elements might be added or removed from the DOM, impacting XPath expressions that rely on specific structures.
- **Timing Issues**: Dynamic elements often require synchronization to ensure they are present and interactable before interaction.

Strategies for Handling Dynamic Elements

- **Relative XPath**: This approach provides flexibility by avoiding reliance on fixed paths, allowing XPath expressions to adapt to changing structures.
- **XPath Functions for Flexibility**: Functions like `contains()`, `starts-with()`, and `substring()` can help create flexible XPath expressions that adapt to dynamic content.
- **Combining Multiple Attributes**: This approach increases robustness by using multiple criteria to locate elements, reducing ambiguity.
- **Explicit Waits**: Synchronization techniques, like explicit waits, ensure elements are ready before interaction, reducing timing-related issues.

Using XPath Functions to Adapt to Dynamic Content

- **Partial Matches with `contains()`**: This function allows for adaptable XPath expressions, useful for dynamic elements with varying attributes or text.
- **`starts-with()` for Consistent Prefixes**: Useful for handling dynamic content with consistent starting patterns.
- **Combining Functions**: Multiple XPath functions can be combined to create robust expressions that handle dynamic content.

Dealing with AJAX-based Changes

- **Explicit Waits for Synchronization**: Essential for ensuring elements are ready before interaction when dealing with AJAX-based updates.
- **Combining Text and Attributes**: This approach can increase robustness and reduce ambiguity in dynamic scenarios.
- **Monitoring DOM Changes**: Helps identify dynamic behavior and informs XPath strategies to handle changing structures.

Best Practices for XPath with Dynamic Elements

- **Flexible Strategies**: Using relative XPath, combining attributes, and leveraging XPath functions for adaptable expressions.
- **Testing and Validation**: Regularly test XPath expressions to ensure they work with dynamic elements. Use tools like SelectorsHub for real-time validation.
- **Documenting XPath Expressions**: Keeping a record of XPath expressions makes maintenance and troubleshooting easier.

Conclusion

Overall, this chapter provided comprehensive strategies for handling dynamic elements with XPath. By understanding the challenges posed by dynamic content and applying best practices, you can create robust and reliable XPath expressions for web automation and testing. The chapter concluded with an emphasis on the importance of flexibility, adaptability, and consistent testing to ensure XPath expressions remain effective in dynamic environments.

Section 3:
Navigating XPath Relationships

XPath for Parent-Child Structures

Outline

1. Understanding Parent-Child Relationships in XPath
2. Navigating the DOM with Parent-Child Relationships
3. Using Direct Child (/) and Descendant (//) Operators
4. Creating XPath Expressions with Parent-Child Relationships
5. Leveraging Parent-Child Structures for Complex XPath
6. Best Practices for Parent-Child XPath
7. Chapter Summary

Understanding Parent-Child Relationships in XPath

XPath (XML Path Language) is used to navigate and query XML and HTML documents, and one of its foundational concepts is parent-child relationships. Understanding these relationships is key to creating XPath expressions that accurately locate elements in the Document Object Model (DOM). This section explores what parent-child relationships are, why they matter, and how to navigate them with XPath.

What Are Parent-Child Relationships?

In XML and HTML documents, elements are structured in a hierarchical way, with each element having a parent element and potentially multiple child elements. A parent-child relationship exists when one element (the parent) directly contains another element (the child). This structure is fundamental to understanding the DOM and navigating it with XPath.

The Hierarchical Nature of the DOM

The DOM represents the structure of a web page or XML document as a tree. Each node in this tree represents an element, and nodes can have parent, child, and sibling relationships. Navigating the DOM with XPath involves understanding these relationships and creating expressions that traverse the tree to find specific elements.

Parent-Child Relationships in XPath

In XPath, parent-child relationships are used to navigate the DOM. The primary operators for working with these relationships are:

- **Direct Child Operator (/)**: Selects direct children of a given element. This operator requires a strict parent-child relationship, meaning it will only match elements that are immediate children.
- **Descendant Operator (//)**: Selects all descendants of a given element, regardless of depth. This operator allows you to traverse the DOM more flexibly, selecting elements at any level of depth.

Why Parent-Child Relationships Matter in XPath

Parent-child relationships are central to XPath for several reasons:

- **Precise Navigation**: By targeting direct children, you can create specific XPath expressions that avoid ambiguity and prevent unintended matches.
- **Flexible Traversal**: Using the descendant operator, you can navigate the DOM more freely, allowing XPath expressions to find elements across multiple levels of depth.
- **Hierarchical Context**: Parent-child relationships provide context within the DOM, helping XPath expressions focus on specific sections or regions.

Navigating Parent-Child Relationships with XPath

To navigate parent-child relationships with XPath, consider the following:

- **Using the Direct Child Operator (/)**: This operator is used when you want to select direct children, ensuring that the XPath expression stays within a specific level of the DOM.
- **Using the Descendant Operator (//)**: This operator is useful when you need to traverse the DOM more flexibly, allowing you to locate elements across multiple levels.

Example: Selecting all `<li>` elements that are direct children of a `<ul>`:

```
//ul/li
```

Example: Locating all `<span>` elements within a `<div>`, regardless of depth:

```
//div[@id='container']//span
```

Understanding parent-child relationships in XPath is fundamental to creating robust XPath expressions. By grasping the hierarchical nature of the DOM and using the appropriate operators, you can navigate the DOM with precision and flexibility. In the following sections, we'll explore more advanced techniques for working with parent-child relationships and discuss best practices for creating reliable XPath expressions that leverage these relationships.

Navigating the DOM with Parent-Child Relationships

Navigating the Document Object Model (DOM) using parent-child relationships is a crucial skill for creating effective XPath expressions. Understanding the structure of the DOM and the relationship between parent and child elements allows you to build XPath expressions that can precisely locate elements in XML or HTML documents. This section explores how to navigate the DOM with parent-child relationships and provides insights into the different approaches to achieve it.

What Are Parent-Child Relationships in the DOM?

In XML and HTML documents, elements are structured in a hierarchical manner, where a parent element contains one or more child elements. This hierarchy creates a tree-like structure, with each node in the tree representing an element in the document. Navigating the DOM with XPath involves understanding these parent-child relationships and using them to move through the structure.

Operators for Navigating Parent-Child Relationships

XPath provides two primary operators for navigating parent-child relationships in the DOM:

- **Direct Child Operator (/)**: This operator selects direct children of a given element. It is used when you need to navigate one level down the hierarchy, ensuring strict parent-child relationships.

- **Descendant Operator (//)**: This operator selects all descendants of a given element, regardless of depth. It allows you to traverse multiple levels of the hierarchy, making it more flexible but potentially less precise.

Navigating the DOM with Direct Child Relationships

When using the direct child operator (/), you are selecting elements that are immediate children of a given parent. This approach is useful for creating specific XPath expressions that avoid ambiguity and maintain a clear structure.

Example: Selecting all direct `<li>` children of a `<ul>`:

```
//ul/li
```

Example: Locating all direct `<div>` children within a parent `<div>` with a specific `id`:

```
//div[@id='container']/div
```

Navigating the DOM with Descendant Relationships

The descendant operator (//) allows for more flexible traversal of the DOM, as it selects all descendants of a given element, regardless of how many levels down they are. This approach is useful when you need to find elements that might be nested within deeper levels of the DOM.

Example: Finding all `<span>` elements within a `<div>`, regardless of depth:

```
//div[@id='content']//span
```

Example: Locating a specific `<button>` within a nested structure:

```
//div[@id='form']//button[text()='Submit']
```

Common Scenarios for Navigating Parent-Child Relationships

Navigating parent-child relationships with XPath is common in various scenarios, including:

- **Finding Direct Children**: When you need to select elements that are direct children of a specific parent, such as list items within a `<ul>`.
- **Navigating Nested Structures**: When you need to traverse deeper into the DOM to find elements at varying levels of depth.
- **Selecting Specific Sections**: When you want to focus on a specific section of the DOM and locate elements within it.

Navigating the DOM with parent-child relationships is a fundamental skill for creating XPath expressions. By understanding the direct child and descendant operators, you can build XPath expressions that precisely locate elements in a hierarchical structure. In the following sections, we'll explore more advanced techniques for creating XPath expressions using parent-child relationships and discuss best practices for maintaining reliable XPath-based automation scripts and tests.

Using Direct Child (/) and Descendant (//) Operators

XPath provides powerful operators to navigate the parent-child relationships in the Document Object Model (DOM). Among these operators, the direct child operator (/) and the descendant operator (//) are critical for creating XPath expressions. Understanding when to use each operator is essential for navigating the DOM efficiently and building robust XPath expressions. This section explores the differences between the direct child and descendant operators, offers examples of their use, and discusses best practices for using them.

The Direct Child Operator (/)

The direct child operator (/) is used to navigate a single level in the DOM, selecting elements that are immediate children of a given parent. This operator is useful when you want to create precise XPath expressions that avoid ambiguity and ensure a strict parent-child relationship.

Example: Selecting all `<li>` elements that are direct children of a `<ul>`:

```
//ul/li
```

Example: Finding all direct `<div>` children of a parent `<div>` with a specific id:

```
//div[@id='container']/div
```

When to Use the Direct Child Operator

The direct child operator is ideal when you need to maintain strict parent-child relationships, ensuring your XPath expressions don't traverse too deeply into the DOM. It is especially useful for:

- **Selecting Immediate Children**: When you want to locate elements that are direct children of a given parent.
- **Maintaining Specificity**: By using the direct child operator, you avoid unintentional matches with descendants or deeper elements.
- **Navigating Predictable Structures**: When the DOM structure is consistent, the direct child operator provides a reliable way to navigate it.

The Descendant Operator (//)

The descendant operator (//) selects all descendants of a given element, regardless of how many levels deep they are. This operator is more flexible than the direct child operator, allowing you to traverse the DOM at multiple levels.

Example: Locating all `<span>` elements within a `<div>`, regardless of depth:

```
//div[@id='content']//span
```

Example: Finding a specific `<button>` within a nested structure:

```
//div[@id='form']//button[text()='Submit']
```

When to Use the Descendant Operator

The descendant operator is ideal for more flexible XPath expressions that need to traverse multiple levels in the DOM. It is useful for:

- **Navigating Complex Structures**: When the DOM has deep or nested structures, the descendant operator allows you to navigate them easily.
- **Handling Unpredictable Structures**: If the DOM structure changes frequently, the descendant operator provides flexibility to adapt to these changes.
- **Creating Flexible XPath Expressions**: The descendant operator allows for broader XPath expressions that can select elements across various levels.

Best Practices for Using Direct Child and Descendant Operators

To use the direct child and descendant operators effectively, consider these best practices:

- **Use Direct Child for Specificity**: The direct child operator is ideal when you need to be precise and avoid ambiguity in XPath expressions.
- **Use Descendant for Flexibility**: The descendant operator allows you to traverse multiple levels, providing flexibility for XPath expressions.
- **Combine with Attributes**: Adding attribute-based conditions can increase specificity and robustness, especially when using the descendant operator.
- **Test and Validate XPath**: Regular testing ensures that your XPath expressions work as expected and are not selecting unintended elements.

The direct child operator (/) and the descendant operator (//) are fundamental tools for navigating the DOM with XPath. Understanding when to use each operator allows you to create robust and flexible XPath expressions. By following best practices and combining these operators with other XPath techniques, you can build reliable expressions that support effective automation, testing, and web development.

Creating XPath Expressions with Parent-Child Relationships

Creating XPath expressions with parent-child relationships is a fundamental skill in web automation and testing. These relationships allow you to navigate the Document Object Model (DOM) and locate elements based on their hierarchical connections. This section explores how to create XPath expressions that leverage parent-child relationships and provides examples to illustrate their practical application.

Understanding Parent-Child Relationships in XPath

Parent-child relationships refer to the structure of the DOM, where a parent element contains one or more child elements. XPath provides operators to navigate these relationships, allowing you to select elements based on their position within the hierarchy.

- **Direct Child Operator (/)**: Selects direct children of a given element. This operator is used when you want to maintain a strict parent-child relationship.
- **Descendant Operator (//)**: Selects all descendants of a given element, regardless of depth. This operator allows for more flexible navigation across multiple levels.

Creating XPath Expressions with Direct Child Relationships

To create XPath expressions with direct child relationships, use the / operator to navigate one level down in the DOM. This approach is useful for creating specific XPath expressions that avoid ambiguity.

Example: Selecting all <li> elements that are direct children of a <ul>:

```
//ul/li
```

Example: Finding direct <div> children within a parent <div> with a specific id:

```
//div[@id='container']/div
```

Creating XPath Expressions with Descendant Relationships

To create XPath expressions with descendant relationships, use the // operator to navigate across multiple levels. This approach is more flexible but may require additional conditions to avoid unintended matches.

Example: Locating all <span> elements within a <div>, regardless of depth:

```
//div[@id='content']//span
```

Example: Finding a specific <button> within a nested structure:

```
//div[@id='form']//button[text()='Submit']
```

Combining Parent-Child Relationships with Attributes

To increase specificity, consider combining parent-child relationships with attribute-based conditions. This approach reduces ambiguity and creates robust XPath expressions.

Example: Finding a specific <button> within a known section with a unique class:

```
//div[@id='controls']//button[contains(@class, 'primary') and text()='Submit']
```

Example: Locating a particular item within a table's rows based on text and index:

```
//table[@id='myTable']/tbody/tr/td[text()='Item 3']
```

Creating XPath expressions with parent-child relationships is key to navigating the DOM and locating elements in a structured way. By understanding the difference between direct child and descendant operators, you can create robust XPath expressions that meet your automation and testing needs. Combining parent-child relationships with attribute-based conditions and following best practices ensures your XPath expressions remain reliable and adaptable.

Leveraging Parent-Child Structures for Complex XPath

Leveraging parent-child structures for complex XPath expressions is essential for handling intricate or nested Document Object Model (DOM) structures. By using parent-child relationships effectively, you can create robust XPath expressions that traverse complex hierarchies to find specific elements. This section explores techniques for using parent-child structures to build complex XPath expressions and provides examples to illustrate their use.

Understanding Parent-Child Structures in the DOM

The DOM represents HTML or XML documents as a tree-like structure, where parent elements contain child elements. Navigating this hierarchy with XPath involves understanding the relationships between parents and children, allowing you to traverse the DOM to locate specific elements.

Using the Direct Child Operator for Precise Navigation

The direct child operator (/) selects immediate children of a given element. It is useful for building specific XPath expressions that maintain a strict parent-child relationship. This precision helps avoid ambiguity and prevents unintentional matches.

Example: Selecting all direct <li> children of a <ul>:

```
//ul/li
```

Example: Finding all direct <div> children of a parent <div> with a specific id:

```
//div[@id='container']/div
```

Using the Descendant Operator for Flexibility

The descendant operator (//) selects all descendants of a given element, regardless of depth. This operator is more flexible, allowing you to traverse the DOM across multiple levels. It is useful for navigating complex structures where elements might be nested.

Example: Locating all <span> elements within a specific section, regardless of depth:

```
//div[@id='content']//span
```

Example: Finding a specific <button> within a nested structure:

```
//div[@id='form']//button[text()='Submit']
```

Combining Parent-Child Structures with Attributes

Combining parent-child structures with attribute-based conditions creates more robust XPath expressions. This approach provides additional specificity and reduces ambiguity, especially in complex DOM structures.

Example: Finding a specific <button> within a known section, using class and text:

```
//div[@id='controls']//button[contains(@class, 'primary') and text()='Submit']
```

Example: Locating a specific item within a table's rows based on text and index:

```
//table[@id='myTable']/tbody/tr[3]/td[text()='Desired Item']
```

Using Parent-Child Structures for Deeply Nested XPath Expressions

Parent-child structures are useful for creating XPath expressions that navigate deep into the DOM. This approach is valuable when working with complex or nested hierarchies.

Example: Locating a specific <a> tag within a complex navigation structure:

```
//nav[@id='main-nav']//ul/li/ul/li/a[text()='Subsection']
```

Example: Finding a nested <div> with specific attributes and text:

```
//div[@id='outer']//div[@class='inner']//span[text()='Important Information']
```

Best Practices for Leveraging Parent-Child Structures

To create effective XPath expressions with parent-child structures, consider these best practices:

- **Use Direct Child for Specificity**: The direct child operator (/) is ideal when you need to navigate a specific level without ambiguity.
- **Use Descendant for Flexibility**: The descendant operator (//) provides flexibility for navigating across multiple levels, useful in complex or nested structures.
- **Combine with Attributes**: Adding attribute-based conditions increases specificity and reduces ambiguity, especially in complex XPath expressions.
- **Test and Validate XPath**: Regularly test and validate your XPath expressions to ensure they work as expected in different scenarios.

Leveraging parent-child structures for complex XPath expressions allows you to navigate intricate DOM hierarchies effectively. By using the direct child operator for precision and the descendant operator for flexibility, you can create XPath expressions that meet a variety of automation and testing needs. Combining parent-child structures with attribute-based conditions and following best practices ensures that your XPath expressions are robust and adaptable.

Best Practices for Parent-Child XPath

Creating XPath expressions with parent-child relationships is essential for navigating the Document Object Model (DOM) effectively. This approach allows you to traverse the hierarchical structure of the DOM, locating elements based on parent-child connections. However, to create robust and reliable XPath expressions, you need to follow best practices that ensure flexibility, accuracy, and adaptability. This section explores the best practices for using parent-child relationships in XPath, providing tips to create effective XPath expressions for web automation and testing.

1. Use the Direct Child Operator for Specificity

The direct child operator (/) is ideal for creating specific XPath expressions that maintain strict parent-child relationships. It helps avoid ambiguity and ensures you are selecting direct children of a given element.

Example: Selecting all `<li>` elements that are direct children of a `<ul>`:

```
//ul/li
```

2. Use the Descendant Operator for Flexibility

The descendant operator (//) is useful when you need to traverse the DOM across multiple levels. This operator is more flexible than the direct child operator, allowing XPath expressions to adapt to changing structures.

Example: Finding all `<span>` elements within a specific section, regardless of depth:

```
//div[@id='content']//span
```

3. Combine Parent-Child Relationships with Attributes

To increase specificity and robustness, combine parent-child relationships with attribute-based conditions. This approach reduces ambiguity and creates more reliable XPath expressions.

Example: Finding a specific `<button>` within a nested structure with a unique class and text:

```
//div[@id='form']//button[contains(@class, 'primary') and text()='Submit']
```

4. Leverage XPath Functions for Adaptability

XPath functions like `contains()`, `starts-with()`, and `substring()` offer flexibility when creating parent-child XPath expressions. These functions allow you to create adaptable expressions that can handle changing attributes or text content.

Example: Finding a `<div>` where the class contains "dynamic":

```
//div[contains(@class, 'dynamic')]
```

5. Avoid Over-Specification

While specificity is important, over-specification can lead to brittle XPath expressions that break if the DOM structure changes. Aim for a balance between specificity and flexibility to ensure your XPath expressions are robust.

6. Test and Validate XPath Regularly

Testing and validating your XPath expressions is crucial, especially when working with parent-child relationships. Use tools like SelectorsHub or browser developer tools to validate XPath in real-time. Regular testing ensures your XPath expressions work as expected and don't select unintended elements.

7. Document Your XPath Expressions

Documenting your XPath expressions, including their intended purpose and structure, makes it easier to maintain and troubleshoot them. This practice is especially useful when working with complex parent-child relationships.

Using parent-child relationships in XPath is a powerful technique for navigating the DOM. By following best practices like using the direct child operator for specificity, the descendant operator for flexibility, and combining parent-child relationships with attributes, you can create robust XPath expressions. Leveraging XPath functions for adaptability and avoiding over-specification further enhances the reliability of your XPath expressions. Regular testing and validation, along with proper documentation, ensure your XPath expressions remain effective and maintainable.

Chapter Summary

This chapter focused on navigating parent-child relationships in XPath. Parent-child structures are a fundamental concept in XPath, allowing you to navigate the Document Object Model (DOM) to locate specific elements based on their hierarchical relationships. This summary encapsulates the key points covered in the chapter:

Understanding Parent-Child Relationships in XPath

- **Definition**: Parent-child relationships refer to the hierarchical structure of the DOM, where parent elements contain child elements. XPath uses these relationships to navigate and query XML and HTML documents.
- **Operators**: The direct child operator (/) selects immediate children of a given element, while the descendant operator (//) selects all descendants, allowing for more flexible navigation.

Navigating the DOM with Parent-Child Relationships

- **Direct Child Navigation**: The direct child operator (/) is ideal for precise XPath expressions, ensuring strict parent-child relationships.
- **Descendant Navigation**: The descendant operator (//) allows for flexible XPath expressions, enabling traversal across multiple levels of the DOM.

Using Direct Child (/) and Descendant (//) Operators

- **When to Use Direct Child**: This operator is best when specificity is required, focusing on immediate children without traversing too deeply.
- **When to Use Descendant**: This operator is useful for broader navigation, especially when the DOM structure is complex or changes frequently.

Creating XPath Expressions with Parent-Child Relationships

- **Direct Child for Precision**: XPath expressions that use the direct child operator are more precise, avoiding ambiguity.
- **Descendant for Flexibility**: The descendant operator allows XPath expressions to adapt to changes in the DOM structure, useful for locating elements across multiple levels.
- **Combining with Attributes**: To increase specificity, you can combine parent-child structures with attribute-based conditions, creating robust XPath expressions.

- **Using Parent-Child Relationships in Complex XPath**: Complex XPath expressions can leverage parent-child structures to navigate deep into the DOM, useful for intricate or nested hierarchies.

Best Practices for Parent-Child XPath

- **Balance Specificity and Flexibility**: Use the direct child operator for precision and the descendant operator for flexibility, avoiding over-specification.
- **Leverage XPath Functions**: Functions like `contains()`, `starts-with()`, and `substring()` offer flexibility, allowing XPath expressions to adapt to changing content.
- **Test and Validate Regularly**: Regular testing ensures your XPath expressions work as expected and do not select unintended elements. Tools like SelectorsHub or browser developer tools can help validate XPath in real-time.
- **Document Your XPath Expressions**: Proper documentation makes it easier to maintain and troubleshoot XPath expressions, especially in complex parent-child structures.

Conclusion

Overall, this chapter provided comprehensive guidance on leveraging parent-child relationships in XPath. By understanding the difference between direct child and descendant operators and following best practices, you can create robust XPath expressions that navigate the DOM with precision and flexibility. Combining parent-child structures with attribute-based conditions, regular testing, and documentation ensures your XPath expressions are reliable and adaptable for a variety of automation and testing scenarios.

XPath for Ancestor-Descendant Relationships

Outline

1. Understanding Ancestor-Descendant Relationships
2. Navigating the DOM with Ancestor-Descendant Relationships
3. Using Ancestor-Descendant Relationships in XPath Expressions
4. Combining Ancestor-Descendant Relationships with Attributes
5. Leveraging Ancestor-Descendant Relationships for Complex XPath
6. Best Practices for Ancestor-Descendant XPath
7. Chapter Summary

Understanding Ancestor-Descendant Relationships

Ancestor-descendant relationships are central to navigating the Document Object Model (DOM) with XPath. This relationship describes the structure in which an ancestor element contains one or more descendant elements, regardless of the number of levels separating them. Understanding ancestor-descendant relationships is crucial for building robust XPath expressions that can traverse complex or nested hierarchies. In this section, we will explore the concept of ancestor-descendant relationships, explain how they differ from parent-child relationships, and discuss their significance in XPath.

What Are Ancestor-Descendant Relationships?

In XML or HTML documents, the DOM represents elements in a hierarchical structure, similar to a tree. An ancestor-descendant relationship exists when one element (the ancestor) contains other elements (the descendants), which can be children, grandchildren, or further down the hierarchy. This relationship is not limited to direct parent-child connections; it encompasses all levels of the hierarchy.

Ancestor-Descendant vs. Parent-Child Relationships

While both ancestor-descendant and parent-child relationships describe hierarchical structures, they differ in scope:

- **Parent-Child Relationships**: This refers to direct connections where an element is the immediate child of a parent. XPath uses the direct child operator (/) to navigate these relationships.
- **Ancestor-Descendant Relationships**: This encompasses all levels of the hierarchy, allowing for deeper navigation. XPath uses the descendant operator (//) to navigate these relationships.

Why Ancestor-Descendant Relationships Are Important in XPath

Ancestor-descendant relationships are essential in XPath for several reasons:

- **Flexibility**: The descendant operator (//) allows XPath expressions to traverse the DOM without needing to specify exact parent-child connections. This flexibility is useful for navigating complex or nested structures.
- **Adaptability**: XPath expressions that use ancestor-descendant relationships can adapt to changes in the DOM structure, making them more robust in dynamic environments.
- **Contextual Navigation**: Ancestor-descendant relationships provide a broader context, enabling XPath expressions to locate elements based on their position within a larger structure.

Common Scenarios for Ancestor-Descendant Relationships

Ancestor-descendant relationships are common in various scenarios, such as:

- **Complex Navigation Structures**: When you need to navigate deeply nested hierarchies to find specific elements.
- **Dynamic Content**: When elements can appear or change position due to AJAX or JavaScript events, ancestor-descendant relationships offer flexibility.
- **Finding Elements Across Multiple Levels**: When you need to select elements that are not direct children but are part of a broader structure.

Understanding ancestor-descendant relationships in XPath is crucial for creating flexible and robust XPath expressions. By leveraging the descendant operator, you can navigate the DOM across multiple levels, allowing for more adaptable XPath expressions. In the following sections, we'll explore how to create XPath expressions with ancestor-descendant relationships and discuss best practices to ensure your XPath expressions are effective and reliable in a variety of scenarios.

Navigating the DOM with Ancestor-Descendant Relationships

Navigating the Document Object Model (DOM) with ancestor-descendant relationships is a powerful technique in XPath. This approach allows you to traverse multiple levels within the DOM, finding elements regardless of their depth. Understanding how to navigate the DOM using ancestor-descendant relationships is crucial for building robust XPath expressions, especially when dealing with complex or dynamic structures. This section explores the key concepts and techniques for navigating the DOM with ancestor-descendant relationships, providing examples and best practices.

What Are Ancestor-Descendant Relationships in the DOM?

In HTML and XML documents, the DOM represents elements in a hierarchical tree structure. An ancestor-descendant relationship exists when an ancestor element contains one or more descendant elements, regardless of how many levels separate them. This structure enables XPath to navigate the DOM with flexibility.

The Descendant Operator (//)

The descendant operator (//) is used to navigate ancestor-descendant relationships in XPath. It selects all descendants of a given element, regardless of depth. This operator allows XPath expressions to traverse the DOM across multiple levels, offering flexibility when navigating complex or nested structures.

Using the Descendant Operator for Flexibility

The descendant operator is ideal when you need to navigate the DOM without specifying exact parent-child relationships. This flexibility is useful for finding elements in dynamic or unpredictable structures.

Example: Finding all `<span>` elements that are descendants of a `<div>`, regardless of depth:

```
//div[@id='content']//span
```

Example: Locating a specific `<button>` within a nested structure:

```
//div[@id='form']//button[text()='Submit']
```

Common Scenarios for Ancestor-Descendant Navigation

Ancestor-descendant relationships are common in various scenarios, providing flexibility and adaptability in XPath expressions:

- **Navigating Nested Structures**: When you need to traverse deep or complex hierarchies to locate specific elements.
- **Dynamic Content**: When elements can change position or structure due to AJAX or JavaScript events, the descendant operator offers flexibility.
- **Locating Elements Across Multiple Levels**: The descendant operator allows you to find elements without knowing their exact depth in the hierarchy.

Best Practices for Navigating the DOM with Ancestor-Descendant Relationships

To create effective XPath expressions with ancestor-descendant relationships, consider these best practices:

- **Use Descendant for Flexibility**: The descendant operator (//) allows you to navigate multiple levels, providing flexibility in complex or dynamic DOM structures.
- **Combine with Attributes**: To increase specificity and reduce ambiguity, combine ancestor-descendant navigation with attribute-based conditions.
- **Test and Validate Regularly**: Regular testing ensures your XPath expressions work as expected. Use tools like SelectorsHub or browser developer tools to validate XPath in real-time.

Navigating the DOM with ancestor-descendant relationships is a versatile approach in XPath. By using the descendant operator, you can create flexible XPath expressions that traverse multiple levels, making it easier to locate elements in complex or dynamic structures. Combining ancestor-descendant navigation with attribute-based conditions can increase specificity, leading to robust and reliable XPath expressions. Following best practices and regularly testing your XPath expressions will ensure they remain effective in a variety of automation and testing scenarios.

Using Ancestor-Descendant Relationships in XPath Expressions

Ancestor-descendant relationships in XPath provide a flexible and powerful way to navigate the Document Object Model (DOM). These relationships describe connections between elements where one element (the ancestor) contains one or more elements (the descendants), regardless of the number of levels separating them. This section explores how to create XPath expressions using ancestor-descendant relationships and offers practical examples and best practices to leverage this powerful feature.

The Descendant Operator (//)

The primary tool for creating XPath expressions with ancestor-descendant relationships is the descendant operator (//). This operator selects all descendants of a given element, regardless of depth. It is useful for navigating complex or deeply nested structures and allows for flexibility when traversing the DOM.

Example: Finding all `<span>` elements that are descendants of a specific `<div>`:

```
//div[@id='content']//span
```

Example: Locating a specific `<button>` within a nested structure:

```
//div[@id='controls']//button[text()='Confirm']
```

When to Use Ancestor-Descendant Relationships

Ancestor-descendant relationships are ideal for XPath expressions when you need to traverse the DOM across multiple levels or when the structure is dynamic or unpredictable. Here are some scenarios where ancestor-descendant relationships are beneficial:

- **Navigating Nested Structures**: When the DOM has deep or complex hierarchies, the descendant operator provides flexibility to traverse the structure.
- **Handling Dynamic Content**: If elements can move or change due to AJAX or JavaScript events, ancestor-descendant relationships offer a flexible way to adapt to these changes.
- **Creating Flexible XPath Expressions**: The descendant operator allows XPath expressions to navigate across multiple levels, providing flexibility in complex scenarios.

Best Practices for Using Ancestor-Descendant Relationships

To create robust XPath expressions using ancestor-descendant relationships, consider these best practices:

- **Use Ancestor-Descendant for Flexibility**: The descendant operator (//) provides flexibility for navigating complex or unpredictable structures.
- **Combine with Attributes**: Combining ancestor-descendant relationships with attribute-based conditions increases specificity and robustness, reducing ambiguity.
- **Avoid Over-Specification**: While specificity is important, avoid over-specification, which can make XPath expressions brittle.
- **Test and Validate Regularly**: Regular testing ensures your XPath expressions work as expected. Tools like SelectorsHub or browser developer tools can help validate XPath in real-time.
- **Document Your XPath Expressions**: Proper documentation of XPath expressions, including their structure and intended purpose, makes them easier to maintain and troubleshoot.

Ancestor-descendant relationships are a powerful tool in XPath, allowing for flexible navigation across multiple levels of the DOM. By using the descendant operator and combining it with attribute-based conditions, you can create robust and adaptable XPath expressions. Following best practices, avoiding over-specification, and regularly testing and validating your XPath expressions will ensure they remain effective in a variety of automation and testing scenarios.

Combining Ancestor-Descendant Relationships with Attributes

Combining ancestor-descendant relationships with attributes is a powerful technique in XPath that enhances the specificity and flexibility of your expressions. By leveraging the descendant operator (//) to navigate the Document Object Model (DOM) across multiple levels and adding attribute-based conditions, you can create robust XPath expressions that adapt to complex or dynamic structures. This section explores how to combine ancestor-descendant relationships with attributes and provides best practices to ensure reliable XPath expressions.

The Role of Attributes in XPath

Attributes in HTML or XML documents provide additional information about elements, such as id, class, name, and others. These attributes are useful for creating XPath expressions that target specific elements within the DOM. By combining ancestor-descendant relationships with attributes, you can increase the specificity of XPath expressions, reducing ambiguity and improving robustness.

Using the Descendant Operator (//) with Attributes

The descendant operator allows you to traverse the DOM across multiple levels, while attributes provide additional conditions to focus on specific elements. This combination is useful when you need to locate elements within complex or nested structures.

Example: Finding all <span> elements that are descendants of a <div> with a specific id, focusing on those with a particular class:

```
//div[@id='content']//span[@class='highlight']
```

Example: Locating a specific <button> within a nested structure, using text and attributes:

```
//div[@id='controls']//button[text()='Submit' and @class='primary']
```

Combining Ancestor-Descendant Relationships with Multiple Attributes

To increase specificity, consider combining ancestor-descendant relationships with multiple attribute-based conditions. This approach helps reduce ambiguity and creates more robust XPath expressions.

Example: Finding a specific <a> element within a nested navigation structure, using text and attributes:

```
//nav[@id='main-nav']//ul/li//a[text()='Home' and @class='nav-link']
```

Example: Locating an item within a table, using ancestor-descendant relationships and a combination of attributes and text:

```
//table[@id='myTable']//tr/td[text()='Desired Item' and @class='highlighted']
```

Handling Dynamic Structures with Ancestor-Descendant Relationships and Attributes

When dealing with dynamic or unpredictable DOM structures, combining ancestor-descendant relationships with attributes can provide flexibility and adaptability. This combination allows you to create XPath expressions that can adapt to changes in the DOM structure.

Example: Finding a nested <div> with a specific class and text content, allowing for flexibility:

```
//div[@id='outer']//div[contains(@class, 'inner')]//span[text()='Important
Information']
```

Best Practices for Combining Ancestor-Descendant Relationships with Attributes

To create effective XPath expressions with ancestor-descendant relationships and attributes, consider these best practices:

- **Use the Descendant Operator for Flexibility**: The descendant operator provides flexibility for navigating across multiple levels in the DOM.
- **Combine with Attributes for Specificity**: Adding attribute-based conditions increases specificity and robustness, reducing ambiguity.
- **Avoid Over-Specification**: While specificity is important, avoid over-specification, which can make XPath expressions brittle or prone to breaking if the DOM structure changes.
- **Test and Validate Regularly**: Regular testing and validation ensure your XPath expressions work as expected. Tools like SelectorsHub or browser developer tools can help validate XPath in real-time.
- **Document Your XPath Expressions**: Proper documentation of XPath expressions, including their intended purpose, makes them easier to maintain and troubleshoot.

Combining ancestor-descendant relationships with attributes in XPath is a powerful technique that provides both flexibility and specificity. By using the descendant operator to navigate across multiple levels and adding attribute-based conditions, you can create robust XPath expressions that adapt to complex or dynamic DOM structures. Following best practices, such as avoiding over-specification, testing regularly, and documenting your XPath expressions, will help ensure they remain reliable and effective for various automation and testing scenarios.

Leveraging Ancestor-Descendant Relationships for Complex XPath

Ancestor-descendant relationships are a powerful tool in XPath for navigating complex or deeply nested Document Object Model (DOM) structures. Leveraging these relationships allows you to create flexible XPath expressions that traverse multiple levels in the DOM, offering a more adaptable approach to locating elements. This section explores how to leverage ancestor-descendant relationships for complex XPath expressions and provides practical examples to illustrate their use.

Using the Descendant Operator for Complex XPath

The descendant operator (//) is the primary tool for leveraging ancestor-descendant relationships in complex XPath expressions. It allows you to traverse the DOM without specifying exact parent-child connections, providing flexibility when navigating nested or complex structures.

Example: Locating all <span> elements that are descendants of a specific <div>, regardless of depth:

```
//div[@id='content']//span
```

Example: Finding a specific <button> within a nested structure:

```
//div[@id='form']//button[text()='Submit']
```

Leveraging Ancestor-Descendant Relationships for Deeply Nested Structures

Ancestor-descendant relationships are particularly useful for creating XPath expressions that need to navigate deeply nested structures. This flexibility allows you to build XPath expressions that can traverse multiple levels, even when the structure is complex or dynamic.

Example: Finding a nested <div> with specific attributes and text content:

```
//div[@id='outer']//div[@class='inner']//span[text()='Important Information']
```

Example: Locating a specific <a> tag within a complex navigation structure, using ancestor-descendant relationships and text:

```
//nav[@id='main-nav']//ul/li//a[text()='Subsection']
```

Combining Ancestor-Descendant Relationships with Attributes

Combining ancestor-descendant relationships with attribute-based conditions increases specificity and reduces ambiguity in complex XPath expressions. This approach creates more robust XPath expressions, especially when dealing with deeply nested or unpredictable DOM structures.

Example: Finding a specific <a> element within a complex navigation structure, using text and attributes:

```
//nav[@id='main-nav']//ul/li//a[text()='Home' and @class='main-link']
```

Example: Locating an item within a table, using ancestor-descendant relationships and a combination of attributes and text:

```
//table[@id='myTable']//tr//td[text()='Desired Value' and
@class='highlighted']
```

Leveraging ancestor-descendant relationships for complex XPath allows for flexible and adaptable navigation across the DOM. By using the descendant operator and combining it with attribute-based conditions, you can create robust XPath expressions that handle complex or deeply nested structures. Following best practices, such as avoiding over-specification, testing regularly, and documenting your

XPath expressions, ensures your XPath expressions remain reliable and effective for a variety of automation and testing scenarios.

Best Practices for Ancestor-Descendant XPath

Ancestor-descendant relationships in XPath offer a flexible approach for navigating the Document Object Model (DOM), allowing you to traverse multiple levels within the hierarchical structure. While this flexibility is advantageous, it also requires careful consideration to avoid unintended matches, over-specification, or fragile XPath expressions. This section provides best practices for creating robust and reliable XPath expressions with ancestor-descendant relationships, helping you make the most of this versatile XPath feature.

1. Use the Descendant Operator for Flexibility

The descendant operator (//) allows you to navigate the DOM across multiple levels, providing flexibility in complex or nested structures. This operator is useful when you need to traverse deeply or when the DOM structure is dynamic or unpredictable.

Example: Finding all <span> elements that are descendants of a specific <div>, regardless of depth:

```
//div[@id='content']//span
```

2. Combine Ancestor-Descendant Relationships with Attributes

Combining ancestor-descendant relationships with attribute-based conditions increases specificity and reduces ambiguity. This approach is especially useful when the DOM structure has many similar elements, allowing you to create more targeted XPath expressions.

Example: Finding a specific <a> tag within a complex navigation structure, using text and attributes:

```
//nav[@id='main-nav']//ul/li//a[text()='Home' and @class='nav-link']
```

3. Avoid Over-Specification

While specificity is important, over-specification can lead to brittle XPath expressions that break if the DOM structure changes. Aim for a balance between specificity and flexibility, using attributes to increase robustness without over-constraining your XPath expressions.

Example: Avoiding over-specification by using a broader attribute condition:

```
//div[contains(@class, 'content')]//span
```

4. Test and Validate XPath Regularly

Regular testing and validation are essential for ensuring that your XPath expressions work as expected. Tools like SelectorsHub or browser developer tools can help validate XPath in real-time, allowing you to check if your expressions select the correct elements.

5. Consider Timing and Synchronization

When dealing with dynamic content, such as AJAX-based updates, ensure your XPath expressions account for timing and synchronization. Explicit waits in Selenium, for example, can help ensure that elements are present before interacting with them.

6. Document Your XPath Expressions

Proper documentation makes it easier to maintain and troubleshoot XPath expressions. Describe the purpose of the XPath expression and provide context for its structure. This practice is especially useful for complex XPath expressions that leverage ancestor-descendant relationships.

7. Use Relative XPath for Robustness

Relative XPath expressions are generally more robust than absolute XPath expressions. By focusing on relative paths, you can create XPath expressions that are less likely to break if the DOM structure changes.

Example: Using relative XPath to locate a specific `<button>` within a section:

```
//div[@id='controls']//button[text()='Submit']
```

Best practices for ancestor-descendant XPath focus on flexibility, specificity, and robustness. By using the descendant operator to navigate across multiple levels and combining ancestor-descendant relationships with attribute-based conditions, you can create robust XPath expressions. Avoiding over-specification, regularly testing and validating XPath, and documenting your expressions are key practices to ensure reliability. Following these best practices will help you create effective XPath expressions that handle a variety of automation and testing scenarios, especially when dealing with complex or dynamic DOM structures.

Chapter Summary

This chapter delved into the use of ancestor-descendant relationships in XPath, exploring how to navigate complex or deeply nested Document Object Model (DOM) structures. Ancestor-descendant relationships offer flexibility and adaptability, allowing XPath expressions to traverse multiple levels within the DOM. Here is a summary of the key topics covered in this chapter:

Understanding Ancestor-Descendant Relationships

- **Definition**: Ancestor-descendant relationships describe the structure in which one element (the ancestor) contains other elements (the descendants), regardless of how many levels separate them.
- **Operators**: The descendant operator (//) is used to navigate ancestor-descendant relationships, allowing XPath expressions to traverse the DOM across multiple levels.

Navigating the DOM with Ancestor-Descendant Relationships

- **Flexibility**: The descendant operator provides flexibility when navigating complex or unpredictable DOM structures. It allows XPath expressions to traverse multiple levels without requiring specific parent-child connections.
- **Common Scenarios**: Ancestor-descendant relationships are useful for navigating deeply nested structures, handling dynamic content, and creating flexible XPath expressions that adapt to changing DOM structures.

Using Ancestor-Descendant Relationships in XPath Expressions

- **Creating Flexible XPath Expressions**: The descendant operator is used to traverse the DOM, allowing XPath expressions to locate elements at various depths.
- **Combining with Attributes**: Combining ancestor-descendant relationships with attribute-based conditions increases specificity and reduces ambiguity, creating robust XPath expressions.
- **Examples**: Practical examples demonstrated how to create XPath expressions using ancestor-descendant relationships, with additional conditions for specificity and robustness.

Leveraging Ancestor-Descendant Relationships for Complex XPath

- **Handling Complex Structures**: Ancestor-descendant relationships are ideal for navigating complex or deeply nested structures. This flexibility allows you to create XPath expressions that adapt to changing DOM environments.
- **Creating Robust XPath Expressions**: By combining ancestor-descendant relationships with attributes and text-based conditions, you can create robust XPath expressions that are less likely to break due to DOM changes.

Best Practices for Ancestor-Descendant XPath

- **Use Descendant for Flexibility**: The descendant operator allows you to navigate across multiple levels, providing adaptability for complex structures.
- **Combine with Attributes for Specificity**: Adding attribute-based conditions increases specificity and reduces ambiguity.
- **Avoid Over-Specification**: While specificity is important, avoid over-specification, which can lead to brittle XPath expressions.
- **Test and Validate Regularly**: Regular testing and validation are crucial to ensure your XPath expressions work as expected.
- **Document Your XPath Expressions**: Proper documentation makes it easier to maintain and troubleshoot XPath expressions, especially in complex scenarios.

Conclusion

Overall, this chapter provided comprehensive guidance on using ancestor-descendant relationships in XPath. By leveraging the descendant operator for flexibility and combining it with attribute-based conditions, you can create robust XPath expressions that adapt to complex or deeply nested DOM structures. Following best practices, such as avoiding over-specification, testing regularly, and documenting your XPath expressions, helps ensure your XPath expressions remain reliable and effective in a variety of automation and testing scenarios. The chapter concluded by encouraging further exploration of advanced XPath techniques to build a deeper understanding of XPath's capabilities.

Using Preceding and Following Nodes with XPath

Outline

1. Understanding Preceding and Following Nodes in XPath
2. Locating Elements Using Preceding Nodes
3. Locating Elements Using Following Nodes
4. Common Use Cases for Preceding and Following XPath
5. Handling Dynamic Changes with Preceding and Following
6. Troubleshooting Common XPath Errors
7. Practical Examples and Exercises
8. Chapter Summary

Understanding Preceding and Following Nodes in XPath

XPath is a powerful language used to navigate through elements and attributes in an XML document, which in the context of Selenium, is often the Document Object Model (DOM) of a web page. Among the various XPath axes, "preceding" and "following" play a crucial role in identifying elements relative to a reference node. Here's a breakdown of what these terms mean and how they can be utilized in XPath:

What are Preceding and Following Nodes?

- **Preceding Nodes**: These are all the nodes in the document that appear before the current node, excluding its ancestors (parents, grandparents, etc.). The "preceding" axis encompasses all such nodes in a document that precede the context node in the source order.
- **Following Nodes**: These are all the nodes in the document that come after the current node, excluding its descendants (children, grandchildren, etc.). The "following" axis includes all nodes in a document that follow the context node in the source order.

Using Preceding and Following Axes in XPath

XPath allows you to navigate through the DOM and select elements based on their relationships with other elements. The following axes are useful for referencing nodes that are before or after a specific node:

- **preceding**: Selects all nodes in the document that come before the context node in the document order, excluding the node's ancestors.
- **preceding-sibling**: Selects all sibling nodes that come before the context node.
- **following**: Selects all nodes in the document that come after the context node in the document order, excluding the node's descendants.
- **following-sibling**: Selects all sibling nodes that come after the context node.

Examples

Here's an example of how you might use these axes to locate elements in a web page:

- **preceding-sibling example**: If you're on a node representing a list item (`<li>`) in a menu, and you want to find the previous list item, you could use:

  ```
  //li[@id='target-item']/preceding-sibling::li[1]
  ```

  This would find the immediate preceding sibling `<li>` before the `target-item`.

- **following example**: If you have a node representing a table row (`<tr>`) and want to find the next row, you could use:

```
//tr[@id='current-row']/following::tr[1]
```

This would locate the next row in the table that comes after the `current-row`.

Use Cases

Preceding and following nodes are useful in many scenarios, such as:

- Navigating through complex structures like tables and lists.
- Locating elements relative to known points in a page.
- Finding elements within a specific range or section of a page.

By understanding how to use these axes effectively, you can improve the robustness and flexibility of your XPath selectors, enabling more reliable web element location in Selenium and similar automation frameworks.

Locating Elements Using Preceding Nodes

In XPath, "preceding" refers to all the nodes that appear before a given context node, excluding any ancestors. This concept allows you to locate elements in a document by searching backward from a specific point. This approach is particularly useful when navigating complex or dynamic structures where the order of elements is important. Here's a deeper look into how to locate elements using preceding nodes in XPath.

Understanding Preceding Nodes

- **Definition**: The "preceding" axis includes all nodes in the document that appear before the current node, excluding the node's ancestors.
- **Scope**: This includes siblings, preceding siblings' descendants, and other elements earlier in the document.

Using Preceding Nodes in XPath

The "preceding" axis is used to locate elements that come before a specific node. This can be helpful in various scenarios where you need to find elements based on their position relative to another element.

- **Syntax**: The basic syntax for the "preceding" axis in XPath is:

```
preceding::node_type
```

Locating Specific Elements

Here are some common use cases for locating elements using the "preceding" axis:

1. **Finding Elements Before a Specific Node**: If you're on a particular node and want to find a specific type of element that comes before it, you can use the "preceding" axis. For example, to find the first preceding paragraph (`<p>`) before a given node, you could use:

```
//div[@id='target']/preceding::p[1]
```

2. **Identifying Previous Siblings**: To find all preceding siblings of a specific node, you can use the "preceding-sibling" axis. For example, to find the first preceding sibling before a list item, you could use:

```
//li[@id='item-3']/preceding-sibling::li[1]
```

Advanced Usage

Preceding nodes can also be used to create more complex queries. For instance, if you have a hierarchical structure like a nested list or table, you can find elements that precede a given node but meet additional criteria.

1. **Finding Specific Preceding Elements**: To locate a preceding element that matches a specific condition, you could use an attribute filter. For example, to find the preceding div with a specific class, you might use:

```
//div[@id='target']/preceding::div[@class='highlighted'][1]
```

2. **Handling Dynamic Content**: When dealing with dynamic content, preceding nodes are helpful in ensuring robust element location, especially when element order changes. Using a unique identifier as a reference point, you can find elements in relation to it.

Best Practices

- **Avoid Absolute XPath**: When using preceding nodes, try to avoid absolute XPath, as it might not be reliable in a dynamic environment.
- **Use Relative Reference Points**: Find stable reference points in the DOM and build XPath expressions relative to those points.
- **Test XPath Selectors**: Given the complexity of using preceding nodes, always test XPath selectors to ensure they work in different scenarios.

By mastering the "preceding" axis in XPath, you can navigate complex document structures with precision and flexibility, allowing for robust automation scripts in Selenium WebDriver or similar frameworks.

Locating Elements Using Following Nodes

In XPath, "following" refers to all the nodes in the document that come after a given context node, excluding its descendants. This concept is useful for finding elements relative to a known point by searching forward in the document structure. Let's explore how to use following nodes in XPath for element location.

Understanding Following Nodes

- **Definition**: The "following" axis includes all nodes in the document that appear after the current node, excluding its descendants.
- **Scope**: This axis encompasses sibling elements and other nodes further down in the document hierarchy.

Using Following Nodes in XPath

The "following" axis is used to locate elements that come after a specific point. This is useful in various scenarios, particularly when traversing structured data or finding elements in a specific order.

- **Syntax**: The basic syntax for the "following" axis in XPath is:

```
following::node_type
```

Locating Specific Elements

Here are common use cases for locating elements using the "following" axis:

1. **Finding Elements After a Specific Node**: To find an element or a set of elements that come after a particular node, you can use the "following" axis. For instance, to locate the first <p> element following a specific <div>, you might use:

    ```
    //div[@id='start']/following::p[1]
    ```

2. **Identifying Following Siblings**: To find sibling elements that come after a specific node, you can use the "following-sibling" axis. For example, to locate the first list item that follows a given list item, the XPath expression would be:

    ```
    //li[@id='first-item']/following-sibling::li[1]
    ```

Advanced Usage

Using the following nodes axis, you can create more complex XPath queries to handle various scenarios:

1. **Finding Specific Following Elements**: To locate a particular type of node that appears after a reference point but satisfies certain conditions, you can add filters to your XPath expression. For example, to find the following <div> with a specific class, you could use:

    ```
    //div[@id='start']/following::div[@class='highlighted'][1]
    ```

2. **Navigating Tables and Lists**: When working with structured data like tables or nested lists, the "following" axis can be valuable. To locate the next row in a table that meets specific criteria, you could use:

    ```
    //tr[@id='current-row']/following::tr[@class='data-row'][1]
    ```

Best Practices

- **Relative Paths over Absolute**: When using the "following" axis, rely on relative paths to increase resilience to DOM changes.
- **Identify Stable Reference Points**: Select nodes that are unlikely to change position or structure as your starting points.
- **Test and Validate XPath Expressions**: Due to the variability in the document structure, always test your XPath expressions to ensure they are robust in various scenarios.

By mastering the "following" axis in XPath, you gain greater flexibility in navigating complex document structures, allowing you to locate elements with precision. This knowledge is invaluable in Selenium WebDriver and other automation frameworks, helping ensure robust and maintainable test scripts.

Common Use Cases for Preceding and Following XPath

XPath is a flexible and powerful tool for navigating XML and HTML documents. The "preceding" and "following" axes allow you to locate elements relative to other known points in a document. This can be particularly useful in a variety of automation and data extraction scenarios. Let's explore some common use cases where the "preceding" and "following" axes in XPath are especially valuable.

1. Navigating Through Tables

Tables are a common structure in web documents, often used to display data in a grid format. The "preceding" and "following" axes can help navigate through tables to find specific rows or cells relative to a known position.

- **Example**: To find the row after a specific header row in a table, you can use:

  ```
  //tr[@id='header-row']/following::tr[1]
  ```

- **Example**: To locate a cell before a known cell, you might use:

  ```
  //td[@id='target-cell']/preceding::td[1]
  ```

2. Finding Related Siblings

In HTML structures with sibling relationships, such as list items or form fields, you can use the "preceding-sibling" and "following-sibling" axes to navigate between related elements.

- **Example**: To find the list item that comes immediately before another item:

  ```
  //li[@id='target-item']/preceding-sibling::li[1]
  ```

- **Example**: To locate a form field that comes after a specific label:

  ```
  //label[@for='username']/following-sibling::input[1]
  ```

3. Navigating Through Sections and Headings

In documents with multiple sections, you can use the "preceding" and "following" axes to navigate through headings and related content.

- **Example**: To find the section heading before a specific subheading, you could use:

  ```
  //h2[@id='subheading']/preceding::h1[1]
  ```

- **Example**: To locate the first paragraph after a specific heading:

  ```
  //h2[@id='section-heading']/following::p[1]
  ```

4. Working with Dynamic Content

In dynamic web applications, elements might change positions, making static XPath less reliable. The "preceding" and "following" axes can help locate elements even when the structure is dynamic.

- **Example**: To find a button that comes after a dynamically loaded section, you could use:

  ```
  //div[@id='dynamic-section']/following::button[1]
  ```

- **Example**: To locate the previous dynamic element from a given point:

  ```
  //div[@id='reference-point']/preceding::div[1]
  ```

5. Finding Contextual Elements

When you know the relative position of elements but not their exact IDs or classes, you can use the "preceding" and "following" axes to locate contextual elements.

- **Example**: To find a link that appears after a specific image:

  ```
  //img[@alt='example']/following::a[1]
  ```

- **Example**: To locate a specific type of element that appears before another known element:

  ```
  //div[@class='content']/preceding::span[1]
  ```

These are just a few examples of how the "preceding" and "following" axes can be used in XPath to navigate and locate elements in various contexts. By mastering these axes, you can create more robust and flexible XPath expressions for automation, testing, and data extraction.

Handling Dynamic Changes with Preceding and Following

When dealing with dynamic web content, element structures and orders may shift based on user interactions, AJAX updates, or other events. In such cases, using static locators can lead to unreliable results, as elements may no longer be in their expected positions. The "preceding" and "following" axes in XPath provide a flexible way to handle these dynamic changes by allowing you to locate elements relative to other stable elements. Here's how you can effectively use these axes to manage dynamic changes in a web environment.

Understanding the Challenges of Dynamic Content

Dynamic content can introduce various challenges for locating elements:

- **Changing Order**: Elements might move, be inserted, or removed, leading to shifting document structure.
- **Variable Content**: Elements with dynamic data may not have consistent attributes or IDs.
- **AJAX and JavaScript**: Asynchronous updates can change the document after the initial page load.

Using Preceding and Following to Maintain Robust XPath

To cope with dynamic changes, you can use the "preceding" and "following" axes to create relative XPath expressions. This approach allows you to anchor your XPath to stable elements and navigate to other elements as needed.

Preceding Nodes

The "preceding" axis can be used to find elements that occur before a reference point. This is useful for navigating backward from a known element or when the order of elements can change.

- **Finding Stable Reference Points**: Identify elements that are unlikely to change, such as unique headings, labels, or static sections, and use them as reference points.
- **Navigating Backward**: If you know an element's relative position to a stable point, use the "preceding" axis to find it. For example, to locate the previous sibling list item:

  ```
  //li[@id='reference-item']/preceding-sibling::li[1]
  ```

- **Combining with Filters**: Add conditions to the XPath expression to ensure the correct selection, such as specific attributes, text content, or positions.

Following Nodes

The "following" axis helps locate elements that occur after a given reference point. This is useful when navigating forward or finding elements in dynamic content where order might change.

- **Navigating Forward**: Use the "following" axis to find elements that come after a known point. For example, to find the next button after a specific section:

```
//div[@id='section']/following::button[1]
```

- **Handling Multiple Elements**: If the document structure has repetitive patterns, use indexing to select the desired element. For example, to get the second following paragraph after a given heading:

```
//h2[@id='section-heading']/following::p[2]
```

Strategies for Handling Dynamic Content

To ensure reliable XPath expressions in dynamic environments, consider these strategies:

- **Relative XPath**: Always use relative XPath expressions based on stable elements instead of absolute paths.
- **Fallback Mechanisms**: Create backup strategies in case the primary XPath expression fails, such as trying alternate paths.
- **Testing and Validation**: Regularly test XPath expressions across different scenarios to ensure they work with dynamic changes.
- **Resilient Locators**: Use robust locators, such as unique IDs or custom attributes, where possible.

By following these approaches and leveraging the "preceding" and "following" axes, you can create reliable XPath expressions that adapt to dynamic changes in web content, ensuring robust automation and testing scripts.

Troubleshooting Common XPath Errors

XPath is a versatile language for navigating XML and HTML structures. However, it can sometimes lead to errors due to various reasons like incorrect syntax, changing document structures, or misinterpretation of the DOM. This guide discusses common XPath errors and provides tips on how to troubleshoot and resolve them.

Common XPath Errors

1. Incorrect XPath Syntax

One of the most frequent errors with XPath is due to incorrect syntax, leading to invalid XPath expressions or unexpected results.

- **Symptoms**: Errors during XPath evaluation, null results, or selecting wrong elements.
- **Solutions**:
    - **Check for Typos**: Review your XPath expression for typos, especially in slashes (/), brackets ([ ]), or at-symbols (@).
    - **Use a Validator**: Use XPath validators or browser developer tools to test your XPath expression.
    - **Consistent Quotes**: Ensure consistent use of single (') or double (") quotes for attribute values.

2. Incorrect Use of XPath Axes

Misunderstanding how different axes work can lead to errors or unintended results.

- **Symptoms**: Selecting incorrect nodes, missing expected elements, or getting more results than intended.
- **Solutions**:
    - **Review Axis Usage**: Ensure you're using the correct axis (e.g., `preceding`, `following`, `ancestor`, etc.) for your use case.
    - **Understand Relationships**: Make sure you understand the document structure and relationships between nodes.
    - **Use Explicit Indices**: When dealing with multiple siblings or dynamic content, consider using explicit indices to ensure you get the correct element.

3. Absolute vs. Relative XPath

Absolute XPath expressions can become brittle, especially in dynamic content scenarios where the document structure may change.

- **Symptoms**: XPath expression breaks when the page layout changes, leading to errors or null results.
- **Solutions**:
    - **Use Relative XPath**: Prefer relative XPath expressions that start from known reference points rather than absolute paths.
    - **Identify Stable Anchors**: Choose stable elements as starting points for your relative XPath expressions.
    - **Avoid Deep XPath Chains**: If your XPath expression is too long or has too many intermediate nodes, it might be more prone to breaking.

4. Incorrect Attribute Selection

Selecting elements based on incorrect or ambiguous attributes can lead to XPath errors or unexpected results.

- **Symptoms**: Selecting the wrong element or getting multiple elements instead of one.
- **Solutions**:
    - **Check Attribute Names and Values**: Ensure you're using the correct attribute names and values in your XPath expressions.
    - **Use Unique Attributes**: Where possible, select elements with unique attributes like `id` or unique class names.
    - **Combine Conditions**: If needed, combine multiple conditions in your XPath expression to ensure you're selecting the correct element.

5. Incorrect Document Context

Misunderstanding the context of your XPath evaluation can lead to errors.

- **Symptoms**: XPath works in some cases but not others, or different outcomes in different environments.
- **Solutions**:
    - **Check Document Context**: Ensure you're evaluating XPath in the correct context, especially if the document structure is dynamic or uses frames/iframes.
    - **Handle Different Document Structures**: If your XPath needs to work across different structures, consider using flexible patterns or conditional checks.

Troubleshooting Tips

1. **Use Browser Developer Tools**: Most browsers offer developer tools to inspect elements and test XPath expressions. Use these tools to validate your XPath.
2. **Add Debugging Information**: When evaluating XPath in code, add debugging information to identify where the XPath fails or returns unexpected results.
3. **Check for Dynamic Changes**: If the document structure changes after a certain event, ensure your XPath can adapt to those changes.
4. **Experiment with Simple Expressions**: Start with simple XPath expressions and gradually build complexity to identify where errors might be occurring.

By following these troubleshooting techniques, you can identify and resolve common XPath errors, ensuring more reliable and robust XPath expressions for automation, testing, and data extraction.

Practical Examples and Exercises

To gain a deeper understanding of how to use XPath with the "preceding" and "following" axes, it's helpful to work through practical examples and exercises. This section provides a series of scenarios where these XPath axes are applicable, along with exercises to test your skills. The exercises are designed to be solved in an environment with access to an XML/HTML document and an XPath evaluator, such as a web browser's developer tools or an online XPath testing tool.

Example 1: Navigating a List

Consider an HTML structure representing a list of items, where each list item contains some text and additional elements like buttons.

```
<ul>
  <li id="item1">Item 1 <button class="edit">Edit</button></li>
  <li id="item2">Item 2 <button class="edit">Edit</button></li>
  <li id="item3">Item 3 <button class="edit">Edit</button></li>
  <li id="item4">Item 4 <button class="edit">Edit</button></li>
</ul>
```

Exercise 1: Find the list item immediately preceding "Item 3".

- **Expected XPath**:

    ```
    //li[text()="Item 3"]/preceding-sibling::li[1]
    ```

Exercise 2: Locate the button following the "Item 2" list item.

- **Expected XPath**:

    ```
    //li[text()="Item 2"]/following::button[1]
    ```

Example 2: Navigating a Table

Tables often contain a structured layout of rows and columns, with headers, data cells, and potentially other nested elements.

```
<table>
  <tr id="row1">
    <td>Row 1, Cell 1</td>
    <td>Row 1, Cell 2</td>
  </tr>
  <tr id="row2">
    <td>Row 2, Cell 1</td>
```

```
    <td>Row 2, Cell 2</td>
  </tr>
  <tr id="row3">
    <td>Row 3, Cell 1</td>
    <td>Row 3, Cell 2</td>
  </tr>
</table>
```

Exercise 3: Find the row that comes immediately after "Row 1".

- **Expected XPath**:

  ```
  //tr[@id="row1"]/following-sibling::tr[1]
  ```

Exercise 4: Locate the table cell that comes before "Row 2, Cell 2".

- **Expected XPath**:

  ```
  //tr[@id="row2"]/preceding::td[1]
  ```

Example 3: Navigating a Document with Sections

In a document with sections and headings, you can use XPath to find elements based on their relative position to known reference points.

```
<div id="section1">
  <h2>Section 1</h2>
  <p>This is the first section.</p>
</div>
<div id="section2">
  <h2>Section 2</h2>
  <p>This is the second section.</p>
</div>
<div id="section3">
  <h2>Section 3</h2>
  <p>This is the third section.</p>
</div>
```

Exercise 5: Find the paragraph following "Section 2".

- **Expected XPath**:

  ```
  //div[@id="section2"]/following::p[1]
  ```

Exercise 6: Locate the section heading that comes before "Section 3".

- **Expected XPath**:

  ```
  //div[@id="section3"]/preceding::h2[1]
  ```

These practical examples and exercises offer hands-on experience with XPath's "preceding" and "following" axes. By solving these exercises, you can strengthen your understanding of XPath and improve your ability to create robust XPath expressions for a variety of use cases.

Chapter Summary

In this chapter, we explored the concepts of "preceding" and "following" nodes in XPath and discussed how to use them to navigate XML and HTML documents. These axes allow you to locate elements based on their relative position to other known elements, providing flexibility in locating web elements for automation and testing scenarios.

Key Takeaways

- **Understanding Preceding and Following Nodes**: We defined the "preceding" axis as encompassing all nodes in the document that appear before the current node, excluding its ancestors. Similarly, the "following" axis includes all nodes that come after the current node, excluding its descendants.
- **Locating Elements with Preceding Nodes**: We discussed how to use the "preceding" and "preceding-sibling" axes to find elements before a given point. This approach is helpful in scenarios where you need to navigate backward from a known element.
- **Locating Elements with Following Nodes**: Similarly, we explored the "following" and "following-sibling" axes, which allow you to navigate forward from a given point. This technique is particularly useful when you want to locate elements in a specific order or when dealing with dynamic content.
- **Common Use Cases for Preceding and Following XPath**: We presented various use cases where these axes are beneficial, such as navigating tables, finding related siblings, and handling dynamic content. The examples demonstrated how these axes could be used to simplify complex XPath queries.
- **Handling Dynamic Changes with Preceding and Following**: This section provided strategies for dealing with dynamic web content, where the document structure can change due to user interactions or AJAX updates. By using stable reference points and relative XPath, we can create more robust locators to handle dynamic changes.
- **Troubleshooting Common XPath Errors**: We identified common errors that occur with XPath and offered troubleshooting techniques to resolve them. These included incorrect syntax, misuse of XPath axes, and absolute vs. relative XPath. We emphasized the importance of testing and validating XPath expressions to ensure reliability.
- **Practical Examples and Exercises**: To solidify the concepts covered in the chapter, we presented practical examples and exercises that used the "preceding" and "following" axes in various scenarios. These exercises provided hands-on experience in locating elements with XPath and helped reinforce the key concepts.

Conclusion

By mastering the use of "preceding" and "following" nodes in XPath, you can create more flexible and reliable XPath expressions for web automation, testing, and data extraction. This chapter equipped you with the knowledge and techniques to navigate complex document structures and handle dynamic changes effectively. As you continue to work with XPath, remember to apply the best practices discussed in this chapter to ensure robust and maintainable XPath expressions.

Comparing Absolute and Relative XPath

Outline

1. Understanding Absolute XPath
2. Understanding Relative XPath
3. Key Differences Between Absolute and Relative XPath
4. Examples of Absolute XPath
5. Examples of Relative XPath
6. Choosing the Right XPath Approach
7. Common Mistakes and How to Avoid Them
8. Real-World Applications of Absolute and Relative XPath
9. Chapter Summary

Understanding Absolute XPath

Absolute XPath is a specific way to locate elements on a web page by following a precise, unambiguous path from the root of the document to the desired element. This type of XPath is straightforward in its structure, providing a clear "roadmap" through the document's hierarchy. However, it comes with some limitations, mainly related to its rigidity.

What is Absolute XPath?

Absolute XPath begins with a single forward slash /, indicating the path starts from the root element of the document (typically <html>). It proceeds through the document structure using a series of node names, along with optional index numbers to specify which child node to select if there are multiple elements with the same tag name.

For example, consider the following HTML structure:

```
<html>
  <body>
    <div>
      <ul>
        <li>Item 1</li>
        <li>Item 2</li>
        <li>Item 3</li>
      </ul>
    </div>
  </body>
</html>
```

An absolute XPath to select the second <li> element might be:

```
/html/body/div/ul/li[2]
```

This path begins at the root (/html), then moves through the body (/body), then the first <div>, and the first <ul>, before selecting the second <li>. It is precise but also fragile—any change in the structure can break this path.

When to Use Absolute XPath

Absolute XPath is useful in a few specific cases:

- **Static Structure**: When you are sure the document's structure won't change, absolute XPath can provide reliable results.
- **Testing**: It can be useful in testing environments with fixed page structures, where changes are infrequent.
- **Quick Prototyping**: When building a prototype or simple automation script, absolute XPath can be a quick way to navigate the document.

Drawbacks of Absolute XPath

The rigid structure of absolute XPath can be its biggest drawback:

- **Prone to Breakage**: If the document structure changes, the XPath can become invalid.
- **Difficult to Maintain**: For larger projects or applications with frequent updates, maintaining absolute XPath can be cumbersome.
- **Limited Flexibility**: Absolute XPath relies on a specific path, limiting its ability to adapt to different situations or varying element structures.

Examples of Absolute XPath

Here are a few examples demonstrating how absolute XPath works:

- **Selecting a Specific Element**: To select a specific element with a known path, absolute XPath is ideal. For example:

```
/html/body/div/ul/li[3]
```

- **Navigating Nested Structures**: Absolute XPath can traverse nested elements easily. For example, to select the second `<div>` within the `<body>`:

```
/html/body/div[2]
```

- **Selecting Attributes**: Absolute XPath can also select specific attributes along the path. For example, to find an `<a>` tag with a specific `href` attribute:

```
/html/body/div/ul/li/a[@href='example.com']
```

Best Practices for Absolute XPath

Despite its limitations, there are a few best practices to make the most of absolute XPath:

- **Use for Stable Structures**: Apply absolute XPath in environments where the document structure is unlikely to change.
- **Avoid Excessive Nesting**: Absolute XPath can become cumbersome with deep nesting, making it harder to read and maintain.
- **Minimize Indexing**: Try to avoid using too many index numbers, as it can increase the risk of breakage if the order of elements changes.

Absolute XPath has its place in automation and web scraping, especially when a stable and precise path is required. However, it's essential to balance its use with other, more flexible approaches like relative XPath to ensure robustness and maintainability in dynamic environments.

Understanding Relative XPath

Relative XPath is a more flexible and adaptable way to locate elements on a web page compared to absolute XPath. Instead of following a rigid path from the root to the desired element, relative XPath allows you to search for elements based on various attributes, relationships, or other contextual information. This flexibility makes it a preferred choice in dynamic or complex web structures where the document's hierarchy may change over time.

What is Relative XPath?

Relative XPath starts with a double slash //, indicating that the path can start from anywhere in the document, not just the root. This approach allows you to find elements without needing to traverse a specific path, making it versatile for locating elements in different contexts.

For example, consider the following HTML structure:

```html
<html>
  <body>
    <div class="content">
      <p>This is a paragraph.</p>
      <p>Another paragraph.</p>
      <div class="footer">
        <p>Footer content.</p>
      </div>
    </div>
  </body>
</html>
```

To select the first paragraph within the <div class="content">, you could use:

```
//div[@class='content']/p[1]
```

This XPath finds any <div> with a class of "content" and then selects the first paragraph within it. This relative approach is more robust than absolute XPath because it is not tied to a specific hierarchical path from the root.

Advantages of Relative XPath

Relative XPath offers several benefits:

- **Flexibility**: It can find elements based on attributes, text content, relationships, or other contextual clues, making it adaptable to changes in the document structure.
- **Resilience to Changes**: Relative XPath is less likely to break if the web page structure changes, as it does not rely on a specific path from the root.
- **Conciseness**: Because it does not need to traverse the entire document hierarchy, relative XPath can be more concise and easier to read.

Common Uses of Relative XPath

Relative XPath can be used in a variety of scenarios:

- **Attribute-Based Selection**: You can select elements based on specific attributes like id, class, name, or custom attributes. For example, to select an element with an id of "header":

  ```
  //*[contains(@id, 'header')]
  ```

- **Text-Based Selection**: You can locate elements based on text content. For example, to find a paragraph containing the text "Welcome":

  ```
  //p[contains(text(), 'Welcome')]
  ```

- **Hierarchical Relationships**: Relative XPath allows you to navigate parent-child and ancestor-descendant relationships. For example, to find a `<span>` within any `<div>` with a specific class:

```
//div[@class='main']//span
```

Best Practices for Relative XPath

To get the most out of relative XPath, consider these best practices:

- **Use Attributes for Clarity**: When possible, select elements using unique attributes to avoid ambiguity. This makes the XPath more robust and easier to maintain.
- **Minimize Complex Relationships**: While relative XPath can navigate complex relationships, too much reliance on parent-child or ancestor-descendant relationships can reduce readability.
- **Use Functions for Precision**: XPath functions like `contains()`, `starts-with()`, and `text()` can help improve the precision of relative XPath without relying on rigid paths.
- **Test for Robustness**: Test your relative XPath expressions in different scenarios to ensure they remain valid even if the web page structure changes slightly.

Examples of Relative XPath

Here are a few examples to illustrate the versatility of relative XPath:

- **Selecting Elements by Attribute**: To find all `<a>` tags with a specific class:

```
//a[@class='nav-link']
```

- **Selecting Based on Text Content**: To find an element containing specific text:

```
//h1[text()='Welcome to the Website']
```

- **Navigating Parent-Child Relationships**: To find a specific child element within a parent:

```
//div[@class='main']//p
```

- **Selecting Elements with Multiple Attributes**: To find elements with multiple attribute criteria:

```
//input[@type='text' and @name='username']
```

Relative XPath offers flexibility and adaptability, making it a preferred choice in many web automation and scraping scenarios. It is resilient to structural changes and provides a concise, efficient way to locate elements based on various attributes and relationships. By following best practices and understanding its key applications, you can leverage relative XPath to build robust automation scripts and web scraping tools.

Key Differences Between Absolute and Relative XPath

Absolute and relative XPath are both crucial tools for navigating and locating elements in XML and HTML documents. However, they differ significantly in terms of structure, flexibility, and use cases. Understanding these differences is key to selecting the most appropriate XPath approach for your automation or web scraping needs.

Definition and Structure

- **Absolute XPath**: This type of XPath follows a specific, unchanging path from the root to the desired element. It starts with a single forward slash /, indicating it begins at the root element. The path explicitly lists each node along the way, including index numbers if necessary, to pinpoint the exact element. The structure is linear and strict.
- **Relative XPath**: This XPath type allows you to find elements from anywhere in the document. It starts with a double forward slash //, indicating it does not need to follow a specific path from the root. Relative XPath can locate elements based on various attributes, text content, or hierarchical relationships, providing greater flexibility.

Flexibility and Adaptability

- **Absolute XPath**: Due to its rigid structure, absolute XPath is less flexible. It relies on a fixed path, making it prone to breakage if the document structure changes. This characteristic makes it less suitable for dynamic or frequently updated web pages.
- **Relative XPath**: This type is more adaptable because it does not depend on a specific root-based path. It allows you to locate elements in various ways, including attribute-based selection, text-based selection, and hierarchical relationships. This flexibility makes it ideal for dynamic environments.

Use Cases

- **Absolute XPath**: Best suited for scenarios where the document structure is stable and unlikely to change. Common use cases include:
  - Testing environments with fixed web page structures.
  - Prototyping or simple scripts where precision is key.
  - Applications where exact paths are necessary.
- **Relative XPath**: Recommended for situations requiring flexibility and adaptability. Common use cases include:
  - Dynamic web pages with changing structures.
  - Applications with complex or nested element hierarchies.
  - Automation frameworks where robustness is crucial.

Performance and Maintainability

- **Absolute XPath**: Performance can be impacted due to its strict path-based structure, especially in large documents. Maintainability is challenging because changes in the document structure can render the XPath invalid, requiring frequent updates.
- **Relative XPath**: Generally offers better performance because it doesn't need to traverse a specific path from the root. Its flexibility also contributes to easier maintainability, as it's less likely to break when the document structure changes. However, excessive reliance on complex relationships can impact performance.

Examples
- **Absolute XPath**: An example of absolute XPath, following a precise path from the root, is:

```
/html/body/div[1]/p[2]
```

- **Relative XPath**: An example of relative XPath, finding an element based on attributes or relationships, is:

```
//div[@class='content']//p
```

In summary, the key differences between absolute and relative XPath are flexibility, adaptability, use cases, performance, and maintainability. Absolute XPath is more rigid and best for stable structures, while relative XPath is more flexible and suitable for dynamic environments. When choosing between the two, consider the document's complexity, stability, and the need for adaptability. By understanding these differences, you can select the right XPath approach to suit your automation or web scraping needs.

Examples of Absolute XPath

Absolute XPath is a precise way to navigate through an HTML or XML document. It starts from the root and follows a specific path, listing each node explicitly until reaching the desired element. Because it is based on a fixed structure, it's ideal for cases where you know the exact layout and want precise targeting. However, its rigidity makes it prone to breakage if the document structure changes.

Here are some examples of absolute XPath, demonstrating how it's used in various scenarios to locate elements.

Example 1: Basic HTML Structure

Consider this basic HTML structure:

```
<html>
  <head>
    <title>Example Page</title>
  </head>
  <body>
    <h1>Welcome</h1>
    <p>First paragraph.</p>
    <p>Second paragraph.</p>
  </body>
</html>
```

To select the first paragraph (`<p>First paragraph.</p>`), you would use absolute XPath:

```
/html/body/p[1]
```

This path starts from the root (`/html`), moves to the `<body>`, and selects the first `<p>` tag. Because it's absolute, any change in the document structure can break this XPath.

Example 2: Nested Elements

Here's a slightly more complex HTML structure with nested elements:

```
<html>
  <body>
    <div class="container">
      <h2>Section Header</h2>
      <div class="content">
        <p>This is a paragraph in the content div.</p>
      </div>
    </div>
  </body>
</html>
```

To locate the paragraph within the `<div class="content">`, the absolute XPath would be:

```
/html/body/div[1]/div[2]/p
```

This path starts from the root, moves through the first and second `<div>` tags, and selects the `<p>` tag within the second `<div>`. Again, if any of these elements change position, the XPath will break.

Example 3: Using Index Numbers

When there are multiple similar elements, you can use index numbers to select a specific instance. Here's an example HTML structure:

```html
<html>
  <body>
    <ul>
      <li>Item 1</li>
      <li>Item 2</li>
      <li>Item 3</li>
    </ul>
  </body>
</html>
```

To select the third list item (`<li>Item 3</li>`), you'd use:

```
/html/body/ul/li[3]
```

The index [3] specifies which item to select, but if the list order changes, this absolute XPath becomes invalid.

Example 4: Navigating Through Attributes

Although absolute XPath primarily follows a fixed path, you can still use attributes to identify elements along the way. Here's an example with attributes:

```html
<html>
  <body>
    <div id="main">
      <a href="home">Home</a>
      <a href="about">About Us</a>
    </div>
  </body>
</html>
```

To select the "About Us" link, you could use:

```
/html/body/div[@id='main']/a[2]
```

This absolute XPath selects the `<div>` with the id of "main" and then the second `<a>` tag within it. Although it uses an attribute, it's still rigid because it follows a specific path.

Absolute XPath is a useful tool when you need precise targeting in a stable document structure. However, its rigidity makes it less adaptable to changes, which is why it is often used in specific scenarios where the structure is unlikely to change. The examples provided demonstrate its use in simple and complex structures, with and without attributes, and using index numbers for specific element targeting.

Examples of Relative XPath

Relative XPath offers a flexible and adaptable way to locate elements in XML and HTML documents. Unlike absolute XPath, which starts from the root and follows a rigid path, relative XPath can start from anywhere in the document and use various strategies to find elements based on attributes, text content, or hierarchical relationships. This flexibility makes it suitable for dynamic web environments and complex document structures.

Here are some examples of relative XPath to demonstrate its use in different scenarios.

Example 1: Selecting Elements by Attribute

Consider the following HTML structure:

```html
<html>
  <body>
    <div class="header">
      <h1>Welcome to My Website</h1>
    </div>
    <div class="content">
      <p>This is the first paragraph.</p>
      <p>This is the second paragraph.</p>
    </div>
  </body>
</html>
```

To select the <h1> tag within the "header" class, you can use relative XPath:

```
//div[@class='header']/h1
```

This path starts anywhere in the document (//) and finds the <div> with the "header" class, then selects the <h1> tag within it. It doesn't depend on a specific path from the root, making it more robust against structural changes.

Example 2: Selecting Elements by Text Content

In the same HTML structure, to select a paragraph that contains specific text, you can use a text-based relative XPath:

```
//p[contains(text(), 'first paragraph')]
```

This XPath finds any <p> tag containing the text "first paragraph." It's a flexible way to locate elements based on their content without relying on a fixed path.

Example 3: Navigating Parent-Child Relationships

In a structure with nested elements, relative XPath can navigate through parent-child relationships. Consider this example:

```html
<html>
  <body>
    <div class="main">
      <div class="nested">
        <span>Nested span content.</span>
      </div>
    </div>
  </body>
</html>
```

To locate the <span> within the "nested" class, you could use relative XPath:

```
//div[@class='main']/div[@class='nested']/span
```

This XPath selects the <span> within a specific nested structure without needing to follow a rigid path from the root.

Example 4: Using Functions to Enhance Flexibility

Relative XPath can use functions to add flexibility to element selection. Here are a couple of examples:

- **Using `contains()` to Find Attributes**: To find an <a> tag with an "href" attribute containing "about":

```
//a[contains(@href, 'about')]
```

- **Using `starts-with()` for Prefix Matching**: To find an <input> field where the id starts with "user":

```
//input[starts-with(@id, 'user')]
```

These functions allow relative XPath to locate elements with specific attribute patterns, providing more flexibility than a fixed path.

Example 5: Selecting Multiple Elements

Relative XPath can also be used to select multiple elements at once. Consider this HTML structure:

```
<html>
  <body>
    <ul>
      <li>Item 1</li>
      <li>Item 2</li>
      <li>Item 3</li>
    </ul>
  </body>
</html>
```

To select all <li> elements within the <ul>, you could use relative XPath:

```
//ul/li
```

This XPath finds all <li> tags within the <ul>, regardless of their position or order.

Relative XPath offers flexibility and adaptability, allowing you to locate elements based on attributes, text content, and relationships. It is less prone to breakage than absolute XPath, making it ideal for dynamic web environments. The examples provided demonstrate its versatility in various scenarios, from attribute-based selection to navigating complex relationships and using functions for enhanced flexibility.

Choosing the Right XPath Approach

XPath is a powerful tool for navigating and locating elements in XML and HTML documents, widely used in web automation, scraping, and testing. When choosing the right XPath approach, you must consider several factors, including the structure of the web page, the frequency of updates, and the specific use case. The primary approaches are absolute XPath and relative XPath, each with its benefits and drawbacks. Let's explore how to choose the right XPath approach for your scenario.

Absolute XPath

Absolute XPath provides a precise path from the root to the desired element. It is reliable in stable environments but lacks flexibility, making it susceptible to breakage if the web page structure changes. Here's when you might consider absolute XPath:

- **Stable Structures**: If the document structure is stable and unlikely to change, absolute XPath can provide an exact and reliable path to your elements.
- **Precise Targeting**: In cases where you need exact precision, such as when automating fixed workflows, absolute XPath is ideal.
- **Simple Scripts**: For quick prototypes or simple scripts where the structure is consistent, absolute XPath can be easier to understand and implement.

Use cases: Absolute XPath is often used in static testing environments, prototyping, and situations requiring precise, fixed targeting.

Pros:

- Predictable and unambiguous.
- Ideal for stable document structures.
- Good for targeting specific elements.

Cons:

- Prone to breakage if the document structure changes.
- Less flexible and adaptable.
- Can become lengthy and complex with deep nesting.

Relative XPath

Relative XPath starts from anywhere in the document and allows flexible element location. It is more adaptable, making it suitable for dynamic or complex environments. Consider relative XPath in the following scenarios:

- **Dynamic Structures**: If the web page structure is subject to change, relative XPath is more resilient, as it doesn't rely on a fixed path.
- **Complex Hierarchies**: Relative XPath can navigate complex relationships, making it ideal for nested elements or dynamic content.
- **Attribute-Based Selection**: When locating elements based on attributes, text, or relationships, relative XPath offers greater flexibility.

Use cases: Relative XPath is widely used in dynamic web environments, complex structures, and automation frameworks like Selenium WebDriver, where flexibility and adaptability are crucial.

Pros:

- More flexible and adaptable.
- Resilient to structural changes.
- Ideal for dynamic or complex environments.
- Allows attribute-based and text-based selection.

Cons:

- Can lead to ambiguity if not used carefully.
- Might require additional testing to ensure robustness.
- Performance may vary based on complexity and document size.

Choosing the Right Approach

To choose the right XPath approach, consider the following factors:

1. **Document Stability**: If the document structure is stable, absolute XPath can be a good choice. If it is dynamic or subject to change, relative XPath is better.

2. **Precision and Flexibility**: If precision is paramount, absolute XPath provides a clear path. If you need flexibility and adaptability, relative XPath is more suitable.
3. **Maintenance and Scalability**: Absolute XPath can be difficult to maintain in changing environments. If scalability and ease of maintenance are important, relative XPath is preferable.
4. **Complexity and Performance**: Absolute XPath can become complex with deep nesting. If performance is a concern, relative XPath's flexibility might offer a better balance, but consider performance testing to avoid slowdowns.

Best Practices

Regardless of the XPath approach you choose, follow these best practices:

- **Use Attributes for Clarity**: Attribute-based XPath is generally more robust and less prone to ambiguity.
- **Avoid Excessive Nesting**: Deeply nested absolute XPath can be cumbersome. For relative XPath, excessive parent-child relationships can affect performance.
- **Test and Validate**: Test your XPath expressions to ensure they are robust against changes and work across different scenarios.
- **Balance Flexibility and Precision**: Find the right balance between flexibility and precision to ensure your XPath expressions are both robust and efficient.

Choosing the right XPath approach involves understanding your specific needs and the environment in which you're working. Absolute XPath is best for stable structures with fixed targeting, while relative XPath offers flexibility and adaptability for dynamic environments. By considering factors like document stability, precision, flexibility, and maintainability, you can select the approach that best suits your use case.

Common Mistakes and How to Avoid Them

XPath is a powerful tool for navigating and selecting elements in XML and HTML documents, but it can also be complex, leading to common mistakes. These mistakes can impact the reliability, performance, and maintainability of automation scripts and web scraping tasks. This guide covers typical errors made when using XPath and provides tips on how to avoid them.

Mistake 1: Using Absolute XPath in Dynamic Environments

Problem: Absolute XPath follows a specific path from the root, making it susceptible to breakage if the document structure changes. In dynamic environments where elements move or change frequently, this can lead to brittle scripts.

Solution: Use relative XPath when working with dynamic or changing web structures. Relative XPath is more adaptable, allowing you to locate elements without depending on a fixed path.

Mistake 2: Relying Too Heavily on Indexes

Problem: Index-based XPath expressions can be fragile, especially when used in lists or repeating structures. If the order of elements changes, the XPath may no longer point to the correct item.

Solution: Favor attribute-based selection instead of index-based. Use attributes like id, class, name, or other unique identifiers to locate elements. If indexes must be used, ensure they're based on consistent patterns.

Mistake 3: Overusing Nested Relationships

Problem: Deeply nested XPath expressions can be challenging to read and maintain, leading to complexity and increased risk of errors. Overusing parent-child relationships can also impact performance.

Solution: Keep XPath expressions as simple and direct as possible. If you need to navigate complex hierarchies, consider using relative XPath with specific attributes to reduce the nesting depth.

Mistake 4: Inadequate Testing and Validation

Problem: XPath expressions might work in one environment but fail in others due to variations in document structure or browser behavior. Inadequate testing can lead to unreliable scripts.

Solution: Test XPath expressions in different scenarios to ensure robustness. Use tools like browser developer consoles, XPath testers, and automation frameworks to validate your XPath across various conditions.

Mistake 5: Ambiguity in XPath Expressions

Problem: Ambiguous XPath expressions can lead to unexpected results, especially when elements have similar characteristics. This can cause automation scripts to select the wrong elements.

Solution: Use specific attributes to reduce ambiguity. If there's a chance of multiple matches, ensure the XPath expression is precise enough to identify the correct element. Functions like `contains()`, `starts-with()`, and `text()` can help improve specificity.

Mistake 6: Ignoring Performance Considerations

Problem: Complex XPath expressions with deep nesting or excessive relationships can impact performance, leading to slowdowns in automation scripts or web scraping tasks.

Solution: Optimize XPath expressions by simplifying structure, reducing nesting, and avoiding unnecessary relationships. Test for performance impacts, especially in large or complex documents.

Mistake 7: Not Handling Dynamic Content

Problem: Some web pages use AJAX or other dynamic content techniques, leading to elements appearing after the initial page load. If XPath expressions don't account for this, automation scripts can fail to find elements.

Solution: Implement waits in your automation scripts to handle dynamic content. Use explicit waits with conditions that check for the presence of elements before attempting to interact with them. Functions like `normalize-space()` can help manage content that changes dynamically.

Avoiding common XPath mistakes requires a combination of best practices, thorough testing, and careful consideration of the document structure. By using relative XPath for dynamic environments, favoring attribute-based selection, minimizing complex nesting, and testing for robustness and performance, you can ensure your XPath expressions are reliable and efficient. With these strategies, you can reduce the risk of errors and improve the stability of your automation and web scraping tasks.

Real-World Applications of Absolute and Relative XPath

XPath is a fundamental technology used in web scraping, automation testing, data extraction, and more. In practice, both absolute and relative XPath can be employed for various purposes, depending on the structure of the document and the context of use. This guide discusses real-world applications of both absolute and relative XPath and how they fit into common automation and data extraction scenarios.

Absolute XPath Applications

Absolute XPath is typically used in scenarios where the document structure is stable and exact precision is required. Although it's less flexible, its reliability in fixed environments makes it valuable for certain use cases.

- **Web Automation Testing**: Absolute XPath is often used in automated testing scenarios where the structure of the web page is consistent. For example, in a test script that verifies the presence of specific UI elements, absolute XPath can ensure precision by following a defined path. This is common in end-to-end testing frameworks like Selenium, where elements are located based on a specific path.
- **Data Extraction from Fixed Layouts**: When extracting data from documents with a consistent structure, absolute XPath provides an exact way to locate elements. This can be useful for extracting data from structured reports, invoices, or other documents where the layout does not change. For example, in a PDF-to-HTML conversion scenario, absolute XPath can pinpoint specific data points.
- **Automated Workflow Testing**: In automated workflows with predefined steps, absolute XPath can be used to validate the correct sequence of elements. This is common in test cases where the order of operations matters, such as in e-commerce checkout processes or form submissions.

Relative XPath Applications

Relative XPath is more flexible and adaptable, making it suitable for dynamic or evolving environments. It is the preferred choice for automation frameworks and web scraping tasks where document structures may change or contain complex hierarchies.

- **Web Scraping**: Relative XPath is widely used in web scraping, where documents are dynamic and subject to change. It allows for robust element selection without relying on a specific path. For example, scraping a news website for headlines can benefit from relative XPath, as it can locate elements based on attributes, text content, or relationships, even if the page layout changes.
- **Dynamic Content Automation**: Relative XPath is ideal for automating web interactions with dynamic content. For example, in Selenium WebDriver scripts that interact with AJAX-based elements or single-page applications, relative XPath can locate elements as they load dynamically. This adaptability is crucial for scripts that must work across different environments and handle changing structures.
- **Complex Web Structures**: Relative XPath excels in complex web structures with nested elements. It can navigate parent-child relationships, ancestor-descendant relationships, and other hierarchical connections. This is useful in scenarios like locating elements within nested tables or complex form structures.

Choosing the Right Application

Choosing between absolute and relative XPath depends on the context and the specific requirements of the task. Here are some guidelines:

- **Stability**: If the structure is stable, absolute XPath can provide precision. If the structure is dynamic, relative XPath is a safer choice.
- **Flexibility**: For tasks requiring flexibility and adaptability, such as web scraping or dynamic content automation, relative XPath is ideal.
- **Precision**: When exact precision is needed, such as in testing or fixed workflows, absolute XPath may be more suitable.
- **Complexity**: For complex web structures, relative XPath's flexibility can navigate through multiple levels of nesting, while absolute XPath might become cumbersome.

Absolute and relative XPath serve distinct purposes in real-world applications. Absolute XPath is useful in scenarios requiring precision and stability, while relative XPath is best for flexibility and adaptability. By understanding the strengths and limitations of each approach, you can choose the most appropriate XPath strategy for your web automation, testing, or data extraction needs.

Chapter Summary

In this chapter, we explored the key aspects of XPath and the common approaches to element selection, focusing on absolute and relative XPath. Here's a summary of the key points discussed in the chapter:

Absolute XPath

- Absolute XPath follows a fixed path from the root to the desired element. It is reliable in stable environments but lacks flexibility.
- Ideal for scenarios where the document structure is consistent and requires precise targeting.
- Commonly used in automated testing and workflow validation, where the exact order of operations is crucial.
- Prone to breakage if the document structure changes, leading to reduced maintainability.

Relative XPath

- Relative XPath starts from anywhere in the document, allowing flexible navigation and element selection. It is more adaptable to changing structures.
- Suitable for dynamic or complex web environments, where document structures can change over time.
- Commonly used in web scraping, dynamic content automation, and complex web structures.
- Offers greater flexibility and resilience, allowing selection based on attributes, text content, or hierarchical relationships.

Choosing the Right XPath Approach

- When selecting the appropriate XPath approach, consider factors like document stability, flexibility, precision, and complexity.
- Absolute XPath is suitable for stable environments requiring precise targeting, while relative XPath is better for dynamic or evolving structures.
- Test XPath expressions in different scenarios to ensure they are robust against changes.

Common Mistakes and How to Avoid Them

- Common mistakes with XPath include using absolute XPath in dynamic environments, over-reliance on indexes, overusing nested relationships, and inadequate testing.
- To avoid these mistakes, use relative XPath for dynamic structures, attribute-based selection instead of index-based, and minimize complex nesting.
- Test XPath expressions thoroughly to ensure robustness and avoid ambiguity in element selection.

Conclusion

In conclusion, understanding the differences between absolute and relative XPath is crucial for successful web automation, testing, and data extraction. Absolute XPath provides precision in stable environments, while relative XPath offers flexibility in dynamic or complex scenarios. By considering the context and following best practices, you can choose the right XPath approach and avoid common mistakes. With this knowledge, you can create robust and reliable XPath expressions for various real-world applications.

Section 4:
CSS Selectors Basics

Introduction to CSS and Selectors

Outline

1. What is CSS?
2. Importance of CSS Selectors in Web Development
3. Overview of Basic CSS Selectors
4. Using CSS Selectors to Locate Web Elements
5. Benefits and Limitations of CSS Selectors
6. Chapter Summary

What is CSS?

CSS stands for Cascading Style Sheets. It is a style sheet language used to describe the presentation of a document written in a markup language, like HTML or XML. CSS allows you to control the appearance of web pages, including layout, colors, fonts, spacing, and other visual aspects.

With CSS, you can separate content (HTML) from design and layout, providing flexibility and making it easier to maintain and update websites. CSS can be used to style individual elements, classes of elements, or entire pages, and can be applied inline within HTML, internally within the `<style>` tag, or externally through separate CSS files. It is a fundamental technology for building modern web pages and applications, enabling developers to create visually appealing and responsive designs.

Importance of CSS Selectors in Web Development

CSS selectors play a crucial role in web development by allowing developers to apply styles to specific elements or groups of elements within an HTML document. They are an essential tool for creating visually appealing and well-organized web pages. Here's why CSS selectors are important in web development:

1. **Separation of Content and Presentation**:
   - CSS selectors enable the separation of content (HTML) from presentation (CSS). This separation promotes a cleaner, more maintainable codebase, allowing developers to focus on design and layout without altering the content structure.
2. **Flexible Styling**:
   - CSS selectors provide flexibility in styling. With a variety of selector types, you can target specific elements, classes, or IDs, and even use attribute-based selectors to apply styles conditionally. This flexibility allows for highly customized designs.
3. **Consistency Across Web Pages**:
   - By using CSS selectors, you can apply consistent styling across multiple pages or throughout an entire website. This consistency improves the user experience and ensures that changes to the design can be made quickly without affecting the content.
4. **Improved Maintainability**:

- o Since CSS allows for centralized styling, you can update the look and feel of a website by modifying a single CSS file or selector. This reduces redundancy and makes it easier to maintain large-scale websites.
5. **Responsive Design**:
   - o CSS selectors are integral to responsive web design. Using media queries and specific selectors, developers can create web pages that adapt to different screen sizes and devices, providing a seamless experience for users on desktops, tablets, and smartphones.
6. **Enhanced Accessibility**:
   - o By using CSS selectors to manage layout and design, developers can ensure that content remains accessible. Proper use of CSS selectors can contribute to a better experience for users with disabilities by enabling clear structure and logical organization.
7. **Enabling Interactivity and Animation**:
   - o CSS selectors are used to define styles for interactive elements and animations. This capability allows developers to create engaging user interfaces with transitions, hover effects, and other dynamic features without relying solely on JavaScript.
8. **Performance Optimization**:
   - o CSS selectors can impact website performance. Efficient use of selectors can lead to faster rendering times and smoother user experiences. Selecting elements using efficient techniques helps reduce the computational load on the browser.

In summary, CSS selectors are foundational to modern web development. They provide a versatile and efficient means to control the visual presentation of a website, enabling consistent styling, improved maintainability, responsive design, enhanced accessibility, and interactive experiences. Understanding and mastering CSS selectors is crucial for any web developer or designer.

Overview of Basic CSS Selectors

CSS selectors are the backbone of applying styles to specific elements in an HTML document. They define which elements are selected for styling, enabling developers to create consistent and visually appealing web designs. Let's explore some of the basic CSS selectors and their uses:

1. Type Selector

- **Description**: Selects all elements of a specific type or tag name, like all <p>, <div>, or <h1> elements.
- **Example**:

```
p {
  color: blue;
}
```

2. Class Selector

- **Description**: Selects elements based on a specified class attribute. It allows you to target multiple elements with the same class.
- **Example**:

```
.highlight {
  background-color: yellow;
}
```

3. ID Selector

- **Description**: Selects a single element based on its unique id attribute. IDs should be unique within a document.
- **Example**:

```
#header {
  font-size: 24px;
}
```

4. Universal Selector

- **Description**: Selects all elements within the document. It can be used to apply global styles or to reset default browser styling.
- **Example**:

```
* {
  margin: 0;
  padding: 0;
}
```

5. Attribute Selector

- **Description**: Selects elements based on specific attributes or attribute values. Useful for targeting elements with certain characteristics.
- **Example**:

```
[type="text"] {
  border: 1px solid black;
}
```

6. Descendant Selector

- **Description**: Selects elements that are descendants of a specified parent element. This allows for more targeted styling within a hierarchy.
- **Example**:

```
.content p {
  font-style: italic;
}
```

7. Child Selector

- **Description**: Selects elements that are direct children of a specified parent element. It provides a more specific level of control.
- **Example**:

```
.menu > li {
  display: inline-block;
}
```

8. Sibling Selectors

- **Description**: Select elements that are siblings of other elements. There are two types: general sibling (~) and adjacent sibling (+).
- **Example**:

```
/* Adjacent sibling selector */
h2 + p {
  margin-top: 10px;
}

/* General sibling selector */
h2 ~ p {
  color: gray;
}
```

9. Pseudo-classes and Pseudo-elements

- **Description**: Pseudo-classes apply styles based on the state or position of an element, while pseudo-elements apply styles to a specific part of an element.
- **Example**:

```
/* Pseudo-class example */
a:hover {
  color: red;
}

/* Pseudo-element example */
p::first-line {
  font-weight: bold;
}
```

These basic CSS selectors provide a comprehensive toolbox for selecting and styling elements within a web page. By combining them, you can achieve intricate designs and robust layouts, forming the basis for more advanced CSS techniques.

Using CSS Selectors to Locate Web Elements

CSS selectors are powerful tools for locating and interacting with elements on a webpage. In the context of web automation and testing, such as with Selenium WebDriver, CSS selectors offer a concise and efficient way to find elements for further actions like clicking, typing, or verifying content. Here's an overview of how to use CSS selectors to locate web elements:

1. Simple Element Selection

- **Description**: Target elements by their tag name, ID, or class.
- **Examples**:
  - **By Tag Name**:

    ```
    div
    ```

    This selects all `<div>` elements.

  - **By ID**:

    ```
    #header
    ```

    This selects the element with the `id="header"`.

  - **By Class**:

```
.button
```

This selects all elements with the `class="button"`.

2. Attribute-Based Selection

- **Description**: Find elements based on their attributes or attribute values.
- **Examples**:
  - **Specific Attribute Value**:

```
[type="submit"]
```

  This selects all elements with a `type` attribute set to "submit".

  - **Partial Attribute Match**:

```
[title^="Hello"]
```

  This selects elements where the `title` attribute starts with "Hello".

3. Descendant and Child Selectors

- **Description**: Target elements based on their relationship to other elements, either as descendants or direct children.
- **Examples**:
  - **Descendant Selector**:

```
.menu li
```

  This selects all `<li>` elements within a parent with the `class="menu"`.

  - **Child Selector**:

```
.content > p
```

  This selects direct child `<p>` elements within a parent with the `class="content"`.

4. Sibling Selectors

- **Description**: Locate elements that are siblings of other elements. There are two types: adjacent and general siblings.
- **Examples**:
  - **Adjacent Sibling Selector**:

```
h2 + p
```

  This selects the first `<p>` element immediately following an `<h2>`.

  - **General Sibling Selector**:

```
h2 ~ p
```

  This selects all `<p>` elements that follow an `<h2>`, regardless of whether they are direct or indirect siblings.

5. Pseudo-classes and Pseudo-elements

- **Description**: Use pseudo-classes to select elements based on their state or position, and pseudo-elements to target specific parts of an element.
- **Examples**:
  - **Pseudo-class Selector**:

    ```
    a:hover
    ```

    This selects all `<a>` elements when the mouse hovers over them.

  - **Pseudo-element Selector**:

    ```
    p::first-line
    ```

  - This targets the first line within a paragraph.

6. Combining Selectors

- **Description**: Combine multiple selectors to create complex selection logic.
- **Example**:

  ```
  #main .content > h2 + p
  ```

  This selects the first `<p>` element that is an adjacent sibling to an `<h2>`, which is a direct child of an element with the `class="content"`, contained within an element with the `id="main"`.

By understanding and mastering these various types of CSS selectors, you can effectively locate and interact with specific elements on a webpage. In automated testing or web scraping scenarios, this knowledge is crucial for creating reliable and efficient test scripts or data extraction processes.

Benefits and Limitations of CSS Selectors

CSS selectors offer a range of benefits that make them indispensable for styling web pages and locating elements in automated testing. However, they also have some limitations. Here's a comprehensive overview of the benefits and limitations of CSS selectors.

Benefits of CSS Selectors

1. **Simplicity and Readability**:
   - CSS selectors are generally simpler and more readable than other selector-based mechanisms like XPath. Their straightforward syntax helps developers quickly understand how elements are being targeted.
2. **Performance**:
   - CSS selectors tend to perform better in web browsers compared to XPath. Browsers are optimized for CSS parsing, allowing CSS-based operations to be faster and more efficient.
3. **Consistency with Web Standards**:
   - CSS is a widely accepted standard for web design. Using CSS selectors aligns with best practices in web development, ensuring compatibility across different browsers and platforms.
4. **Versatility and Flexibility**:
   - CSS selectors can be used in a variety of scenarios, from styling web pages to locating elements in automated tests with frameworks like Selenium. They support various methods for targeting elements, such as by class, ID, attribute, or position.
5. **Broad Applicability**:

- CSS selectors can be used to style elements based on their state (using pseudo-classes), structure (using descendant, child, or sibling selectors), or attributes (using attribute-based selectors). This broad applicability makes them suitable for a range of tasks.

6. **Responsiveness and Interactivity**:
   - CSS selectors are integral to creating responsive and interactive designs. They enable dynamic styling based on user interaction, screen size, or other conditions, allowing developers to create engaging user experiences.

7. **Centralized Control**:
   - CSS selectors allow developers to control styles centrally, promoting a clean separation between content and presentation. This centralization makes it easier to maintain and update styles across a website.

Limitations of CSS Selectors

1. **Limited Traversal Capabilities**:
   - Unlike XPath, CSS selectors cannot traverse the DOM in complex ways. They are limited in terms of ancestor-based traversal and do not support backward traversal (e.g., finding a parent element).

2. **No Text-based Selection**:
   - CSS selectors cannot select elements based on their text content. This is a significant limitation compared to XPath, which can find elements based on partial or exact text matches.

3. **Less Flexibility in Dynamic Scenarios**:
   - In highly dynamic web applications, CSS selectors might struggle with complex DOM manipulations. XPath's flexibility can be more suitable for handling intricate structures or frequent changes in the DOM.

4. **Potential Conflicts with Specificity**:
   - CSS specificity can cause unintended styling conflicts. If selectors are not designed with careful consideration of specificity rules, unexpected behavior can occur, leading to challenging debugging scenarios.

5. **No Built-in Functions**:
   - Unlike XPath, CSS does not offer built-in functions for operations like counting elements, text extraction, or mathematical operations. This limitation can make XPath more appealing for advanced use cases.

CSS selectors are a fundamental tool in web development and testing, offering simplicity, performance, and broad applicability. However, they have limitations in traversal capabilities and lack support for text-based selection. When choosing between CSS and XPath, it's essential to consider the specific requirements of the project or task at hand. Understanding the benefits and limitations of CSS selectors helps you make informed decisions and build efficient, maintainable solutions.

Chapter Summary

In this chapter, we explored the role of CSS (Cascading Style Sheets) in web development, focusing on how CSS selectors are used to locate and style elements on a web page. Here's a brief summary of the key points covered:

1. **What is CSS?**
   - CSS is a language for controlling the presentation of HTML or XML documents, allowing for flexible styling, layout management, and design consistency across web pages.

2. **Importance of CSS Selectors in Web Development**
   - CSS selectors play a critical role in defining how elements are styled, enabling a separation between content and presentation. This separation facilitates maintainable code and consistent design throughout a website.

3. **Overview of Basic CSS Selectors**
   - We introduced various types of CSS selectors, including type selectors, class selectors, ID selectors, attribute selectors, descendant and child selectors, sibling selectors, and pseudo-classes. Each type offers different capabilities for targeting specific elements or groups of elements.

4. **Using CSS Selectors to Locate Web Elements**
   - We discussed how CSS selectors are used in web automation and testing to locate elements for interaction, like in Selenium WebDriver. The flexibility of CSS selectors allows for a range of selection strategies, from simple tag-based selection to more complex combinations of selectors.

5. **Benefits and Limitations of CSS Selectors**
   - CSS selectors offer benefits such as simplicity, performance, consistency with web standards, and centralized control of styles. However, they also have limitations, including limited traversal capabilities, no text-based selection, and potential conflicts due to CSS specificity.

Conclusion

CSS selectors are essential tools for web developers and testers. They enable flexible and consistent styling while also providing a robust way to locate elements for web automation. Understanding the different types of CSS selectors, their benefits, and their limitations will empower you to use them effectively in your web projects and automation scripts. As you continue through this book, you'll delve deeper into advanced CSS selector techniques and learn how to apply them in real-world scenarios, setting the stage for a comprehensive understanding of web element location with CSS.

Crafting CSS Selectors with Attributes

Outline

1. Understanding CSS Selectors with Attributes
2. Common Attribute Types for CSS Selection
3. Selecting Elements by ID and Class
4. Using Attribute Value Matchers
5. Leveraging Advanced Attribute Selectors
6. Building Resilient CSS Selectors
7. Chapter Summary

Understanding CSS Selectors with Attributes

Attributes are a key component in web development, serving as identifiable markers for HTML elements. They provide additional information about an element, allowing developers to manipulate or style elements based on these attributes. CSS (Cascading Style Sheets) selectors utilize attributes to target specific elements for styling or scripting. This section focuses on how attributes can be used to craft effective CSS selectors.

What Are Attributes in HTML?

An attribute in HTML is a key-value pair within an opening tag that provides more information about an element. Common attributes include id, class, name, href, src, and others. Attributes often play a critical role in defining the behavior, appearance, or content of an HTML element. Here's an example of an HTML tag with several attributes:

```
<input type="text" id="username" class="input-field" name="username">
```

This input tag has three attributes: type, id, and class. These attributes can be used to target the element with CSS selectors.

CSS Selectors: The Basics

CSS selectors are patterns used to select elements from the Document Object Model (DOM) and apply styles to them. They can select elements by tag name, class, ID, or attribute. Selectors are versatile, allowing for complex queries to target specific elements on a page.

Common CSS selectors include:

- **Type selectors**: Select elements by their tag name.
- **Class selectors**: Select elements by their class attribute.
- **ID selectors**: Select elements by their id attribute.
- **Attribute selectors**: Select elements based on their attributes.

Attribute-Based CSS Selectors

Attribute-based CSS selectors allow you to target elements by specific attributes or combinations of attributes. These selectors are especially useful for targeting elements when other identifiers like ID or class are not unique enough.

Here are some examples of attribute-based selectors:

- **Selecting by attribute name**: [attribute] selects all elements with the specified attribute.
- **Selecting by attribute value**: [attribute="value"] selects elements where the attribute has the specified value.
- **Selecting by partial attribute value**: [attribute*="part"] selects elements where the attribute value contains a certain substring.
- **Selecting by attribute prefix/suffix**: [attribute^="start"] and [attribute$="end"] select elements where the attribute value starts or ends with a certain string.

Attribute-based CSS selectors provide flexibility, allowing developers to craft complex queries to target specific elements. This capability is particularly useful when working with dynamic web pages or complex HTML structures where traditional selectors may fall short.

The Role of Attributes in CSS Selectors

Attributes serve as a bridge between HTML structure and CSS styling. By using attributes in CSS selectors, developers can target elements with a higher degree of precision. This allows for more robust and maintainable stylesheets, reducing the risk of unintentional styling or script conflicts.

Attributes also play a crucial role in automation and testing frameworks like Selenium WebDriver, where locating elements accurately is essential. By mastering attribute-based CSS selectors, developers can create robust automation scripts and enhance their testing capabilities.

In summary, understanding and leveraging CSS selectors with attributes is a fundamental skill for web developers, enabling them to create more maintainable, robust, and flexible stylesheets and scripts. As we explore more advanced topics in the coming sections, you'll gain a deeper appreciation for the power of attribute-based CSS selectors in real-world applications

Common Attribute Types for CSS Selection

Attributes are fundamental elements of HTML, providing metadata and context to web elements. In CSS, you can use these attributes to create selectors that target specific elements on a web page. This section explores the most common attribute types used for CSS selection, giving you the tools to create precise and efficient CSS selectors.

Overview of Attribute-Based CSS Selectors

Attribute-based CSS selectors allow you to target elements based on their attribute name, value, or even a combination of both. This type of selector is invaluable when you need more specificity than tag or class-based selectors offer. Attribute selectors can be combined with other selectors for greater flexibility.

Commonly Used Attribute Types

Let's delve into the most frequently used attribute types in HTML and understand how they can be utilized in CSS selectors.

1. ID Attribute

The id attribute is a unique identifier for HTML elements. It's intended to be unique within a page, allowing you to target a specific element.

- **CSS Selector**: To select an element by its id, use the # symbol followed by the id value.
- **Example**: To select an element with an id of "header", you'd use the following CSS selector:

```css
#header {
  background-color: blue;
```

```
}
```

2. Class Attribute

The class attribute allows you to group elements together. An element can have multiple classes, and a class can be used across multiple elements.

- **CSS Selector**: To select by class, use the . symbol followed by the class name.
- **Example**: To select elements with a class of "button", you'd use:

```
.button {
  color: red;
}
```

3. Name Attribute

The name attribute is commonly used in form elements to specify a unique identifier for form data handling. It's often utilized in web applications and automation scenarios.

- **CSS Selector**: To select elements by name, you can use attribute-based selectors.
- **Example**: To select an input element with the name "username", you'd use:

```
input[name="username"] {
  border: 1px solid green;
}
```

4. Data Attributes

Data attributes allow you to store additional information on HTML elements. They are generally prefixed with data-, enabling custom metadata storage on elements without affecting the element's original functionality.

- **CSS Selector**: You can use attribute-based selectors to target elements by data-* attributes.
- **Example**: To select elements with a data-role attribute of "admin", you could use:

```
[data-role="admin"] {
  background-color: yellow;
}
```

5. Attribute Combinations

CSS selectors can target elements based on multiple attributes or attribute-value combinations. This offers a higher level of specificity, useful in complex structures.

- **Example**: To select an element with both id="unique" and class="important", you'd use:

```
#unique.important {
  font-weight: bold;
}
```

Advanced Attribute Matching Techniques

Beyond basic matching, CSS offers advanced techniques for working with attributes, such as matching partial values, prefixes, or suffixes. These techniques are covered in detail in subsequent chapters, providing you with the flexibility to create complex CSS selectors.

Understanding these common attribute types for CSS selection is the first step toward mastering attribute-based CSS selectors. By familiarizing yourself with these attributes and how to create selectors for them, you gain the foundational knowledge needed to tackle more complex scenarios in your web development journey.

Selecting Elements by ID and Class

In CSS, selecting elements by their ID or class is a fundamental technique. It provides a straightforward way to style or interact with specific elements on a web page. In this section, we'll explore the concepts of ID and class attributes, and how to create CSS selectors that use these attributes for selecting elements.

Overview of ID and Class Attributes

The ID and class attributes in HTML serve as identifiers for elements. They are key to building consistent and maintainable web pages, and they play a crucial role in styling, scripting, and automation frameworks like Selenium WebDriver.

ID Attribute

The id attribute is meant to be unique within a page or a document. This means you can use it to target a single specific element. If there are multiple elements with the same id, it violates the HTML specification, leading to unexpected behavior in CSS and JavaScript.

- **Uniqueness**: An ID should be unique, providing a precise identifier for an element.
- **Usage in CSS**: The id attribute is used with the # symbol to create CSS selectors.
- **Usage in JavaScript**: In scripting, an ID is often used with methods like document.getElementById().

Class Attribute

The class attribute is not unique, allowing multiple elements to share the same class. This is useful for applying the same styles or behaviors to a group of elements.

- **Shared Class**: Elements with the same class attribute can be targeted simultaneously.
- **Usage in CSS**: The class attribute is used with the . symbol to create CSS selectors.
- **Usage in JavaScript**: Methods like document.getElementsByClassName() or document.querySelectorAll('.classname') can be used to access elements by class.

Selecting Elements by ID

Selecting elements by ID is straightforward due to the unique nature of IDs. Here's how to create CSS selectors using IDs.

- **CSS Selector for ID**: To select an element by its ID, use the # symbol followed by the ID value.
- **Example**: If an element has an ID of "main-header", the CSS selector to target it would be:

```
#main-header {
  font-size: 24px;
  color: blue;
}
```

This example applies a larger font size and a blue color to an element with the ID "main-header."

Selecting Elements by Class

Selecting elements by class is useful when you want to style or interact with multiple elements sharing the same class.

- **CSS Selector for Class**: To select elements by class, use the . symbol followed by the class name.
- **Example**: If several elements have the class "highlight", the CSS selector to target them would be:

```
.highlight {
  background-color: yellow;
}
```

This example sets a yellow background for all elements with the class "highlight."

Combining ID and Class Selectors

You can combine ID and class selectors to achieve more specific targeting. This is useful when you have an element with a unique ID and a specific class, allowing you to refine the selection.

- **Combining ID and Class**: To combine these selectors, use the # and . symbols as needed.
- **Example**: To select an element with ID "content" and class "active", the CSS selector would be:

```
#content.active {
  border: 2px solid red;
}
```

This example applies a red border to an element with ID "content" and class "active."

Best Practices for Using ID and Class Selectors

- **Use IDs Sparingly**: Since IDs are meant to be unique, use them only when you need to target a single specific element.
- **Prefer Classes for Reusability**: Classes offer flexibility and reusability, making them a preferred choice for most styling scenarios.
- **Combine Selectors for Specificity**: When needed, combine ID and class selectors to target elements more precisely.
- **Avoid Multiple Elements with the Same ID**: This can lead to unpredictable behavior and conflicts in CSS and JavaScript.

Selecting elements by ID and class is a fundamental skill in web development. Understanding these concepts allows you to create robust CSS selectors and ensures that your styling and scripting are consistent and maintainable. By mastering these basic selectors, you'll be well-prepared to tackle more complex scenarios in web development and automation.

Using Attribute Value Matchers

Attribute value matchers are a powerful feature in CSS that allow you to select elements based on specific attribute values, giving you greater flexibility and control over your styles. This section explores various methods for matching attribute values in CSS selectors, helping you create precise and adaptable styles for your web projects.

Introduction to Attribute Value Matchers

Attribute value matchers are CSS selectors that select elements based on the value of a particular attribute. They are especially useful when you need to find elements with specific characteristics or when simple ID or class-based selectors are not sufficient.

The basic syntax for an attribute-based selector is:

```
[element[attribute="value"] {
  /* style rules */
}
```

Here, `[attribute="value"]` selects all elements with the specified attribute value. Let's delve into different types of attribute value matchers and how to use them effectively.

Exact Match

The most straightforward way to match an attribute value is by exact match. This selector targets elements with an attribute having the exact specified value.

- **Example**: To select all input elements with a `type` of "text":

```
input[type="text"] {
  background-color: lightgray;
}
```

This applies a light gray background to all text input fields.

Partial Match

Partial match selectors allow you to select elements where the attribute value contains a specific substring. This is useful when the exact value can vary but contains a common pattern.

- **Contains Match (*=)**: This selects elements where the attribute value contains a specific substring.
  - **Example**: To select all elements with a `class` containing "nav":

```
[class*="nav"] {
  font-weight: bold;
}
```

This example makes the font bold for all elements with classes like "navbar", "navigation", or "nav-link".

Prefix Match

Prefix match selectors are used to select elements where the attribute value starts with a specified substring.

- **Prefix Match (^=)**: Targets elements where the attribute value starts with a specific string.
  - **Example**: To select all input fields where the name attribute starts with "user":

```
input[name^="user"] {
  border: 2px solid green;
}
```

This applies a green border to all inputs with name attributes like "username" or "useremail".

Suffix Match

Suffix match selectors allow you to target elements where the attribute value ends with a specified substring.

- **Suffix Match ($=)**: Selects elements where the attribute value ends with a specific string.

○ **Example**: To select all elements with `href` attributes ending in ".pdf":

```
a[href$=".pdf"] {
  text-decoration: underline;
}
```

This underlines all links pointing to PDF files.

Matching Multiple Attribute Values

You can also match elements based on multiple attribute values, creating more specific and complex selectors.

• **Example**: To select all elements with both `data-role="admin"` and `data-active="true"`:

```
[data-role="admin"][data-active="true"] {
  background-color: yellow;
}
```

This applies a yellow background to elements with both `data-role` set to "admin" and `data-active` set to "true".

Best Practices for Attribute Value Matchers

• **Use Exact Match When Possible**: It's more specific and reduces the risk of unintended side effects.
• **Leverage Partial Match for Dynamic Content**: Use partial, prefix, or suffix matchers to handle dynamic or varying attribute values.
• **Test for Edge Cases**: Ensure that your selectors work as expected in different scenarios, especially when dealing with complex attribute-based selectors.
• **Combine Matchers for Specificity**: Combine multiple attribute matchers to create precise selectors without over-specifying.

Attribute value matchers are a versatile tool in CSS that allow you to create detailed and adaptable selectors based on attribute values. By mastering these matchers, you can select elements with greater precision and build stylesheets that are both robust and flexible.

Leveraging Advanced Attribute Selectors

Advanced attribute selectors in CSS provide a powerful mechanism for selecting elements based on a variety of complex conditions. By leveraging these selectors, you can build more precise and dynamic styles for your web applications. This section explores advanced attribute selectors and how to use them to create flexible and robust CSS rules.

Introduction to Advanced Attribute Selectors

Attribute selectors allow you to select elements based on their attributes and attribute values. While basic attribute selectors focus on exact matches or simple patterns, advanced attribute selectors offer a broader range of matching options, enabling you to select elements based on partial matches, attribute existence, or attribute value variations.

Here's an overview of different types of advanced attribute selectors and their common use cases.

Existence Selector

The existence selector allows you to select elements that have a specified attribute, regardless of its value.

- **Selector Syntax**: [attribute]
- **Example**: To select all elements with a title attribute:

```
[title] {
  text-decoration: underline;
}
```

This example underlines all elements that have a title attribute, regardless of its content.

Matching Multiple Attribute Conditions

You can combine multiple attribute conditions to create more specific selectors. This can be useful when you need to target elements that meet multiple criteria.

- **Selector Syntax**: [attribute1="value1"][attribute2="value2"]
- **Example**: To select all buttons with a data-action of "submit" and a disabled attribute:

```
button[data-action="submit"][disabled] {
  opacity: 0.5;
}
```

This reduces the opacity of all submit buttons that are disabled.

Attribute Value Variants

Advanced attribute selectors allow you to create CSS rules that target elements with attribute values that start, end, or contain specific strings.

- **Prefix Match (^=)**: Targets elements where the attribute value starts with a specific substring.
- **Example**: To select all input fields with name attributes that start with "user":

```
input[name^="user"] {
  border: 2px solid blue;
}
```

- **Suffix Match ($=)**: Selects elements where the attribute value ends with a specific substring.
- **Example**: To select all elements with href attributes ending in ".jpg":

```
a[href$=".jpg"] {
  border-bottom: 1px solid black;
}
```

- **Contains Match (*=)**: Matches elements where the attribute value contains a specific substring.
- **Example**: To select all div elements with a class that contains "header":

```
div[class*="header"] {
  font-weight: bold;
}
```

Case Sensitivity

CSS attribute selectors are generally case-sensitive. However, some selectors allow case-insensitive matching by appending the i flag to the selector.

- **Case-Insensitive Matching**: [attribute="value" i]
- **Example**: To select elements with a class of "button", ignoring case sensitivity:

```
[class="button" i] {
  color: green;
}
```

This selector will apply green text to any element with a class of "Button", "button", or any other case variant.

Best Practices for Advanced Attribute Selectors

- **Be Mindful of Specificity**: Advanced attribute selectors can become overly specific. Use them judiciously to avoid conflicts and maintain flexibility.
- **Test for Unexpected Results**: Ensure your selectors work as expected in different scenarios, especially when using complex combinations.
- **Use Advanced Selectors to Handle Dynamic Content**: In applications with dynamic or varying attribute values, advanced attribute selectors can be a lifesaver, allowing you to create robust and flexible selectors.
- **Combine with Other Selectors**: Combine advanced attribute selectors with other types of selectors (like class or ID) to create comprehensive and resilient rules.

Advanced attribute selectors in CSS offer a wealth of possibilities for creating flexible and precise CSS rules. By leveraging these selectors, you can build more robust stylesheets that handle a variety of complex conditions. With these techniques, you're well-equipped to create adaptable CSS rules for even the most complex web development scenarios.

Building Resilient CSS Selectors

Creating CSS selectors that are resilient to changes and capable of withstanding a variety of conditions is essential in modern web development. A resilient selector remains functional despite changes in the HTML structure or the addition/removal of elements. This section explores strategies and best practices for building robust CSS selectors that are adaptable, maintainable, and less prone to breakage.

Why Resilient CSS Selectors Matter

In a fast-evolving web environment, where elements might be added, modified, or removed, CSS selectors must be flexible enough to handle these changes without causing unintended side effects. Resilient selectors help maintain consistent styling and reduce the risk of CSS conflicts.

Characteristics of Resilient CSS Selectors

Resilient CSS selectors possess the following characteristics:

- **Flexibility**: The selector can adapt to changes in the HTML structure without losing its effectiveness.
- **Maintainability**: It's easy to understand, modify, and troubleshoot.
- **Low Specificity**: It avoids overly specific rules that may break if the underlying structure changes.
- **Consistent Behavior**: It behaves predictably across different scenarios and browsers.

Strategies for Building Resilient CSS Selectors

1. Use Attribute-Based Selectors Judiciously

Attribute-based selectors are a powerful tool for building flexible CSS rules, but overusing them can lead to brittle selectors. Instead of hardcoding attribute values, consider using more general patterns.

- **Example**: Instead of targeting a specific id, use a more general attribute or class:

```css
.menu-item {
  color: blue;
}
```

Here, .menu-item is less specific than targeting an id, allowing for greater flexibility if the HTML structure changes.

2. Prefer Class Selectors Over ID Selectors

Class selectors are more flexible than ID selectors because they can be applied to multiple elements. They also have lower specificity, which is useful in complex CSS hierarchies.

- **Example**: Use class selectors for general styling:

```css
.btn-primary {
  background-color: blue;
}
```

This example uses a class selector to style primary buttons, allowing for greater reusability across different components.

3. Combine Selectors for Specificity

Combining selectors allows you to achieve a balance between specificity and flexibility. This technique helps ensure that the selector targets the intended elements without being overly specific.

- **Example**: To target specific elements within a broader context, you can combine selectors:

```css
.form .input-group .input-field {
  padding: 10px;
}
```

This selector applies padding to .input-field elements within the context of .form and .input-group.

4. Use Pseudo-Classes for State-Based Styling

Pseudo-classes can help create resilient selectors by targeting elements based on their state or position within the DOM, rather than relying on specific IDs or classes.

- **Example**: Use pseudo-classes to target elements in specific states:

```css
.button:hover {
  background-color: lightblue;
}
```

Here, the hover pseudo-class is used to change the background color when a button is hovered, providing interactive feedback without hardcoding specific elements.

5. Leverage Cascading and Inheritance

Cascading and inheritance are fundamental concepts in CSS that can help create more resilient selectors. By leveraging these concepts, you can create consistent styling with fewer explicit selectors.

- **Example**: Use inheritance to apply styles to a broader context:

```css
.container {
  color: black;
}
.container .sub-container {
  padding: 10px;
}
```

This example sets the text color for a whole container, ensuring that child elements inherit the color without needing explicit selectors.

Best Practices for Building Resilient CSS Selectors

- **Avoid Over-Specificity**: High-specificity selectors are more prone to breakage if the HTML structure changes.
- **Use Classes for Reusability**: Class-based selectors are more flexible and can be reused across different elements and components.
- **Test for Consistency**: Ensure your selectors work across different browsers and devices to avoid inconsistencies.
- **Document Your CSS Structure**: Proper documentation can help maintain resilience by providing a clear understanding of the CSS architecture.

Building resilient CSS selectors is crucial in modern web development, where flexibility and maintainability are key. By following these strategies and best practices, you can create selectors that are adaptable to change and capable of withstanding the evolving nature of web development. With resilient selectors, you'll reduce the risk of styling conflicts and create a more maintainable CSS architecture.

Chapter Summary

This chapter delved into the essentials of crafting CSS selectors using attributes. By understanding how attributes work in HTML and how CSS selectors can target them, you can create more specific and flexible styling rules for your web applications. Here's what you learned:

Understanding Attributes in HTML

Attributes in HTML provide metadata about elements and can be used to uniquely identify or group elements. The most common attributes for CSS selectors include id, class, name, and custom data attributes like data-*.

Types of CSS Selectors with Attributes

There are various ways to craft CSS selectors using attributes:

- **Exact Match**: Selects elements where the attribute has a specific value.
- **Partial Match**: Selects elements where the attribute value contains a specified substring.
- **Prefix and Suffix Match**: Selects elements where the attribute value starts or ends with a specific substring.
- **Existence Selector**: Targets elements that contain a specific attribute, regardless of its value.
- **Combining Multiple Attributes**: Allows for complex selectors by combining several attribute-based conditions.

Common Attribute-Based CSS Selectors

This section explained how to use common attributes to craft CSS selectors:

- **Selecting by ID**: Using #id to select an element with a specific id.
- **Selecting by Class**: Using .class to select elements sharing the same class.
- **Selecting by Attribute**: Using [attribute="value"] or similar patterns to target elements by specific attributes.
- **Using Attribute Combinations**: Combining multiple attribute-based selectors for more precise targeting.

Building Resilient CSS Selectors with Attributes

This chapter also highlighted best practices to ensure your CSS selectors are resilient and maintainable:

- **Avoid Over-Specificity**: Overly specific selectors can become brittle and prone to breaking with changes in the HTML structure.
- **Use Attribute-Based Selectors Wisely**: When crafting attribute-based selectors, consider flexibility and avoid hardcoding specific values whenever possible.
- **Combine Selectors for Specificity**: Balance between general and specific selectors to achieve optimal results.
- **Leverage Pseudo-Classes**: Use pseudo-classes like :hover, :focus, and others to add interactivity and style based on element states.
- **Test Your Selectors**: Regularly test your CSS selectors to ensure they work across various scenarios and browsers.

Conclusion

Crafting CSS selectors with attributes is a fundamental skill in web development. By understanding the various types of attribute-based selectors and applying best practices, you can create resilient, maintainable, and flexible CSS rules for your projects. This chapter equipped you with the knowledge to use attribute-based CSS selectors effectively, setting a solid foundation for building robust stylesheets and automation frameworks.

CSS Selectors for Dynamic Content

Outline

1. Understanding Dynamic Content
2. Using Attribute Selectors for Changing Attributes
3. Employing Pseudo-Classes to Target States
4. Finding Elements by Data Attributes
5. Handling Changing Element Structures
6. Practical Examples of CSS Selectors for Dynamic Content
7. Common Challenges and Solutions
8. Chapter Summary

Understanding Dynamic Content

Dynamic content refers to web page elements that change their structure, attributes, or appearance in response to user interactions, JavaScript events, AJAX calls, or other dynamic processes. These changes can include adding new elements, removing existing ones, altering styles, or updating text and attributes based on user inputs or other conditions.

Examples of Dynamic Content

Here are some common examples of dynamic content on modern web pages:

- **Dynamic Navigation Menus**: Menus that expand or collapse when clicked, revealing new elements or hiding others.
- **Interactive Forms**: Forms that adjust their fields, validations, or styling based on user input or choices.
- **AJAX-based Updates**: Elements updated without a page reload, such as chat messages, notifications, or product suggestions.
- **Carousel or Slideshow Components**: Changing images or content in response to user interactions or auto-scrolling.
- **Popup Modals and Dialog Boxes**: Dynamic windows that appear in response to user actions like clicking a button.
- **Real-Time Data**: Elements that reflect live data, such as stock prices, sports scores, or online user statuses.

Challenges of Locating Dynamic Content

Locating dynamic content can be challenging because the structure or attributes of elements can change at runtime. Common issues include:

- **Changing DOM Structure**: Elements might be added, removed, or moved within the Document Object Model (DOM).
- **Attribute Changes**: IDs, classes, or other attributes may be altered in response to events.
- **Dynamic Visibility**: Elements might become visible or hidden based on user interactions or logic.
- **Timing Issues**: Asynchronous updates can lead to timing-related issues, where elements are not available when needed.

Strategies for Handling Dynamic Content

To effectively locate dynamic elements, you need flexible and robust CSS selectors that can adapt to these changes. Key strategies include:

- **Use Attribute Selectors**: Attribute selectors can be helpful when IDs or classes change frequently, allowing you to target elements based on known patterns.
- **Leverage Pseudo-Classes**: Pseudo-classes such as `:hover`, `:active`, or `:checked` enable you to target elements based on their state.
- **Utilize Parent-Child and Sibling Relationships**: Using relationships between elements can help locate dynamic content even when the structure changes.
- **Employ Data Attributes**: Data attributes can provide unique identifiers for elements that change or are created dynamically.

Understanding these concepts is critical to creating effective and robust CSS selectors that can withstand the dynamic nature of modern web applications. In the following sections, you'll learn specific techniques and best practices for crafting CSS selectors to handle dynamic content.

Using Attribute Selectors for Changing Attributes

CSS attribute selectors allow you to target elements based on their attributes and values, providing a flexible way to locate elements even when their IDs, classes, or other characteristics change. This makes attribute selectors particularly useful for dealing with dynamic content, where traditional selectors may fail due to shifting structures or changing element properties.

Types of Attribute Selectors

There are several ways to use attribute selectors in CSS, offering various levels of specificity and flexibility:

- **Exact Match**: To select elements with a specific attribute value, use square brackets with the attribute name and its exact value, e.g., `[attribute="value"]`. This is useful when you know the exact value to look for.
- **Partial Match**: For partial matching, you can use wildcard characters to target attribute values that contain or start/end with specific text:
    - `*=`: Selects elements where the attribute contains the given value, e.g., `[attribute*="partial"]`.
    - `^=`: Targets attributes that start with a given value, e.g., `[attribute^="start"]`.
    - `$=`: Matches attributes that end with a specified value, e.g., `[attribute$="end"]`.

Application of Attribute Selectors

Selecting by ID

Using an attribute selector to target elements by ID can be more flexible than traditional ID-based selectors, especially when IDs are dynamically generated or follow a pattern. For example:

- `input[id="username"]` targets an input with an exact ID of "username".
- `div[id^="section-"]` selects all `<div>` elements whose ID starts with "section-".

Targeting Classes

Classes are commonly used to style elements, but dynamic content may change them based on user interactions or state. Attribute selectors let you target elements with specific classes or class patterns:

- `button[class="submit"]` selects buttons with an exact class of "submit".

- `div[class*="warning"]` targets all `<div>` elements whose class contains "warning", useful for alert messages or status indicators.

Selecting Elements by Custom Attributes

Custom attributes, like data attributes, can be a reliable way to locate dynamic content. Using attribute selectors with data attributes, you can find elements with specific data values or custom properties. For example:

- `div[data-role="admin"]` targets `<div>` elements with a "data-role" attribute set to "admin".
- `input[data-status*="active"]` selects input fields with a "data-status" attribute containing "active".

Attribute Selectors in Dynamic Content

Attribute selectors are particularly effective in handling dynamic content because they allow you to create robust and flexible selectors even when elements change attributes or structure. By leveraging these selectors, you can:

- **Handle Dynamic IDs and Classes**: Attribute selectors provide a flexible alternative to traditional selectors, adapting to changes in ID or class naming patterns.
- **Locate Elements with Custom Data Attributes**: Data attributes are often used to store unique identifiers or additional information, providing a reliable way to target elements.
- **Build Resilient Selectors for Dynamic Content**: By using partial match attribute selectors, you can create resilient selectors that are less prone to breaking due to DOM changes or attribute updates.

In the next section, we will explore how to employ pseudo-classes to target specific element states and user interactions.

Employing Pseudo-Classes to Target States

Pseudo-classes in CSS allow you to select elements based on their state, position, or user interaction. They are particularly useful when working with dynamic content, as they can target elements in specific states without relying solely on static attributes like IDs or classes. In this section, you'll learn about common pseudo-classes and how to use them to create selectors that can adapt to changing web page structures and user interactions.

Understanding Pseudo-Classes

Pseudo-classes begin with a colon (`:`) and describe a state or condition that is often dependent on user interaction or the position of elements in the DOM. Here's an overview of some of the most widely used pseudo-classes:

Targeting User Interaction

- `:hover`: This pseudo-class selects elements when the user hovers over them with a mouse pointer. It's commonly used to style interactive elements like buttons or links during hover events.
- `:focus`: It selects elements that are currently focused, often used for input fields or buttons when they receive user focus through clicking or keyboard navigation.
- `:active`: This pseudo-class targets elements that are currently being activated (clicked). It is commonly used to style buttons or links during a click event.

Targeting Element Position and Structure

- **:first-child and :last-child**: These pseudo-classes select the first and last children of a parent element, respectively. They can be useful for targeting specific items in a list or navigation menu.
- **:nth-child(n) and :nth-of-type(n)**: These pseudo-classes select elements based on their position within a parent or among elements of the same type. For example, :nth-child(2) selects the second child, while :nth-of-type(3) selects the third element of a specific type.
- **:only-child and :only-of-type**: These pseudo-classes select elements that are the only child or the only element of a specific type within their parent.

Targeting Specific States

- **:checked**: This pseudo-class selects checkboxes, radio buttons, or other elements that are currently checked.
- **:disabled**: It selects elements that are disabled, such as input fields or buttons that cannot be interacted with.
- **:enabled**: This pseudo-class selects elements that are enabled, providing a way to target interactive elements.

Applying Pseudo-Classes to Dynamic Content

Pseudo-classes are useful in handling dynamic content because they allow you to create selectors that respond to changes in user interaction and element state. Here are some examples of how you can use them to work with dynamic content:

Styling Interactive Elements

Using pseudo-classes like :hover and :active, you can target elements based on user interactions. For example:

- button:hover applies styles to a button when hovered over, which can be useful for dynamic menus or interactive buttons.
- a:active targets a link when it's being clicked, allowing you to adjust styles during a click event.

Locating Specific Elements in a Collection

Pseudo-classes like :first-child or :nth-child allow you to locate specific elements in dynamic collections. This can be useful for working with dynamically generated lists or complex menu structures. Examples include:

- ul > li:first-child selects the first item in an unordered list, useful for targeting specific menu items.
- div:nth-child(3) targets the third child within a parent <div>, allowing you to focus on specific elements in a dynamically changing structure.

Handling Form States

Pseudo-classes are useful for targeting elements in different form states, such as checkboxes, radio buttons, or disabled fields. Consider these examples:

- input:checked selects checkboxes or radio buttons that are checked, allowing you to apply specific styles or behaviors based on the state.
- input:disabled targets input fields that are disabled, helping you work with dynamic forms that may disable fields based on user input or conditions.

By incorporating pseudo-classes into your CSS selectors, you can create flexible and robust selectors that adapt to dynamic content, user interactions, and changing web page structures. This approach enhances your ability to work with Selenium WebDriver and similar frameworks for automated testing and web element location.

Finding Elements by Data Attributes

Data attributes in HTML, prefixed with `data-`, provide a flexible and extensible way to attach additional information to elements. These attributes are useful for various purposes, from adding metadata to enabling JavaScript-based interactions. They are also valuable when working with dynamic content, as they allow you to create robust CSS selectors that target elements based on specific data attributes or values.

Why Use Data Attributes?

Data attributes offer several advantages when dealing with dynamic content:

- **Consistency**: They can be a stable source of information even when other attributes like IDs or classes change dynamically.
- **Flexibility**: You can store a wide range of information in data attributes, from unique identifiers to configuration data, which can be used to locate elements or influence behavior.
- **Maintainability**: Data attributes are less likely to interfere with styling or existing class-based selectors, making them easier to maintain in complex projects.

CSS Selectors for Data Attributes

CSS attribute selectors can be used to target elements with specific data attributes or values. Here's how you can create selectors that use data attributes:

- **Selecting by Data Attribute Name**: To select all elements with a specific data attribute, use a simple attribute selector. For example:
    - `[data-role]` selects all elements with the `data-role` attribute, regardless of its value.
    - `div[data-custom]` targets `<div>` elements with any `data-custom` attribute.
- **Matching Data Attribute Values**: You can select elements based on the exact value of a data attribute:
    - `[data-role="admin"]` selects elements where the `data-role` attribute is "admin".
    - `button[data-action="submit"]` targets buttons with a `data-action` attribute set to "submit".
- **Partial Matches with Data Attributes**: To find elements where a data attribute contains, starts with, or ends with a specific value, you can use partial match attribute selectors:
    - `[data-role*="admin"]` selects elements where `data-role` contains "admin".
    - `[data-type^="btn"]` targets elements with a `data-type` attribute starting with "btn".
    - `[data-category$="main"]` selects elements with a `data-category` attribute ending in "main".

Applying Data Attributes in Dynamic Content

Using data attributes is particularly effective in handling dynamic content because they provide stable references even when the structure or other attributes change. Here are some examples of how to leverage data attributes to locate elements in dynamic content scenarios:

Targeting Unique Identifiers

When IDs are dynamically generated or change frequently, data attributes can provide a stable identifier. Consider these examples:

- `div[data-id="12345"]` selects a `<div>` with a specific `data-id` value.
- `tr[data-row="2"]` targets the second row in a table with a corresponding `data-row` attribute.

Locating Elements in Complex Structures

Data attributes can help navigate complex or dynamic structures where other selectors might fail. For example:

- `ul[data-menu="main"] > li[data-item="3"]` selects the third item in an unordered list where the list has a `data-menu` attribute set to "main".
- `div[data-section="header"]` targets a specific section within a dynamic page structure.

Finding Elements with Custom Data

Data attributes are often used to store custom information, making them ideal for targeting specific elements based on this data. Consider these use cases:

- `input[data-validation="required"]` selects input fields with a `data-validation` attribute set to "required", useful for form validation.
- `button[data-toggle="collapse"]` targets buttons that control collapsible sections, ideal for dynamic content scenarios.

By using data attributes and CSS selectors, you can create robust and flexible ways to locate elements in dynamic content. This approach is especially valuable when working with automation frameworks like Selenium WebDriver, where stability and adaptability are crucial.

Handling Changing Element Structures

In web development, especially when dealing with dynamic content, the structure of a web page can change due to user interactions, JavaScript logic, AJAX calls, or other factors. These changes can make it challenging to locate elements using static CSS selectors. However, with the right techniques, you can create flexible and robust CSS selectors to handle these changing element structures.

Understanding Changing Element Structures

Changing element structures refer to scenarios where elements are added, removed, or rearranged within the Document Object Model (DOM). This can happen due to:

- **User interactions**: Clicking buttons, expanding/collapsing sections, or submitting forms.
- **JavaScript events**: Scripts dynamically adding or removing elements.
- **AJAX calls**: Content updating without a full page reload.
- **Framework-specific behaviors**: Front-end frameworks that update the DOM dynamically (e.g., React, Angular, Vue).

Techniques for Handling Changing Structures

Parent-Child Relationships

Using parent-child relationships is a reliable way to locate elements even when the structure changes. The > selector targets direct children of a parent element. This technique helps you focus on a specific scope within the DOM. Examples include:

- `div > p` selects all `<p>` elements that are direct children of a `<div>`.
- `ul > li:first-child` targets the first list item within an unordered list.

Sibling Relationships

Sibling selectors allow you to locate elements based on their position relative to other elements in the same parent. This approach is useful when elements are dynamically added or removed, changing the sibling structure. Common sibling selectors are:

- `element + sibling` selects the next immediate sibling.
- `element ~ siblings` selects all following siblings.

Examples:

- `h2 + p` selects the first paragraph following an `<h2>`.
- `li ~ li` selects all list items following the first one.

Combined Parent-Child and Sibling Relationships

Combining parent-child and sibling relationships can be useful for navigating complex structures, allowing you to find elements even when their exact position changes. Consider these examples:

- `div > ul > li:first-child` selects the first list item within an unordered list that is inside a `<div>`.
- `div > ul > li:nth-child(2)` selects the second list item, which is useful when the position within the list matters.

Using Specific Attributes or Classes

When elements are dynamically added or removed, using specific attributes or classes can provide stability. Custom data attributes, as discussed earlier, can be particularly useful. Examples include:

- `div[data-role="header"]` selects a `<div>` with a specific `data-role`.
- `input[data-status="active"]` targets input fields with a `data-status` attribute set to "active".

Handling Asynchronous Content

Dealing with asynchronous content updates often requires waiting for elements to appear or ensuring the DOM is in a stable state. To manage this, you can use timing-based techniques or other methods to handle changing structures. Techniques include:

- **Waiting for Content to Load**: Use Selenium WebDriver's explicit waits to ensure the dynamic content is fully loaded before interacting with elements.
- **Resilient Selectors**: Design CSS selectors that are less prone to breaking due to minor changes in structure or attributes.

Examples of Handling Changing Structures

Example 1: Dynamic Lists

Consider a dynamic list where items are added or removed based on user interactions. You can use the following CSS selectors to handle changes:

- `ul > li:last-child` selects the last item, regardless of how many items are added.
- `ul > li:nth-child(odd)` targets odd-numbered items, useful for applying alternating styles.

Example 2: Dynamic Forms

In forms with fields that appear or disappear based on user input, specific CSS selectors can help locate and interact with changing elements:

- `form > input[data-validation="required"]` selects input fields that require validation.
- `form > input:disabled` targets disabled input fields, useful when forms dynamically disable elements based on conditions.

Example 3: Collapsible Sections

For web pages with collapsible sections, you can use parent-child and sibling relationships to locate specific elements within changing structures:

- `div[data-section="main"] > button[data-toggle="collapse"]` targets buttons that control collapsible sections.
- `div > h2 + p` selects paragraphs that follow section headers, useful for dynamic content with varying structures.

By employing these techniques and examples, you can create robust CSS selectors to handle changing element structures effectively. These approaches are especially useful in automation scenarios with Selenium WebDriver, where flexibility and adaptability are crucial for maintaining stable tests.

Practical Examples of CSS Selectors for Dynamic Content

Creating robust CSS selectors for dynamic content can be challenging due to changing element structures, attributes, and asynchronous updates. This chapter section focuses on practical examples to help you understand how to use CSS selectors to locate and interact with dynamic elements on modern web pages.

Example 1: Selecting Elements in Dynamic Lists

Dynamic lists are common in web applications, where items are added or removed based on user interactions or data changes. Here's how to create CSS selectors for such scenarios:

- **Selecting All List Items**:
  - `ul > li` selects all list items within a parent unordered list.
- **Selecting Specific List Items by Index**:
  - `ul > li:nth-child(1)` selects the first item in the list.
  - `ul > li:last-child` targets the last item, regardless of the list's length.
- **Selecting Odd or Even Items**:
  - `ul > li:nth-child(odd)` selects all odd-numbered items.
  - `ul > li:nth-child(even)` targets even-numbered items.
- **Selecting Items Based on Content**:
  - `ul > li[data-status="active"]` selects list items with a specific data attribute, useful for dynamic content with changing statuses.

Example 2: Locating Elements in Dynamic Navigation Menus

Navigation menus often change structure based on user interactions, such as expanding/collapsing sections or adding new items. Here are some examples of CSS selectors for dynamic menus:

- **Selecting All Menu Items**:
  - `nav > ul > li` targets all menu items within a navigation element.

- **Selecting Specific Menu Items by Class or Attribute**:
  - `nav > ul > li.active` selects menu items with a class of "active".
  - `nav > ul > li[data-section="home"]` targets a specific menu item based on a data attribute.
- **Selecting Menu Items by Hierarchical Structure**:
  - `nav > ul > li > ul > li` selects nested menu items within a submenu.

Example 3: Handling Dynamic Forms

Forms with dynamic elements, such as inputs that appear or disappear based on user input, require flexible CSS selectors. Here's how to create selectors for dynamic forms:

- **Selecting All Form Fields**:
  - `form > input` selects all input fields within a form.
- **Selecting Fields by Type**:
  - `form > input[type="text"]` targets text input fields.
  - `form > input[type="checkbox"]` selects checkboxes.
- **Selecting Fields by Data Attributes**:
  - `form > input[data-required="true"]` selects input fields that are marked as required through a data attribute.
- **Selecting Form Buttons**:
  - `form > button[type="submit"]` targets the submit button in a form.
  - `form > button[data-action="cancel"]` selects a button with a specific data action, useful for dynamic forms with multiple actions.

Example 4: Managing Dynamic Content in Collapsible Sections

Collapsible sections often have dynamic content that appears or disappears based on user interactions. These CSS selectors help locate elements in such scenarios:

- **Selecting Collapsible Sections by Data Attributes**:
  - `div[data-section="faq"]` selects a collapsible section with a specific data attribute.
- **Selecting Collapse/Expand Buttons**:
  - `div[data-section="faq"] > button[data-toggle="collapse"]` targets the button used to collapse or expand the section.
- **Selecting Content within Collapsible Sections**:
  - `div[data-section="faq"] > div.content` selects the content within a specific collapsible section.

Example 5: Handling Asynchronous Updates

Asynchronous updates, such as those caused by AJAX, require selectors that account for potential timing issues. Consider these examples for handling dynamic content:

- **Selecting Elements with Specific States**:
  - `div.loading` targets elements with a "loading" class, useful for handling asynchronous content updates.
  - `div[data-status="loaded"]` selects elements that indicate content has been loaded.
- **Selecting Elements After AJAX Updates**:
  - `div[data-update="true"]` targets elements that have been updated asynchronously.
  - `ul > li.new` selects new list items added through AJAX.

These practical examples demonstrate how to use CSS selectors to navigate dynamic content on web pages. By leveraging attribute selectors, parent-child relationships, sibling selectors, and data attributes, you can create robust and flexible selectors to handle various scenarios. These examples are especially useful in automated testing with Selenium WebDriver, where dynamic content is common, and robust selectors are crucial for maintaining stable tests.

Common Challenges and Solutions

Working with CSS selectors in dynamic content scenarios can be challenging due to changing element structures, asynchronous content updates, and evolving web technologies. This section discusses common challenges when dealing with CSS selectors in dynamic content and offers practical solutions to address them.

Challenge 1: Changing DOM Structures

Dynamic content often leads to changing DOM structures. Elements can be added, removed, or moved, making it difficult to create stable CSS selectors.

Solution

- **Use Parent-Child and Sibling Relationships**: Create selectors based on the relative position of elements in the DOM. This approach is more resilient to changes in overall structure.
- **Leverage Attribute Selectors**: Instead of relying solely on IDs or classes, use attribute selectors to target elements with specific attributes or patterns.
- **Consider Data Attributes**: Data attributes offer a consistent way to identify elements even when their structure or position changes.

Challenge 2: Dynamic IDs and Classes

In dynamic web applications, IDs and classes might be generated dynamically, making them unreliable for creating static CSS selectors.

Solution

- **Avoid Relying on Specific IDs**: Instead of targeting specific IDs, use attribute selectors with patterns or parent-child relationships to increase selector robustness.
- **Use Unique Attributes**: Find stable attributes that don't change dynamically. Data attributes can provide a reliable way to locate elements.
- **Combine Multiple Selectors**: Create selectors that combine attributes, parent-child relationships, and sibling selectors to reduce reliance on changing IDs or classes.

Challenge 3: Asynchronous Content Updates

Asynchronous content updates, such as AJAX calls, can lead to timing-related issues where elements are not immediately available when needed.

Solution

- **Implement Explicit Waits**: In automation frameworks like Selenium WebDriver, use explicit waits to ensure elements are loaded before interacting with them.
- **Target Loading States**: Create selectors that target elements indicating a loading state. For example, an element with a class like "loading" can be used to wait for asynchronous updates to complete.
- **Use Dynamic Content Indicators**: Data attributes or specific classes can be used to indicate when content has finished loading, allowing you to create selectors that wait for these indicators.

Challenge 4: Handling Complex Web Page Structures

Modern web pages often have complex structures with nested elements, making it challenging to create stable CSS selectors.

Solution

- **Use Hierarchical Selectors**: Combine parent-child relationships with sibling selectors to navigate complex structures. This approach allows you to create selectors that are more resilient to changes in structure.
- **Target Specific Data Attributes**: Data attributes can be used to identify specific sections or elements within complex structures.
- **Implement Flexible Selectors**: Design selectors that account for potential changes in structure. For example, use `:nth-child()` or `:nth-of-type()` to target specific positions within a parent.

Challenge 5: Handling Dynamic Forms

Dynamic forms may add or remove fields based on user interactions or other conditions, making it difficult to locate specific elements.

Solution

- **Use Form-Specific Selectors**: Create selectors that target elements based on form-specific attributes, such as `form > input` or `form > button`.
- **Target Data Attributes for Validation**: Data attributes can indicate specific validations or requirements, allowing you to create selectors that adapt to changing form fields.
- **Leverage Pseudo-Classes for State-Based Selection**: Pseudo-classes like `:checked`, `:disabled`, or `:focus` can help target specific form states.

Challenge 6: Debugging and Troubleshooting Selector Issues

When CSS selectors fail, it can be challenging to identify the root cause, especially with dynamic content.

Solution

- **Use Browser Developer Tools**: Most modern browsers have developer tools that allow you to inspect elements and test CSS selectors. Use these tools to troubleshoot issues.
- **Log Selector Results**: In automation frameworks like Selenium WebDriver, logging selector results can help identify where the selector fails.
- **Implement Robust Error Handling**: Design error handling mechanisms to address common selector issues, ensuring your scripts are resilient to failures.

These common challenges and solutions provide a foundation for creating robust and flexible CSS selectors in dynamic content scenarios. By understanding these challenges and applying the solutions, you can improve the reliability and stability of your selectors in automated testing and web automation.

Chapter Summary

In this chapter, you learned about various techniques for using CSS selectors to handle dynamic content. Here's a summary of the key points covered in the chapter:

1. **Understanding Dynamic Content**
   - Dynamic content involves web elements that change due to user interactions, JavaScript, AJAX calls, or other factors.

    ○ This can lead to challenges in locating elements because the structure and attributes may shift over time.

2. **Using Attribute Selectors for Changing Attributes**
   - Attribute selectors allow you to target elements based on specific attributes or patterns.
   - They are useful for handling dynamic content because they offer flexibility and resilience even when IDs or classes change.
   - Different types of attribute selectors include exact matches, partial matches, and prefix/suffix-based selectors.

3. **Employing Pseudo-Classes to Target States**
   - Pseudo-classes are used to select elements based on their state, position, or user interaction.
   - Common pseudo-classes include `:hover`, `:focus`, `:checked`, `:first-child`, `:last-child`, and more.
   - These selectors help target elements in changing structures or varying states.

4. **Finding Elements by Data Attributes**
   - Data attributes (prefixed with `data-`) provide a consistent way to identify elements, even in dynamic content scenarios.
   - CSS attribute selectors can be used to target elements based on specific data attributes or values.
   - This approach is particularly useful when other attributes like IDs or classes are dynamically generated or altered.

5. **Handling Changing Element Structures**
   - Dynamic content can lead to changing DOM structures, requiring flexible and robust selectors.
   - Parent-child relationships and sibling selectors are valuable for navigating complex structures.
   - Using stable attributes, like data attributes, helps create resilient selectors for dynamic content.

6. **Practical Examples of CSS Selectors for Dynamic Content**
   - Various examples illustrate how to use CSS selectors in real-world scenarios with dynamic content.
   - These examples include handling dynamic lists, dynamic navigation menus, dynamic forms, collapsible sections, and asynchronous content updates.

7. **Common Challenges and Solutions**
   - Common challenges include changing DOM structures, dynamic IDs and classes, asynchronous content updates, complex web page structures, and dynamic forms.
   - Practical solutions were provided, such as using parent-child relationships, implementing explicit waits, targeting specific attributes, and leveraging pseudo-classes for state-based selection.

By understanding and applying these concepts, you can create CSS selectors that are robust and adaptable, ensuring they remain effective in the face of dynamic content and changing web structures. This knowledge is particularly valuable for automated testing with frameworks like Selenium WebDriver, where selectors play a crucial role in interacting with web elements.

Creating CSS Selectors with Multiple Attributes

Outline

Understanding CSS Selectors with Multiple Attributes

CSS (Cascading Style Sheets) selectors are a fundamental tool for web development and automation testing with Selenium WebDriver. They allow you to target specific elements on a webpage based on their attributes, classes, IDs, or other characteristics. When dealing with complex or dynamic webpages, using multiple attributes to create selectors can be an effective strategy to precisely locate the elements you need.

Why Use Multiple Attribute Selectors?

Using multiple attributes to create CSS selectors is helpful in several scenarios:

- **Precision**: A single attribute like id or class might not be unique enough, leading to incorrect selections. Combining multiple attributes provides more specificity.
- **Handling Similar Elements**: On webpages with repeated elements, like multiple buttons or input fields, combining attributes helps differentiate between them.
- **Working with Dynamic Content**: In cases where content changes dynamically (like with AJAX), multiple attributes can provide more stability in your selectors.

Examples of Multiple Attribute Selectors

Consider a scenario where you have a list of buttons with a common class, but you need to select a specific button based on its role and its associated data attribute:

```
[class="button"][data-role="submit"]
```

This selector targets a button with a class of "button" and a data-role of "submit." It's more precise than simply selecting by class, reducing the risk of unintended matches.

Here's another example for a webpage with complex elements, where you need to target a specific item based on its class and an ID-like attribute:

```
[class="item"][data-id="12345"]
```

Real-World Use Cases

- **Form Fields**: To select a particular input field in a form where class names are similar but other attributes differ.
- **Menu Items**: To target a specific menu item in a dynamic navigation bar by combining class with a custom data attribute.

- **AJAX-based Content**: To find elements that are dynamically generated and require more specific targeting due to similar class structures.

Using multiple attribute selectors is a powerful technique that allows for precise element targeting, which is critical in automation testing and complex web development. This approach reduces ambiguity and increases the reliability of your CSS selectors. Understanding the syntax and real-world applications of this technique will enhance your ability to locate and interact with elements effectively in Selenium WebDriver or other automation frameworks.

Basic Syntax for Multiple Attribute Selectors

CSS selectors are a powerful tool for identifying and interacting with specific elements on a webpage. When working with multiple attributes, the syntax is quite flexible, allowing you to define selectors that precisely match your requirements. Understanding this basic syntax is essential for both web development and automated testing with frameworks like Selenium WebDriver.

Combining Attributes in CSS Selectors

The primary way to create a CSS selector that uses multiple attributes is to place each attribute condition within square brackets [ ]. These attribute conditions are then combined, resulting in a single selector that must meet all specified criteria.

Here's the general syntax for combining multiple attributes:

```
[attribute1="value1"][attribute2="value2"]
```

This selector will match any element that has both specified attributes with the given values. It's useful when you need to target elements with more precision.

Attribute Comparisons

The basic syntax allows for various types of comparisons to match specific patterns or conditions in attribute values. Here are some common comparison operators:

- = (Equals): Matches elements where the attribute equals a specific value.
- ~ (Contains Word): Matches elements where the attribute contains a specific word.
- | (Starts with Value): Matches elements where the attribute is a specific value or begins with that value followed by a hyphen.
- ^ (Begins With): Matches elements where the attribute value starts with a specific pattern.
- $ (Ends With): Matches elements where the attribute value ends with a specific pattern.
- * (Contains Substring): Matches elements where the attribute contains a specific substring.

Examples of Multiple Attribute Selectors

Let's explore a few examples to see how you might use multiple attribute selectors in practice:

- **Example 1: A Button with Specific Class and Data-Attribute**

  ```
  [class="btn"][data-action="submit"]
  ```

  This selector targets a button with a class of "btn" and a data-action attribute with the value "submit".

- **Example 2: An Input Field with a Specific Name and Type**

```
[name="username"][type="text"]
```

This selector locates an input field with the name "username" and a type of "text".

- **Example 3: An Element with Multiple Classes and Specific ID**

```
[class~="item selected"][id="item123"]
```

This selector finds an element with both "item" and "selected" in its class list and a specific ID of "item123".

- **Example 4: A List Item with a Specific Role and Data-Attribute**

```
[role="menuitem"][data-id^="menu"]
```

This selector targets a list item with the role of "menuitem" and a data-id attribute starting with "menu".

Practical Tips for Multiple Attribute Selectors

- **Avoid Excessive Complexity**: While combining multiple attributes is powerful, avoid overly complex selectors that can be hard to maintain.
- **Be Consistent with Attribute Names**: Use consistent naming conventions for attributes to ensure easier selection.
- **Optimize for Performance**: Although CSS selectors are efficient, complex attribute combinations can impact performance. Test your selectors in context to ensure they perform as expected.

Using multiple attributes in CSS selectors is a flexible approach to locating specific elements on a webpage. By understanding the basic syntax and different comparison operators, you can create robust selectors that meet your automation and development needs. These skills are essential for working with dynamic web content and building reliable automated tests.

Combining Attributes for Specific Selections

When building CSS selectors, combining multiple attributes allows for more specific and accurate selections. This technique is particularly useful when individual attributes, such as ID, class, or data attributes, do not uniquely identify an element. By combining attributes, you can create targeted selectors that reduce ambiguity and ensure you're interacting with the intended elements.

Why Combine Attributes?

Combining attributes helps in several scenarios:

- **Unique Identification**: Sometimes a single attribute isn't unique. By combining multiple attributes, you can narrow down your selection to a specific element or group of elements.
- **Dynamic Content**: Dynamic websites often use similar class names or changing IDs. Combining attributes can provide more stable selectors.
- **Avoiding Conflicts**: To avoid selecting unintended elements, combining attributes ensures that the selector is unique and specific.

Basic Syntax for Combining Attributes

The syntax for combining multiple attributes involves enclosing each attribute condition in square brackets [ ]. When using multiple attributes, you join them to form a single selector that must meet all specified conditions. Here's a general example:

```
[attribute1="value1"][attribute2="value2"]
```

This selector targets elements that have both specified attributes with the given values. You can also use a combination of different operators within the attribute conditions.

Using Multiple Attributes in CSS Selectors

Combining attributes provides a versatile way to target elements. Here are some common examples and scenarios where this technique is useful:

- **Selecting Elements by Class and Data-Attribute**

  ```
  [class="btn-primary"][data-action="save"]
  ```

  This selector targets elements with a "btn-primary" class and a data-action attribute with the value "save". It's helpful for distinguishing between buttons with similar class names but different data roles.

- **Combining Attributes to Target Specific Input Fields**

  ```
  [type="text"][name="username"]
  ```

  This selector locates text input fields with the name "username", ensuring that you select the correct form field.

- **Selecting Elements with Multiple Classes and Specific Data Attributes**

  ```
  [class~="item active"][data-id="item123"]
  ```

  This selector identifies elements that have both "item" and "active" in their class list and a specific data-id of "item123". This approach is particularly useful when dealing with collections of elements where uniqueness is critical.

Advanced Scenarios with Multiple Attributes

Combining attributes allows for more complex scenarios. Consider these examples:

- **Locating Nested Elements with Combined Attributes**

  ```
  [data-parent="menu"][class="submenu"]
  ```

  This selector finds elements with a specific data-parent attribute and a "submenu" class, useful for selecting nested menu items or components.

- **Selecting Elements with Multiple Data Attributes**

  ```
  [data-role="button"][data-toggle="collapse"]
  ```

  This selector identifies elements that serve as buttons and have a specific role in toggling a collapse state. It provides greater control over dynamic content selection.

Tips for Combining Attributes

- **Ensure Uniqueness**: When combining attributes, ensure the resulting selector is unique enough to avoid unintended selections.
- **Test in Context**: Always test your selectors within the context of the webpage to ensure they function as expected.

- **Optimize for Performance**: Complex attribute combinations can affect performance, especially in large-scale automation. Keep selectors as efficient as possible.

Combining attributes in CSS selectors is a robust method for creating specific and unique selections. By understanding the syntax and common use cases, you can build effective selectors for automation and development tasks. This approach reduces ambiguity and increases the reliability of your CSS-based interactions, providing a solid foundation for advanced automation frameworks like Selenium WebDriver.

Common Scenarios for Multiple Attribute Selectors

CSS selectors with multiple attributes allow you to locate elements on a webpage with a high degree of specificity. This can be incredibly useful in various situations where elements share common attributes or when the structure is complex. In this section, we'll explore common scenarios where combining multiple attributes is beneficial and why these selectors are valuable in web development and automated testing contexts.

Scenarios Requiring Multiple Attribute Selectors

Let's examine some typical scenarios where combining multiple attributes provides clarity and precision:

1. Identifying Unique Elements in a Collection

When you have a collection of similar elements, such as a list of items or buttons, using multiple attribute selectors can help you identify a specific item. For example, to find a specific button in a set of buttons:

```
[class="btn"][data-action="save"]
```

Here, the selector locates a button with a "btn" class and a data-action attribute set to "save." This technique ensures you're interacting with the right element among many similar ones.

2. Handling Nested Structures

In complex webpage layouts, elements might be nested within parent elements. Using multiple attributes can help you select elements within a specific context. For instance, to find an item within a particular section:

```
[section="main"][class="item"]
```

This selector targets an element with the class "item" that is nested within a section designated as "main." It ensures you are targeting the right context, even in complex nested structures.

3. Working with Forms and User Inputs

Forms often contain multiple input fields with similar attributes. Combining multiple attributes helps identify unique fields. Consider selecting a text input field in a form with a specific placeholder and name:

```
[type="text"][name="username"][placeholder="Enter Username"]
```

This selector allows you to find a text field specifically designed for entering a username, ensuring you don't accidentally select other text fields with similar attributes.

4. Selecting Elements with Common Classes but Different Data Attributes

Web applications often use common class names with differentiating data attributes. Combining these can be useful to select specific elements. Here's an example for selecting a particular navigation item:

```
[class="nav-item"][data-id="nav-123"]
```

This selector helps locate a specific navigation item within a group, where each item has a unique data attribute but shares a common class.

5. Locating Elements in Dynamic Content

Dynamic content, especially in modern single-page applications, can be challenging to navigate. Using multiple attribute selectors provides stability when elements change dynamically. For example, selecting a specific tab in a dynamic navigation:

```
[role="tab"][data-tab="profile"]
```

This selector targets a tab element with a role of "tab" and a data-tab attribute set to "profile." It provides a robust way to select the correct element, even when content updates dynamically.

Tips for Creating Multiple Attribute Selectors

When creating selectors with multiple attributes, consider these tips:

- **Ensure Uniqueness**: Make sure your selector uniquely identifies the desired element(s). Test it within the context of the webpage to confirm its specificity.
- **Use Consistent Naming Conventions**: Consistent attribute naming helps reduce errors and confusion when creating selectors.
- **Avoid Excessive Complexity**: While combining attributes can increase precision, avoid making selectors too complex, as this can reduce readability and increase maintenance effort.
- **Optimize for Performance**: Although CSS selectors are generally efficient, overly complex combinations can impact performance. Test your selectors to ensure they are optimized.

Using multiple attribute selectors is a flexible and powerful technique to address common scenarios in web development and automated testing. By combining attributes, you can navigate complex web structures, handle dynamic content, and ensure precision in your selections. Understanding these scenarios and the best practices for creating effective selectors will enhance your ability to work with CSS and automation frameworks like Selenium WebDriver.

Examples and Practice

In this section, we'll explore various examples that demonstrate how to create CSS selectors with multiple attributes. These examples aim to solidify your understanding of using multiple attributes for precise element selection in different scenarios. After exploring these examples, you'll find some practical exercises to practice building these selectors yourself.

Example 1: Locating a Button with Specific Class and Data-Attribute

In a form, you might have multiple buttons with the same class but different data attributes. Let's say you need to select a "submit" button with a specific class and a unique data attribute. Here's an example of a CSS selector for this scenario:

```
[class="btn-primary"][data-action="submit"]
```

This selector locates a button with the class "btn-primary" and a data-action attribute of "submit." It ensures you are interacting with the correct button among potentially many similar buttons.

Example 2: Selecting a Text Field with Multiple Attributes

Imagine a login form with multiple text input fields, such as "username" and "password." To ensure you're selecting the correct field, you might combine attributes like type, name, and placeholder:

```
[type="text"][name="username"][placeholder="Enter your username"]
```

This selector targets a text input field with the name "username" and a placeholder that matches "Enter your username." It helps avoid accidental selection of the wrong field.

Example 3: Identifying a Specific List Item

Consider a navigation menu with multiple list items. If you need to select a specific item, you might use a combination of class and data attributes. For instance, to select an item based on a unique ID and class:

```
[class="menu-item"][data-id="item-123"]
```

This selector targets a list item with the class "menu-item" and a data-id of "item-123." It ensures precise selection within a collection of similar elements.

Example 4: Finding a Table Cell with Specific Attributes

If you're working with tables, you might need to find a cell with specific attributes. For example, to locate a cell based on row and column attributes:

```
[data-row="2"][data-column="3"]
```

This selector locates a table cell in row 2, column 3, based on custom data attributes. This approach is helpful when you need to interact with specific cells in a table structure.

Practical Exercises

Now that you've seen a few examples, let's put your skills to the test with some practical exercises. For each exercise, try to create a CSS selector using multiple attributes to locate the desired elements.

Exercise 1: Find a Button in a Form

Create a CSS selector to find a button in a form with the following attributes:

- Class: "btn-secondary"
- Data-action: "reset"

Exercise 2: Locate a Specific Div within a Section

In a webpage, you have a section with a unique ID and multiple div elements within it. Create a CSS selector to find a div with the following attributes:

- ID of the section: "main-section"
- Class of the div: "content-block"

Exercise 3: Identify an Input Field with Specific Attributes

To locate a specific input field in a form, create a CSS selector with the following attributes:

- Type: "email"
- Name: "user-email"
- Placeholder: "Enter your email"

Exercise 4: Find an Anchor Tag with Multiple Attributes

In a navigation bar, you have multiple anchor tags. Create a CSS selector to find an anchor tag with the following attributes:

- Role: "navigation"

- Data-link: "home"

These examples and exercises demonstrate the versatility of CSS selectors with multiple attributes. By understanding these concepts and practicing with various scenarios, you can improve your ability to locate and interact with specific elements on a webpage. This skill is essential for both web development and automated testing with frameworks like Selenium WebDriver.

Tips and Best Practices

When creating CSS selectors with multiple attributes, it's important to follow best practices to ensure your selectors are efficient, maintainable, and reliable. This section provides tips and insights for creating robust selectors that are suitable for complex web environments and automation tasks like Selenium WebDriver.

1. Ensure Uniqueness

Combining multiple attributes in CSS selectors allows you to target specific elements with greater precision. However, make sure your selectors uniquely identify the intended elements to avoid ambiguous selections. Always test your selectors within the context of the webpage to confirm they return only the expected elements.

2. Use Consistent Naming Conventions

Consistency in attribute naming makes it easier to create reliable selectors. When working with custom attributes like `data-attributes`, ensure that they follow a consistent naming pattern. This consistency helps in building predictable selectors and reduces the risk of errors.

3. Avoid Overly Complex Selectors

While combining multiple attributes increases specificity, avoid making selectors excessively complex. Complex selectors can become hard to read, maintain, and debug. Aim for simplicity and readability, focusing on essential attributes to achieve the desired precision.

4. Test Selectors for Performance

Complex CSS selectors can impact performance, especially when used in automated testing with Selenium WebDriver. Test your selectors to ensure they execute efficiently and don't cause slowdowns in your automation scripts. Simplify selectors where possible to improve performance.

5. Optimize Selectors for Readability

Readable selectors are easier to maintain and update. Use clear attribute names and avoid excessive chaining of multiple attributes. Consider adding comments in your code to explain complex selectors, especially if they contain specific business logic or dependencies.

6. Use Attribute Operators Wisely

CSS provides various attribute operators for different scenarios. Use the appropriate operator for your needs, but avoid overusing them. Here's a quick overview of common attribute operators:

- = (Equals): Selects elements where the attribute equals a specific value.
- ~ (Contains Word): Selects elements where the attribute contains a specific word.
- | (Starts with Value): Selects elements where the attribute is a specific value or begins with it followed by a hyphen.
- ^ (Begins With): Selects elements where the attribute value starts with a specific pattern.

- $ (Ends With): Selects elements where the attribute value ends with a specific pattern.
- * (Contains Substring): Selects elements where the attribute contains a specific substring.

Use these operators strategically to create efficient selectors that meet your specific requirements.

7. Account for Dynamic Content

In modern web applications, content can change dynamically, affecting the reliability of CSS selectors. When creating selectors for dynamic content, focus on attributes that are less likely to change. Avoid relying solely on `id` or other volatile attributes. Instead, consider using a combination of stable attributes, such as class names and data attributes.

8. Document Your Selectors

Documenting your selectors helps others understand their purpose and logic. When creating complex selectors with multiple attributes, include comments explaining their context, especially if they rely on specific business logic. This practice makes it easier for others to maintain and update your code.

Creating CSS selectors with multiple attributes requires careful consideration to ensure they are unique, efficient, and maintainable. By following these tips and best practices, you can build robust selectors that are suitable for both web development and automated testing with frameworks like Selenium WebDriver. These best practices will help you avoid common pitfalls and ensure your selectors perform well in real-world scenarios.

Chapter Summary

In this chapter, we've explored the concept of creating CSS selectors using multiple attributes, a technique that provides precision and flexibility when selecting elements on a webpage. This approach is particularly useful in complex web environments and automation tasks, like those performed with Selenium WebDriver.

Here's a summary of the key topics covered in this chapter:

Understanding CSS Selectors with Multiple Attributes

- **Purpose and Benefits**: We discussed why combining multiple attributes in CSS selectors is valuable, particularly for targeting specific elements and handling complex or dynamic web content.
- **Basic Syntax**: We explored the syntax for creating CSS selectors with multiple attributes, using square brackets [ ] to encapsulate attribute conditions. Common comparison operators like =, ~, ^, $, and * were also introduced.

Combining Attributes for Specific Selections

- **Precision and Uniqueness**: By combining attributes, selectors can achieve a higher degree of specificity, helping to avoid unintended matches.
- **Handling Common Scenarios**: We examined scenarios where combining attributes is beneficial, such as identifying unique elements in collections, handling nested structures, and working with forms and user inputs.

Examples and Practice

- **Real-World Examples**: We presented various examples demonstrating how to use multiple attributes to select elements in different contexts, such as buttons, input fields, and table cells.
- **Practical Exercises**: Exercises were provided to help you practice creating CSS selectors with multiple attributes, reinforcing your understanding and skill in this area.

Tips and Best Practices

- **Ensuring Selector Uniqueness**: We discussed the importance of ensuring that selectors uniquely identify the intended elements to avoid ambiguity.
- **Avoiding Excessive Complexity**: While combining attributes increases specificity, keeping selectors readable and maintainable is crucial.
- **Performance and Optimization**: We highlighted the need to test selectors for performance and optimize for efficiency.
- **Dynamic Content and Stability**: Given the dynamic nature of modern web applications, we emphasized the importance of choosing stable attributes to create reliable selectors.

Conclusion

Creating CSS selectors with multiple attributes is a powerful technique for web development and automated testing. By combining attributes, you can achieve precise selections and handle complex or dynamic content with greater stability. The examples, exercises, and best practices discussed in this chapter provide a solid foundation for building robust CSS selectors, ensuring they are efficient, maintainable, and optimized for performance. This understanding is critical for success in web automation frameworks like Selenium WebDriver.

Section 5:
Advanced CSS Selectors Techniques

Advanced CSS Selector Techniques

Outline

1. Introduction to Advanced CSS Selectors
2. Understanding Sibling Selectors
3. Using Pseudo-classes and Pseudo-elements
4. Utilizing CSS Combinators
5. Crafting Advanced Attribute Selectors
6. Selecting Based on Position
7. Leveraging Advanced CSS Patterns
8. Examples and Best Practices
9. Common Pitfalls and Debugging
10. Chapter Summary

Introduction to Advanced CSS Selectors

CSS selectors are the core of selecting and manipulating web elements in automation and front-end development. While basic CSS selectors like #id and .class are essential for straightforward scenarios, advanced CSS selector techniques are crucial for navigating complex structures and addressing unique conditions.

In this section, we explore advanced selectors, including pseudo-classes, pseudo-elements, combinators, and advanced attribute selectors. We'll also delve into patterns that help solve specific challenges in web automation and discuss common pitfalls and best practices.

Here's what you can expect from this chapter:

- An overview of advanced CSS selectors and their significance in web automation.
- Deep dives into pseudo-classes and pseudo-elements, explaining their functionality and use cases.
- Techniques for combining selectors to navigate complex relationships.
- Advanced attribute selectors for more precise element targeting.
- Best practices for ensuring reliable and maintainable CSS selectors.
- Common pitfalls and troubleshooting techniques to ensure smooth automation with CSS selectors.

By mastering these techniques, you'll gain the ability to tackle intricate web page layouts, dynamic content, and other challenging scenarios in your automation scripts. These skills are particularly valuable for Selenium WebDriver users seeking greater control and precision in their element location strategies.

Understanding Sibling Selectors

Sibling selectors in CSS are a powerful way to target elements based on their relationships with other elements on the same level in the Document Object Model (DOM). This is especially useful in complex web structures where elements might not have unique IDs or class names, but their relationships with other elements can be leveraged to select them.

In this section, we will explore different types of sibling selectors and their applications. We'll also examine practical examples to illustrate how sibling selectors can be used to navigate the DOM efficiently.

What are Sibling Selectors?

Sibling selectors allow you to select elements that share the same parent and are on the same level in the DOM tree. There are two main types of sibling selectors:

1. **Adjacent Sibling Selector (+)**: Selects an element that is immediately next to a specified element. This is useful when you want to target an element that directly follows another.
2. **General Sibling Selector (~)**: Selects all elements that follow a specified element within the same parent. This selector is broader and allows for selecting multiple elements in a group.

Adjacent Sibling Selector (+)

The adjacent sibling selector (+) selects an element that is the immediate sibling of another element. Here's an example:

```css
h1 + p {
  color: blue;
}
```

In this example, any <p> element that directly follows an <h1> will have its text color changed to blue. This selector is useful when you want to apply styles to an element only if it's immediately adjacent to another specified element.

General Sibling Selector (~)

The general sibling selector (~) selects all elements that follow a specified sibling, regardless of how many elements are in between. Here's an example:

```css
h1 ~ p {
  color: green;
}
```

In this example, all <p> elements that follow an <h1>, even if they're not immediately adjacent, will have their text color changed to green. This selector is useful for applying styles to a group of elements that follow a specific sibling.

Practical Use Cases

Sibling selectors can be useful in various scenarios, such as:

- Applying styles to specific elements in a list based on their position relative to others.
- Targeting form elements that follow specific labels for consistent styling.
- Implementing conditional styling based on the presence of other elements.

Sibling selectors are a flexible tool for targeting elements based on their relationships within the same parent. By understanding the differences between adjacent and general sibling selectors, you can apply these techniques to automate complex scenarios or create robust CSS rules for styling. Whether you're working with Selenium WebDriver or creating CSS stylesheets, mastering sibling selectors opens up new possibilities for navigating and manipulating the DOM.

Using Pseudo-classes and Pseudo-elements

Pseudo-classes and pseudo-elements are two powerful concepts in CSS that enable you to select elements based on their state, position, or other criteria, and to style specific parts of an element without adding additional HTML markup. In this section, we'll explore various pseudo-classes and pseudo-elements, discuss their use cases, and examine practical examples.

Pseudo-classes

A pseudo-class is a keyword that you can add to a CSS selector to target elements based on their state, position, or other characteristics that are not explicitly defined in the HTML. Pseudo-classes typically use a colon (:) before the class name. Here are some common pseudo-classes and their applications:

- **:hover**: Targets an element when the user hovers over it with a pointing device. Example:

```css
a:hover {
  color: red;
}
```

- **:active**: Targets an element when it's being clicked or activated. Example:

```css
button:active {
  background-color: green;
}
```

- **:focus**: Applies styles to an element when it receives focus, such as when a user tabs into an input field. Example:

```css
input:focus {
  border: 2px solid blue;
}
```

- **:nth-child()**: Selects elements based on their position among siblings. You can use specific patterns within the parentheses, like 2n for even elements or 2n-1 for odd elements. Example:

```css
li:nth-child(2n) {
  background-color: lightgray;
}
```

- **:first-child and :last-child**: Selects the first or last child among siblings. Example:

```css
p:first-child {
  font-weight: bold;
}

p:last-child {
  font-style: italic.
}
```

- **:not()**: Excludes certain elements from a selection. This is helpful when you want to target everything except a specific element. Example:

```css
p:not(.exclude) {
```

```
  color: purple;
}
```

Pseudo-elements

Pseudo-elements allow you to style parts of an element that are not explicitly defined in the HTML. They are typically denoted with double colons (: :). Here are some common pseudo-elements:

- **::before**: Inserts content before an element's content. Useful for adding decorative elements or custom text. Example:

```
h1::before {
  content: "Section: ";
  color: gray;
}
```

- **::after**: Inserts content after an element's content. Example:

```
p::after {
  content: " (end of paragraph)";
  color: lightgray;
}
```

- **::first-letter**: Applies styles to the first letter of a block-level element. Example:

```
p::first-letter {
  font-size: 2em;
  color: red;
}
```

- **::first-line**: Styles the first line of a block-level element. Example:

```
p::first-line {
  text-decoration: underline;
}
```

Pseudo-classes and pseudo-elements provide flexible ways to target and style web elements based on their state, position, or content structure without modifying the HTML. Understanding and applying these techniques allows you to create dynamic and interactive web pages or write more efficient automation scripts. These concepts are invaluable for both CSS developers and Selenium WebDriver automation engineers looking to control and interact with web elements in complex scenarios.

Utilizing CSS Combinators

CSS combinators define the relationships between different selectors, allowing you to select elements based on their position in the Document Object Model (DOM) relative to other elements. These combinators are crucial for navigating complex HTML structures in both front-end development and automation contexts, like Selenium WebDriver scripts.

In this section, we'll explore the four primary CSS combinators, discuss their use cases, and provide examples to illustrate how you can use them to locate and style elements based on relationships in the DOM.

What are CSS Combinators?

CSS combinators are symbols used to combine two or more selectors, establishing a relationship between them. The four main CSS combinators are:

- **Descendant combinator ()**
- **Child combinator (>)**
- **Adjacent sibling combinator (+)**
- **General sibling combinator (~)**

Let's delve into each of these combinators to understand their behavior and use cases.

Descendant Combinator ()

The descendant combinator (a space between selectors) selects elements that are descendants of another element, regardless of how deep they are in the DOM tree. This is the most flexible combinator but can lead to broad selections if not used carefully. Example:

```css
div p {
  color: blue;
}
```

In this example, all `<p>` elements within any `<div>` will be selected, no matter how deeply nested they are. This is useful for selecting elements in nested structures like menus, lists, or content sections.

Child Combinator (>)

The child combinator selects elements that are direct children of a specified parent element. This is more precise than the descendant combinator, as it doesn't include deeper descendants. Example:

```css
ul > li {
  list-style: square;
}
```

Here, only `<li>` elements that are direct children of a `<ul>` will have a square list style. This combinator is useful for maintaining strict relationships, like selecting immediate children in a navigation menu or a structured list.

Adjacent Sibling Combinator (+)

The adjacent sibling combinator selects an element that immediately follows another element with the same parent. This combinator is useful for targeting elements based on their immediate neighbor. Example:

```css
h2 + p {
  font-size: 1.2em;
}
```

In this case, any `<p>` element that directly follows an `<h2>` will have a larger font size. This combinator is often used for styling content blocks that follow specific headers or for adding space between sections.

General Sibling Combinator (~)

The general sibling combinator selects all elements that follow another element with the same parent. This combinator is broader than the adjacent sibling combinator, allowing you to select multiple siblings after a given element. Example:

```css
h1 ~ p {
```

```
  color: green;
}
```

Here, all <p> elements that follow an <h1>, even if not immediately adjacent, will be styled with a green color. This combinator is useful for applying styles to a group of related elements or for automation scenarios where a trigger element affects multiple subsequent elements.

CSS combinators offer powerful ways to define relationships between elements in the DOM. Understanding how to use descendant, child, adjacent sibling, and general sibling combinators allows you to navigate complex HTML structures efficiently. In automation contexts, like Selenium WebDriver, these combinators can help you create more targeted and maintainable element locators. By mastering CSS combinators, you can improve the robustness and flexibility of your CSS styling and web automation scripts.

Crafting Advanced Attribute Selectors

Attribute selectors in CSS allow you to select elements based on their attributes and attribute values. While simple attribute selectors like [attribute=value] are common, advanced attribute selectors offer more flexibility, enabling you to target elements in complex ways. This section explores various attribute selectors and provides examples to demonstrate how they can be used to navigate intricate HTML structures.

Understanding Attribute Selectors

Attribute selectors enable you to select elements based on the presence of specific attributes or specific attribute values. This is useful when you want to select elements with certain characteristics without relying solely on class or ID. Here are some basic and advanced attribute selectors:

- **Basic Attribute Selector ([attribute])**: Selects elements with the specified attribute, regardless of its value. Example:

  ```
  a[href] {
    color: blue;
  }
  ```

  This selector targets all anchor (<a>) elements with an href attribute, regardless of the actual link.

- **Exact Match Attribute Selector ([attribute=value])**: Selects elements with a specific attribute value. Example:

  ```
  input[type=text] {
    border: 1px solid black;
  }
  ```

  This selector targets all text input fields.

Advanced Attribute Selectors

Advanced attribute selectors allow for more complex conditions, such as matching parts of attribute values or combining multiple attributes. Let's explore these advanced selectors:

- **Attribute Starts With ([attribute^=value])**: Selects elements where the attribute value starts with a specified string. Example:

  ```
  input[name^="user"] {
  ```

```
    background-color: lightyellow;
  }
```

This selector targets all input fields with a name attribute starting with "user."

- **Attribute Ends With (`[attribute$=value]`):** Selects elements where the attribute value ends with a specified string. Example:

```
img[src$=".jpg"] {
  border: 2px solid red;
}
```

This selector targets all image elements with a `src` attribute ending in ".jpg."

- **Attribute Contains (`[attribute*=value]`):** Selects elements where the attribute value contains a specified substring. Example:

```
div[class*="content"] {
  padding: 10px;
}
```

This selector targets all `<div>` elements whose `class` attribute contains the substring "content."

Combining Attribute Selectors

You can also combine multiple attribute selectors to create more complex selection criteria. This allows for very precise targeting of elements. Example:

```
a[href^="https"][target="_blank"] {
  font-weight: bold;
}
```

In this example, all anchor tags that start with "https" in their `href` attribute and have a `target` of "_blank" are selected, applying bold styling. This combination is useful for locating secure links that open in a new tab.

Practical Applications

Advanced attribute selectors are useful for:

- Finding elements based on complex patterns or partial matches.
- Locating elements in automation scripts where exact matches are required.
- Styling or interacting with elements based on specific attribute configurations.
- Creating more flexible CSS rules that adapt to changing attribute values.

Advanced attribute selectors give you powerful tools to navigate and interact with HTML elements based on attribute patterns, partial matches, or specific combinations. Whether you are styling complex web pages or locating elements in automation scripts like Selenium WebDriver, mastering these advanced selectors will significantly improve your flexibility and precision.

Selecting Based on Position

CSS allows you to select elements based on their position within a parent or relative to other elements. Position-based selectors can be helpful in complex scenarios where you need to apply styles or automate interactions based on the location of an element. This section covers position-based CSS selectors and explores their practical applications.

Types of Position-based Selectors

There are several CSS selectors that allow you to select elements based on their position:

- `:first-child` and `:last-child`: These selectors target the first and last child, respectively, within a parent element.
- `:nth-child(n)`: This selector targets a child element at a specific position within a parent.
- `:nth-of-type(n)`: This is similar to `:nth-child`, but it selects elements of a specific type at a given position.
- `:first-of-type` and `:last-of-type`: These selectors target the first and last child of a specific type within a parent.

`:first-child` and `:last-child`

These selectors are used to select the first or last child in a parent element, regardless of its type.

```css
/* Select the first paragraph in each section */
section p:first-child {
  font-weight: bold;
}

/* Select the last item in a list */
ul li:last-child {
  text-decoration: underline;
}
```

`:nth-child(n)`

This selector allows you to select elements based on their exact position or pattern. The argument n can be a number, a keyword (odd, even), or an expression.

```css
/* Select every second child in a list */
ul li:nth-child(2n) {
  background-color: lightgray;
}

/* Select the third child in any div */
div:nth-child(3) {
  color: red;
}
```

`:nth-of-type(n)`

This selector is similar to `:nth-child`, but it considers only elements of a specific type.

```css
/* Select every second paragraph within a parent */
div p:nth-of-type(2n) {
  margin-bottom: 10px;
}
```

`:first-of-type` and `:last-of-type`

These selectors target the first and last child of a specific type within a parent.

```css
/* Select the first image in a container */
div img:first-of-type {
  border: 2px solid blue;
}

/* Select the last header in a section */
section h2:last-of-type {
  font-style: italic;
}
```

Practical Applications

Position-based selectors are useful in various scenarios:

- **Stylizing Lists and Navigation**: Position-based selectors allow you to style specific items in lists or navigation menus based on their position.
- **Dynamic Content**: When working with dynamically generated content, position-based selectors help you apply styles or interact with specific elements.
- **Automation Scripts**: In Selenium WebDriver, these selectors can be used to locate elements that are dynamically positioned or change based on content updates.

Position-based CSS selectors offer a flexible way to select elements based on their position within a parent or relative to other elements. Understanding these selectors allows you to create dynamic styles and efficient automation scripts. Whether you are styling a complex layout or navigating dynamic content in a Selenium WebDriver script, position-based selectors are valuable tools in your toolkit.

Leveraging Advanced CSS Patterns

Advanced CSS patterns are techniques that go beyond basic selectors to create complex, flexible, and dynamic styling or element selection. These patterns allow you to handle complex scenarios and apply styles or locate elements based on more sophisticated rules. This section explores various advanced CSS patterns, including combining selectors, using complex attribute selectors, and leveraging :not() for exclusion.

Combining Selectors

Combining selectors lets you apply styles to multiple elements or create more specific selections by using logical operators. Common ways to combine selectors include:

- **Grouping Selectors with Comma (,)**: This allows you to apply the same style to multiple different selectors.

  ```css
  /* Style both <h1> and <h2> elements */
  h1, h2 {
    color: blue;
    text-align: center;
  }
  ```

- **Combining Selectors with Space**: This creates a descendant selector, allowing you to target nested elements.

  ```css
  /* Select all <span> elements within a <div> */
  div span {
  ```

```
    font-style: italic;
  }
```

- **Combining Selectors with a Child Combinator (>)**: This targets direct child elements.

```
/* Select direct children <li> within a <ul> */
ul > li {
  list-style-type: square;
}
```

Complex Attribute Selectors

Advanced attribute selectors allow you to create complex conditions for selecting elements based on attribute patterns. These include:

- **Attribute Starts With ([`attribute^=value`])**: Selects elements whose attribute value starts with a specific substring.

```
/* Select input fields with names starting with 'user' */
input[name^="user"] {
  border: 1px solid green;
}
```

- **Attribute Contains ([`attribute*=value`])**: Selects elements whose attribute value contains a specific substring.

```
/* Select links with 'example' in the href */
a[href*="example"] {
  color: orange;
}
```

Using `:not()` for Exclusion

The `:not()` pseudo-class is used to exclude specific elements from a selection. This is useful when you want to apply styles or locate elements, excluding certain patterns.

```
/* Select all <p> elements except those with the class 'exclude' */
p:not(.exclude) {
  color: darkblue;
}

/* Select all <li> except the first child */
ul li:not(:first-child) {
  font-size: 0.9em;
}
```

Practical Applications

Advanced CSS patterns are useful in a variety of scenarios:

- **Flexible Styling**: By combining selectors and using complex attribute patterns, you can create dynamic styles for complex layouts.
- **Targeted Automation**: In automation scripts, like those using Selenium WebDriver, these advanced patterns help you find elements with more precision.
- **Creating Robust CSS**: The ability to exclude elements or use attribute patterns allows for more maintainable CSS, reducing the risk of conflicts and unintended styles.

Leveraging advanced CSS patterns allows you to create more dynamic and flexible styles or locate elements in complex scenarios. Combining selectors, using advanced attribute patterns, and applying the :not() pseudo-class are powerful tools in your CSS toolkit. Whether you're designing complex web layouts or writing robust automation scripts, mastering these advanced patterns can significantly enhance your work.

Examples and Best Practices

Understanding best practices and examining real-world examples can be valuable for creating robust CSS styles and efficient Selenium WebDriver scripts. In this section, we'll look at common scenarios where advanced CSS selectors are applied, and outline best practices to ensure maintainable and efficient code.

Real-World Examples of Advanced CSS Selectors

Here are some examples of how advanced CSS selectors can be used in practice:

- **Dynamic Forms**: When dealing with complex forms where element order might change, attribute selectors and combinators can help locate specific fields.

```
/* Select text inputs whose name starts with 'user_' */
input[type="text"][name^="user_"] {
  background-color: lightyellow;
}

/* Select the first submit button within a form */
form > input[type="submit"]:first-child {
  background-color: lightgreen;
}
```

- **Navigation Menus**: CSS combinators allow for flexible navigation menu styling, regardless of the structure.

```
/* Apply styles to direct child items of a menu */
nav > ul > li {
  padding: 10px;
}

/* Apply hover styles to submenu items */
nav ul > li > ul > li:hover {
  background-color: lightgray;
}
```

- **Card Layouts**: For complex card-based layouts, sibling selectors and attribute selectors can define styles and interactions.

```
/* Select all cards with a specific attribute */
div.card[data-status="active"] {
  border: 2px solid green;
}

/* Select the following sibling card for special styling */
div.card[data-status="active"] ~ div.card {
  opacity: 0.5;
}
```

Best Practices for Using Advanced CSS Selectors

Following best practices ensures that your CSS and automation scripts are maintainable, efficient, and less prone to errors. Here are some key practices to consider:

- **Use Specific Selectors**: Avoid overly broad selectors that can affect unintended elements. Be specific about the parent-child or sibling relationships to avoid conflicts.
- **Combine Selectors Carefully**: When combining selectors, ensure that the combinations are logical and do not create ambiguity. Use group selectors with commas (h1, h2, h3) for shared styles, and combinators for more specific relationships.
- **Leverage Attribute Selectors**: Use attribute selectors for flexible targeting. Consider using exact matches, starts-with (^), ends-with ($), or contains (*) to increase specificity.
- **Limit the Use of :not()**: While the :not() pseudo-class is powerful, overusing it can make the CSS difficult to understand and debug. Use it sparingly to avoid overly complex rules.
- **Optimize Performance**: In large applications, deeply nested selectors can impact performance. Use the least complex selectors that achieve the desired result, and avoid long chains of descendant selectors.
- **Consider Maintainability**: Use comments and structured CSS organization to make your code easier to maintain. Group related styles and separate concerns for clarity.

By exploring real-world examples and adhering to best practices, you can create robust and efficient CSS styles and Selenium WebDriver scripts. Understanding how to use advanced CSS selectors effectively allows you to navigate complex HTML structures, create dynamic layouts, and automate intricate interactions with confidence. Applying best practices ensures that your code is maintainable and optimized for performance, reducing the risk of errors and improving overall quality.

Common Pitfalls and Debugging

Working with advanced CSS selectors can be challenging, especially when dealing with complex web structures or automation scenarios. Understanding common pitfalls and effective debugging strategies can help you avoid issues and quickly resolve problems when they arise. In this section, we'll discuss some common pitfalls when working with CSS selectors and provide tips on debugging techniques.

Common Pitfalls

Here are some of the most common pitfalls encountered with CSS selectors and suggestions on how to avoid them:

- **Overly Broad Selectors**: Using broad selectors can lead to unexpected results, as they might select more elements than intended. To avoid this, be specific and use precise selectors.

```
/* This might select more than intended */
div {
  padding: 10px;
}

/* A more specific approach */
div.container {
  padding: 10px;
}
```

- **Deeply Nested Selectors**: Deep nesting can make the CSS difficult to maintain and impact performance. Aim for shorter selector chains and use class names to simplify selections.

```
/* Deeply nested selectors */
```

```
div > ul > li > a {
  color: blue;
}

/* Simplified approach using class names */
.nav-link {
  color: blue;
}
```

- **Conflicting Styles**: Multiple CSS rules with similar specificity can cause conflicts, resulting in unpredictable styles. To avoid this, understand the CSS specificity hierarchy and use appropriate selectors.

```
/* Conflicting styles due to similar specificity */
.nav-item {
  color: red;
}

.nav-item {
  color: green;
}

/* Resolve conflicts by increasing specificity or organizing styles */
.nav-item.special {
  color: green;
}
```

- **Improper Use of Combinators**: Incorrect use of combinators can lead to unintended selections. Double-check combinators to ensure correct relationships between elements.

```
/* Incorrect combinator */
div + span {
  color: red;
}

/* Correct combinator to select direct children */
div > span {
  color: red;
}
```

Debugging Techniques

When encountering issues with CSS selectors or automated element location, the following debugging techniques can be helpful:

- **Browser Developer Tools**: Use browser developer tools to inspect elements, view applied styles, and identify selector issues. This can help you understand why certain elements are not being styled or located as expected.
- **Experiment with Selectors**: In browser developer tools, experiment with different selectors to identify the correct combination. This helps refine your selection strategy.
- **Check for Specificity Conflicts**: Use browser developer tools to view the specificity of CSS rules. If conflicts occur, try increasing or decreasing specificity to resolve the issue.
- **Use CSS Linters**: CSS linters can help identify common issues, such as unused selectors, deeply nested selectors, and specificity conflicts. This can improve code quality and maintainability.

- **Debugging Automation Scripts**: If you're using Selenium WebDriver, use built-in debugging tools to identify issues with element location. Check for changes in the DOM structure, use explicit waits to ensure elements are present, and double-check selectors for accuracy.

By understanding common pitfalls and applying effective debugging techniques, you can create more robust CSS styles and avoid common mistakes. These strategies are crucial for both front-end developers and automation engineers using advanced CSS selectors to locate and interact with web elements. By focusing on specificity, avoiding deep nesting, and using appropriate combinators, you can reduce errors and improve code maintainability. Effective debugging with browser developer tools and CSS linters can further enhance your workflow, ensuring smooth and efficient development.

Chapter Summary

In this chapter on "Advanced CSS Selector Techniques," we've explored several advanced concepts that allow you to select and style elements in complex scenarios. Here's a summary of the key topics covered and the takeaways from each section:

Key Topics

- **Using Pseudo-classes and Pseudo-elements**: We discussed how pseudo-classes like `:hover`, `:focus`, and `:nth-child()` allow you to target elements based on their state, position, or other characteristics. Pseudo-elements like `::before` and `::after` allow you to style specific parts of an element without adding additional HTML. These techniques enable dynamic and interactive styling.
- **Utilizing CSS Combinators**: We explored combinators that define relationships between elements, including descendant (), child (>), adjacent sibling (+), and general sibling (~). Combinators are crucial for navigating the Document Object Model (DOM) and applying styles based on element relationships.
- **Crafting Advanced Attribute Selectors**: We covered how attribute selectors can be used to select elements based on specific attributes or patterns in their attribute values. Advanced selectors like `[attribute^=value]`, `[attribute$=value]`, and `[attribute*=value]` provide greater flexibility and precision.
- **Selecting Based on Position**: This section focused on selecting elements based on their position within a parent or relative to other elements. Selectors like `:first-child`, `:last-child`, `:nth-child(n)`, and `:nth-of-type(n)` allow for complex position-based selections.
- **Leveraging Advanced CSS Patterns**: We explored more complex CSS patterns, such as combining selectors, using attribute patterns, and leveraging `:not()` for exclusion. These patterns allow for flexible and robust CSS rules.
- **Examples and Best Practices**: We provided real-world examples of advanced CSS selectors in action and outlined best practices for creating maintainable and efficient CSS styles. The best practices included using specific selectors, limiting deep nesting, avoiding conflicts, and optimizing performance.
- **Common Pitfalls and Debugging**: This section addressed common pitfalls encountered with CSS selectors, such as overly broad selectors, conflicting styles, and improper combinators. We also discussed debugging techniques, including using browser developer tools, experimenting with selectors, and CSS linters.

Takeaways

By mastering these advanced CSS selector techniques, you can:

- Create dynamic and interactive styles for complex web pages.
- Navigate and interact with the DOM effectively, which is valuable for both front-end developers and automation engineers.

- Solve complex web automation scenarios with precise selectors, reducing errors and increasing maintainability.
- Avoid common pitfalls and debug issues efficiently, ensuring smooth development workflows.

Conclusion

Advanced CSS selector techniques are essential tools for anyone working with complex web structures, whether for styling or automation. By understanding and applying these concepts, you can enhance your ability to navigate, style, and automate interactions with greater flexibility and precision. The knowledge gained from this chapter will help you tackle real-world scenarios with confidence and ensure that your CSS styles and automation scripts are robust and maintainable.

Using Child-Node Indexing with CSS Selectors

Outline

Understanding the Concept of Child-Node Indexing

Child-node indexing is a method in CSS that allows you to select and style elements based on their position within a parent element's children. This technique is incredibly useful when dealing with complex HTML structures where elements can be in various orders, and you need precise control over which ones to target. Here's a deeper dive into the concept:

What is Child-Node Indexing?

Child-node indexing refers to the practice of selecting specific child elements from a parent element by their index (or position) within the child node list. This concept is commonly applied using two primary CSS selectors: `nth-child()` and `nth-of-type()`.

Why is Child-Node Indexing Important?

- **Precision**: It allows you to target specific elements within a parent, giving you fine-tuned control over your styling or interactions.
- **Dynamic Content Handling**: As web applications become more dynamic, child-node indexing provides a way to navigate and manipulate elements even when their order or structure changes.
- **Reduced Complexity**: By using indexing, you can avoid complex and brittle selectors, reducing the chance of errors and improving maintainability.

Typical Use Cases for Child-Node Indexing

- **Tables and Lists**: When you want to target specific rows or list items.
- **Forms**: To select specific input fields or form elements in complex form structures.
- **Navigation Menus**: When customizing styles or behavior for specific items in a navigation menu.

Key Selectors for Child-Node Indexing

- **`nth-child()`**: Targets a child element by its exact position within its parent, regardless of the type of element.
- **`nth-of-type()`**: Selects a child element by its position among other elements of the same type within its parent.

Basic Syntax of `nth-child()` and `nth-of-type()`

- **Simple Index**: `nth-child(3)` selects the third child within its parent.

- **Even/Odd Index**: nth-child(odd) selects all odd-indexed children, while nth-child(even) selects all even-indexed ones.
- **Formula-Based Index**: nth-child(2n+1) selects every other child, starting from the first one (1, 3, 5, etc.).

Considerations When Using Child-Node Indexing

- **Hierarchy Sensitivity**: Child-node indexing depends on the structure of the parent-child relationship, which can change if new elements are added or removed.
- **Accessibility**: Ensure that using indexing does not affect the accessibility of your content, especially for screen readers or assistive technologies.

By understanding the concept of child-node indexing, you gain a powerful tool for selecting and manipulating web elements in a flexible and maintainable way. This foundational knowledge will prepare you for more advanced techniques and scenarios where precise element selection is required.

Using the nth-child() Selector

The nth-child() selector in CSS allows you to select a child element based on its index or position within a parent element's list of children. This selector is particularly useful for targeting specific children in a dynamic or structured environment, like a list, table, or complex hierarchical HTML. Here's a breakdown of how to use the nth-child() selector effectively:

What is the nth-child() Selector?

The nth-child() selector selects a child element based on its position among its siblings, regardless of type. This position is based on the order in which the children are defined in the parent element.

Basic Syntax of nth-child()

- **Single Index**: :nth-child(3) selects the third child of a parent element.
- **Odd/Even**: :nth-child(odd) selects all odd-numbered children (1, 3, 5, etc.), while :nth-child(even) selects all even-numbered children (2, 4, 6, etc.).
- **Formula-Based Index**: :nth-child(2n+1) selects every other child, starting from the first, while :nth-child(2n+2) selects every other child starting from the second.

Using nth-child() for Simple Indexing

- **Example 1: Selecting a Specific Child**: If you have a list of <li> elements and you want to style the third one differently, you can use ul li:nth-child(3) { color: red; }.
- **Example 2: Highlighting Every Other Child**: To style every other row in a table, you can use table tr:nth-child(odd) { background-color: lightgray; }.

Advanced Usage of nth-child()

- **Using Mathematical Formulas**: The nth-child() selector allows for more complex patterns using mathematical expressions. For example, nth-child(3n) selects every third child (3, 6, 9, etc.), and nth-child(3n+1) selects children at 1, 4, 7, etc.
- **Selecting Multiple Ranges**: To select multiple children within a specific range, you can combine nth-child() with other CSS rules. For example, to style the first three children, you could use ul li:nth-child(-n+3) { font-weight: bold; }.

Pitfalls and Considerations

- **Dynamic Content**: The order of children may change if the content is dynamic, which can affect the expected behavior of nth-child().
- **Cross-Browser Consistency**: While widely supported, some older browsers may not fully support complex nth-child() expressions. Be sure to test in various environments.
- **Accessibility and Readability**: Using nth-child() excessively or in complex combinations may reduce code readability and maintainability. Consider simpler approaches when possible.

Practical Applications

- **Styling Navigation Menus**: nth-child() can help to differentiate specific items in a navigation menu, such as highlighting the first or last item.
- **Form Validation**: To visually indicate specific form fields (like error fields), you could use nth-child() to apply styles.
- **Dynamic Tables and Lists**: The ability to select specific rows or list items is valuable in complex data structures.

Overall, the nth-child() selector is a powerful tool for precise control over CSS styling and element selection. Its flexibility allows for a range of uses, from simple odd/even selections to more complex patterns using formulas. Understanding its basics and potential applications can greatly enhance your CSS skills.

Using the nth-of-type() Selector

The nth-of-type() selector in CSS allows you to select child elements of a specific type based on their position within their parent. It is particularly useful in complex HTML structures where you need to differentiate between elements of the same type but not necessarily the same overall position among all child nodes. This section covers the key concepts, usage, and best practices for the nth-of-type() selector.

What is the nth-of-type() Selector?

The nth-of-type() selector targets elements based on their position among siblings of the same type (e.g., all <div>, all <p>, all <tr>, etc.). Unlike nth-child(), which selects a child by its overall position among all siblings, nth-of-type() selects based on the position among siblings of the same tag or type.

Basic Syntax for nth-of-type()

- **Single Index**: :nth-of-type(3) selects the third child of the same type within its parent.
- **Odd/Even**: :nth-of-type(odd) selects all odd-numbered children of a specific type, while :nth-of-type(even) selects all even-numbered children.
- **Formula-Based Index**: :nth-of-type(2n+1) selects every other child of a specific type, starting from the first.

Using nth-of-type() for Specific Selections

- **Example 1: Selecting a Specific Element Type**: In a structure with mixed child types, you might want to target the third paragraph (p) regardless of other elements. You could use div p:nth-of-type(3) { color: blue; }.

- **Example 2: Highlighting Even or Odd Rows in a Table**: To style even rows in a table without considering non-row elements, you can use `table tr:nth-of-type(even) { background-color: lightgray; }`.

Advanced Usage of `nth-of-type()`

- **Selecting Alternating Elements of a Specific Type**: `nth-of-type()` can select every third `<div>` or every second `<p>`. For example, `div:nth-of-type(3n)` selects every third `<div>` within a parent.
- **Combining with Other Selectors**: You can combine `nth-of-type()` with class or attribute selectors to achieve complex patterns. For instance, `div > p:nth-of-type(odd)` selects odd-numbered paragraphs within a `div`.

Pitfalls and Considerations

- **Mixed Element Types**: If the parent has mixed child types, ensure you're selecting the correct type. `nth-of-type()` might behave unexpectedly if the order of mixed elements changes.
- **Consistency Across Browsers**: While generally supported, some older browsers may not handle complex `nth-of-type()` expressions well. Test in various environments to ensure consistency.
- **Readability and Maintenance**: Using complex patterns or combining with other selectors can affect code readability and maintainability. Aim for clarity when using `nth-of-type()`.

Practical Applications

- **Styling Specific Sections**: In a complex structure with multiple child types, `nth-of-type()` can target specific sections without impacting others.
- **Dynamic Content Handling**: When the number and type of children might change dynamically, `nth-of-type()` helps maintain consistent styling.
- **Table and List Operations**: Ideal for styling specific rows or columns in tables or lists where you want to ignore non-row/list elements.

Overall, the `nth-of-type()` selector offers a powerful method for selecting specific child elements based on type and position. It provides a flexible approach to CSS targeting, enabling precise styling and behavior control in complex and dynamic HTML structures. Understanding its fundamentals and best practices can greatly enhance your CSS capabilities and allow for more robust designs.

Leveraging `nth-child()` and `nth-of-type()` in Practice

In practice, `nth-child()` and `nth-of-type()` are powerful CSS selectors that allow you to target specific elements within a parent based on their index or type. Understanding their nuances and learning how to use them effectively can significantly enhance your ability to style and manipulate web elements. Let's explore various scenarios where you can leverage these selectors and discuss common patterns, practical applications, and potential pitfalls.

`nth-child()` vs. `nth-of-type()`

- **`nth-child()`** selects a child based on its position among all children within a parent. It considers every child, regardless of its type.
- **`nth-of-type()`** selects a child based on its position among children of the same type within a parent. This is useful when there are mixed types of children in a parent.

Common Use Cases for `nth-child()` and `nth-of-type()`

- **Styling Lists and Tables**: `nth-child()` and `nth-of-type()` can be used to create alternating patterns (like striped tables) or to highlight specific items in lists.
- **Navigating Complex Structures**: In scenarios with complex HTML structures, these selectors can help target specific elements for styling or JavaScript interactions.
- **Applying Style to Specific Items**: Use these selectors to highlight certain items in a navigation menu, carousel, or other repetitive structures.

Using `nth-child()` in Practice

- **Alternating Table Rows**: To create a striped table, you can use `table tr:nth-child(odd) { background-color: lightgray; }`. This applies a background color to all odd-numbered rows.
- **Highlighting Specific List Items**: If you want to change the color of every third list item, you could use `ul li:nth-child(3n) { color: red; }`.
- **Targeting Specific Indices**: To style the first three children in a parent, you might use `div:nth-child(-n+3) { font-weight: bold; }`.

Using `nth-of-type()` in Practice

- **Styling Specific Paragraphs**: To target the third paragraph within a section, regardless of other elements, you could use `section p:nth-of-type(3) { color: blue; }`.
- **Applying Patterns to Mixed Content**: If you have a parent with multiple child types, like a mix of div, p, and span, `nth-of-type()` helps focus on specific types. For example, `div:nth-of-type(2n) { font-style: italic; }` applies italic styling to every even div child.
- **Managing Nested Structures**: In complex HTML with multiple levels, `nth-of-type()` can help target specific elements. For instance, `table tr:nth-of-type(2) td:nth-of-type(3) { background-color: yellow; }` targets the second row's third cell.

Tips and Considerations

- **Dynamic Content**: When working with dynamic content, be aware that adding or removing children can change the indices, affecting `nth-child()` or `nth-of-type()`.
- **Readability**: Keep your CSS readable by avoiding overly complex combinations of these selectors.
- **Testing for Consistency**: Ensure your selectors behave as expected across different browsers and environments.
- **Fallback Strategies**: In some cases, especially with complex dynamic content, consider alternative strategies to maintain consistency if `nth-child()` or `nth-of-type()` could lead to unexpected results.

Leveraging `nth-child()` and `nth-of-type()` effectively requires an understanding of their behavior and careful planning. When used correctly, they offer a robust way to target specific elements, create patterns, and style content dynamically.

Working with Combined Child-Node Indexing Techniques

Combining child-node indexing techniques, such as `nth-child()` and `nth-of-type()`, allows you to create complex and powerful CSS selectors. These combinations can be used to target specific elements, apply intricate styles, and manipulate nested structures in a more refined way. This section explores various ways to combine child-node indexing techniques and provides examples of their practical applications.

Why Combine Child-Node Indexing Techniques?

Combining techniques like nth-child() and nth-of-type() gives you more flexibility and control over your CSS selectors. It allows you to target specific patterns, manage complex nested structures, and apply dynamic styling while maintaining a clear and concise codebase.

Basic Combination Techniques

- **Combining nth-child() with Other Selectors**: You can combine nth-child() with class selectors, attribute selectors, or other child-node indexers to target more specific elements. For example, .container > div:nth-child(2) selects the second div within .container.
- **Combining nth-of-type() with nth-child()**: In a structure with mixed child types, you can use nth-of-type() to focus on a specific type and nth-child() to select based on position. For instance, div:nth-of-type(2) > p:nth-child(1) selects the first p in the second div.

Advanced Techniques with Combined Indexing

- **Selecting Specific Children in Nested Structures**: By combining child-node indexers, you can traverse complex structures. For example, table > tr:nth-child(2) > td:nth-child(3) targets the third cell in the second row of a table.
- **Creating Patterns with Formulas**: Using formulas like nth-child(2n+1) or nth-of-type(3n-1), you can create specific patterns. For instance, to style every second li element, you could use ul > li:nth-child(2n) { color: blue; }.
- **Using Ranges with nth-child()**: You can select a range of elements using nth-child(). For example, ul > li:nth-child(n+2):nth-child(-n+4) targets the second through fourth list items.

Practical Applications of Combined Techniques

- **Styling Navigation Menus**: Use combinations to target specific menu items or apply different styles to even and odd items. For instance, .nav > ul > li:nth-child(odd) selects all odd-numbered items in a navigation menu.
- **Creating Striped Tables with Specific Cell Styles**: To create a striped table where specific cells are highlighted, you can combine nth-child() and nth-of-type(). For example, table > tr:nth-child(odd) > td:nth-of-type(2) { background-color: yellow; } applies a yellow background to the second cell in odd-numbered rows.
- **Managing Complex Forms**: In a form with various input fields and elements, you can use combined techniques to style specific fields or label relationships. For example, form > div:nth-of-type(3) > input:nth-child(1) selects the first input in the third div.

Pitfalls and Considerations

- **Overcomplication**: While combined child-node indexing is powerful, it can lead to overly complex CSS selectors, making the code hard to read and maintain.
- **Stability in Dynamic Content**: If the content structure changes frequently, ensure your selectors remain consistent. Test thoroughly in dynamic environments.
- **Cross-Browser Compatibility**: Test in different browsers and environments to ensure consistent behavior, as some older browsers may not fully support complex index combinations.
- **Accessibility**: Ensure that combined child-node indexing doesn't affect the accessibility of your content, particularly for assistive technologies.

Combining child-node indexing techniques offers powerful tools for targeting elements with precision and flexibility. By understanding how to use these combinations effectively, you can create robust, maintainable, and efficient CSS selectors for a wide range of applications.

Troubleshooting Common Issues with Child-Node Indexing

Child-node indexing in CSS, using selectors like nth-child() and nth-of-type(), can be incredibly useful for targeting specific elements within a parent. However, these selectors can sometimes cause unexpected results or behavior due to a variety of factors. This section explores common issues that arise when using child-node indexing and provides solutions and best practices to avoid and resolve these issues.

Common Issues with Child-Node Indexing

1. **Incorrect Targeting Due to Dynamic Content**
   - When elements are dynamically added, removed, or reordered, nth-child() and nth-of-type() selectors might not work as expected. This is particularly true in JavaScript-heavy applications where DOM manipulation is frequent.
2. **Unexpected Results with Mixed Child Types**
   - If a parent has mixed child types (e.g., a combination of div, p, and span), nth-child() might not target what you expect because it considers all children, regardless of type. This can lead to confusion and unexpected styling.
3. **Complex Structures Causing Ambiguity**
   - In nested structures, using nth-child() or nth-of-type() may require additional context to avoid ambiguity. If multiple levels contain similar patterns, selectors might apply styles to the wrong elements.
4. **Cross-Browser Inconsistencies**
   - While nth-child() and nth-of-type() are generally well-supported, certain older browsers or less common environments might not fully support complex selector patterns.
5. **Accessibility Concerns**
   - Using nth-child() and nth-of-type() without consideration for accessibility can lead to issues for users with disabilities. Screen readers and other assistive technologies might not interpret complex selectors as expected.

Solutions and Best Practices for Troubleshooting

1. **Use Explicit Selectors to Reduce Ambiguity**
   - To avoid targeting the wrong elements, be as explicit as possible with your selectors. Combine nth-child() and nth-of-type() with class names, IDs, or other specific attributes to ensure you're targeting the correct elements.
   - For example, instead of div:nth-child(3), use section > div:nth-child(3) to provide more context and reduce ambiguity.
2. **Test in Dynamic Environments**
   - If your content is dynamic, test your CSS thoroughly in scenarios where elements are added, removed, or reordered. This will help identify potential issues with nth-child() and nth-of-type() selectors.
   - Consider using frameworks or libraries that support testing dynamic content, and employ tools that allow you to manipulate the DOM to simulate real-world scenarios.
3. **Use More Stable Selectors for Critical Functionality**
   - For critical functionality or where precision is required, consider using more stable selectors, like IDs or unique class names, to ensure consistency even when content changes.

- Avoid relying solely on `nth-child()` or `nth-of-type()` in areas where content structure may change frequently.
4. **Ensure Cross-Browser Compatibility**
   - Test your CSS selectors across multiple browsers and platforms to ensure consistent behavior. Pay attention to older browsers or less common environments, as they might handle complex patterns differently.
   - Use tools like BrowserStack or CrossBrowserTesting to test your CSS in various environments.
5. **Consider Accessibility and Usability**
   - When using child-node indexing, ensure it doesn't negatively impact accessibility. Test with screen readers and other assistive technologies to ensure proper interpretation of your selectors.
   - Avoid overusing `nth-child()` and `nth-of-type()` in ways that might obscure the logical structure of your content, which could impact accessibility.

Child-node indexing is a powerful tool for targeting specific elements in CSS, but it can lead to common issues if not used carefully. By understanding these issues and applying best practices, you can ensure your CSS selectors are stable, consistent, and accessible. Keep in mind the potential pitfalls and test thoroughly to avoid unexpected behavior and ensure a robust and maintainable codebase.

Chapter Summary

This chapter covered the concept of child-node indexing in CSS, focusing on the `nth-child()` and `nth-of-type()` selectors. These tools enable you to target specific elements based on their position within a parent. Here's a summary of the key points discussed in this chapter:

Overview of Child-Node Indexing

- **What Is Child-Node Indexing?** It's a CSS technique that allows you to select elements based on their order or type within a parent element.
- **Why Is It Useful?** It helps in creating complex patterns, targeting specific elements, and applying styles to dynamic or structured content.

Using `nth-child()`

- **Basic Syntax**: `:nth-child(n)`, where n is the index of the child to be selected.
- **Common Patterns**: You can target every odd or even child, select based on a formula, or focus on specific index ranges.
- **Applications**: Useful for creating striped tables, highlighting specific items in lists, or targeting specific elements in complex structures.

Using `nth-of-type()`

- **Basic Syntax**: `:nth-of-type(n)`, which targets a child of a specific type based on its position.
- ****Difference from `nth-child()`****: While `nth-child()` selects based on overall position, `nth-of-type()` selects based on position among elements of the same type.
- **Common Uses**: Ideal for mixed-content structures where you need to focus on a specific type, like paragraphs or table rows.

Combining Child-Node Indexing Techniques

- **Combining `nth-child()` and `nth-of-type()`**: You can create complex patterns by combining these selectors with other CSS rules or within nested structures.

.

- **Common Examples**: Targeting a specific element type within a nested structure or creating alternating styles with specific patterns.

Best Practices and Troubleshooting

- **Avoiding Overly Complex Selectors**: Complex combinations can lead to confusing code and maintenance issues.
- **Testing in Dynamic Environments**: Since child-node indexing is sensitive to changes in the DOM, always test in dynamic scenarios.
- **Ensuring Accessibility**: Make sure your use of child-node indexing doesn't impact accessibility, especially for assistive technologies.

Conclusion

Child-node indexing with CSS selectors is a powerful tool for targeting specific elements based on their position or type. By understanding the basics, exploring common patterns, and combining these techniques, you can create robust, maintainable CSS. However, it's essential to test your selectors thoroughly and follow best practices to avoid common pitfalls and ensure accessibility.

Retrieving Multiple WebElements with CSS

Outline

1. Overview of CSS Selectors for Multiple Elements
2. Basic Techniques for Retrieving Multiple Elements
3. Combining Selectors for Precise Element Retrieval
4. Using Child and Descendant Selectors
5. Working with Sibling Selectors
6. Locating Multiple Elements Within a Specific Context
7. Iterating and Manipulating Collections in Selenium WebDriver
8. Common Challenges and Troubleshooting
9. Chapter Summary

Overview of CSS Selectors for Multiple Elements

Selecting multiple elements on a web page using CSS selectors is a fundamental skill for automation and testing with Selenium WebDriver. In this overview, we'll explore why selecting multiple elements is important, common use cases, and the different types of CSS selectors that are useful for this purpose.

Importance of Selecting Multiple Elements

In web automation and testing, interacting with multiple elements is often necessary. Whether you're dealing with lists, tables, or other repeated structures, you need a reliable way to select all the relevant elements at once. This ability is critical for:

- Validating content on a web page.
- Automating repetitive interactions.
- Extracting data from web pages.
- Performing bulk operations, like form submissions or batch updates.

Common Use Cases for Selecting Multiple Elements

CSS selectors are widely used to select multiple elements in a variety of contexts, including:

- **Lists:** When dealing with unordered (`<ul>`) or ordered (`<ol>`) lists, you may need to select all list items (`<li>`).
- **Tables:** Selecting rows (`<tr>`) or specific cells (`<td>`) in a table to validate data or perform operations.
- **Forms:** Selecting input fields or buttons within a form for automated filling or submission.
- **Navigation Menus:** Selecting multiple navigation links or buttons to ensure proper navigation.

Types of CSS Selectors for Multiple Elements

CSS offers a range of selectors that can be used to select multiple elements at once. Here are some common types:

1. **Tag Selectors:**
   - Selecting elements by their tag name (e.g., `div`, `span`, `li`). This is a straightforward way to select all elements of a certain type.
2. **Class Selectors:**

- ○ Selecting elements by their class attribute (e.g., `.item`, `.row`). This is useful when elements share a common style or role.
3. **Attribute Selectors:**
   - ○ Selecting elements based on specific attributes or attribute values (e.g., `[type="text"]`, `[data-role="item"]`). This allows for more granular selection.
4. **Combination Selectors:**
   - ○ Combining tag, class, and attribute selectors for more precise selection (e.g., `div.item`, `input[type="text"]`).
5. **Descendant and Child Selectors:**
   - ○ Selecting elements based on their hierarchy in the document. Descendant selectors (`parent child`) select all matching descendants, while child selectors (`parent > child`) select only direct children.
6. **Sibling Selectors:**
   - ○ Selecting adjacent (+) or general (~) siblings. This is useful when elements are arranged in sequences or sets.

Selecting multiple elements using CSS selectors is a critical skill for web automation. By understanding the various types of selectors and their appropriate use cases, you can interact with collections of elements efficiently and effectively. This overview sets the stage for deeper exploration into more advanced techniques and real-world applications in the subsequent sections.

Basic Techniques for Retrieving Multiple Elements

CSS selectors offer a flexible and efficient way to retrieve multiple elements from a web page, a crucial skill when working with Selenium WebDriver for automation and testing. This section explores basic techniques for retrieving multiple elements, focusing on tag-based selectors, class-based selectors, and other fundamental approaches.

Tag-Based Selectors

A straightforward technique to retrieve multiple elements is by using tag-based selectors. This method allows you to select all elements of a specific tag type on a web page. Here's how it works:

- **Selecting All Elements of a Tag:** You can select all elements of a particular tag, such as `div`, `span`, `li`, etc. This is useful when you need to interact with all elements of a certain type. For example:

```
div {
    /* Styles or other operations */
}
```

This CSS selector selects all `<div>` elements on a page.

- **Applying the Tag-Based Selector in Selenium WebDriver:** To retrieve multiple elements with a tag-based selector in Selenium WebDriver, use the `findElements` method. Here's an example in Java:

```
List<WebElement> divElements = driver.findElements(By.tagName("div"));
```

Class-Based Selectors

Class-based selectors are another common technique for selecting multiple elements. They are used when you want to select all elements with a specific class attribute. This technique is useful for interacting with elements that share a common style or role.

- **Selecting All Elements with a Class:** Use the dot . followed by the class name to select elements with that class. For example:

```
.menu-item {
  /* Styles or other operations */
}
```

This CSS selector selects all elements with the class menu-item.

- **Using Class-Based Selectors in Selenium WebDriver:** To retrieve multiple elements with a class-based selector in Selenium WebDriver, you can use the findElements method with By.className or By.cssSelector. Example:

```
List<WebElement> menuItems =
driver.findElements(By.className("menu-item"));
```

Combining Tag and Class-Based Selectors

Combining tag and class-based selectors allows for more specific element retrieval. This technique is useful when you need to target elements with a certain tag and class combination.

- **Combining Tag and Class:** By combining tag names and class selectors, you can narrow down your selection. For example:

```
div.content {
  /* Styles or other operations */
}
```

This selector selects all <div> elements with the class content.

- **Using Combined Selectors in Selenium WebDriver:** To use combined selectors in Selenium WebDriver, you can use the findElements method with By.cssSelector. Example:

```
List<WebElement> contentDivs =
driver.findElements(By.cssSelector("div.content"));
```

Attribute-Based Selectors

Another basic technique is using attribute-based selectors. This method selects elements based on specific attributes or attribute values.

- **Selecting Elements with Attribute Selectors:** You can select elements with specific attributes or attribute values by enclosing the attribute in square brackets. Example:

```
input[type="checkbox"] {
  /* Styles or other operations */
}
```

This selector selects all <input> elements with a type attribute of "checkbox".

- **Using Attribute-Based Selectors in Selenium WebDriver:** To retrieve elements with attribute-based selectors in Selenium WebDriver, use the `findElements` method with `By.cssSelector`. Example:

```
List<WebElement> checkboxes =
driver.findElements(By.cssSelector("input[type='checkbox']"));
```

By using these basic techniques for retrieving multiple elements, you can efficiently interact with various elements on a web page. Whether you use tag-based selectors, class-based selectors, or attribute-based selectors, these approaches form the foundation for more advanced techniques and complex element retrieval scenarios.

Combining Selectors for Precise Element Retrieval

CSS selectors allow you to combine different types of selectors to achieve more precise element retrieval. This capability is crucial when working with complex web pages that contain various elements with similar characteristics. By combining selectors, you can narrow down your searches, target specific elements, and avoid ambiguity. This section explores different techniques for combining selectors and provides practical examples of their use in Selenium WebDriver.

Why Combine Selectors?

Combining selectors helps to:

- Refine element selection by adding specificity.
- Avoid unintended matches caused by broad selectors.
- Navigate complex structures to select the exact elements you need.
- Enhance test stability by targeting more specific elements.

Combining Tag and Class Selectors

One common combination is to use both tag and class selectors. This approach lets you select elements based on their tag and class, providing more specific matches.

- **Combining Tag and Class:** To combine a tag and a class, you use the tag name followed by the class name with a dot `.`. Example:

```
div.content {
  /* CSS for all divs with the class "content" */
}
```

This selector targets all `<div>` elements with the class `content`.

- **Using in Selenium WebDriver:** You can use `By.cssSelector` to retrieve elements using combined tag and class selectors. Example:

```
List<WebElement> contentDivs =
driver.findElements(By.cssSelector("div.content"));
```

Combining Class Selectors

Sometimes, elements have multiple classes. By combining class selectors, you can select elements that have a specific combination of classes.

- **Combining Multiple Classes:** To combine class selectors, list each class with a dot . between them. Example:

```
div.content.highlight {
  /* CSS for divs with both "content" and "highlight" classes */
}
```

This selector targets all `<div>` elements with both `content` and `highlight` classes.

- **Using in Selenium WebDriver:** This can be achieved in Selenium using the same `By.cssSelector` approach. Example:

```
List<WebElement> highlightedContent =
driver.findElements(By.cssSelector("div.content.highlight"));
```

Combining Tag, Class, and Attribute Selectors

For even more precise targeting, you can combine tag, class, and attribute selectors. This technique is useful when elements have unique attributes that help differentiate them.

- **Combining Tag, Class, and Attribute:** Use tag names, class names, and attribute selectors to build complex combinations. Example:

```
div.content[data-role="main"] {
  /* CSS for divs with class "content" and data-role "main" */
}
```

This selector targets all `<div>` elements with the class `content` and a `data-role` attribute with the value `"main"`.

- **Using in Selenium WebDriver:** The same combination logic applies in Selenium WebDriver. Example:

```
List<WebElement> mainContentDivs =
driver.findElements(By.cssSelector("div.content[data-role='main']"));
```

Chaining Selectors to Navigate Structures

Chaining selectors allows you to navigate complex web structures. This approach is useful when you need to select elements within specific parent or container elements.

- **Using Descendant Selectors:** You can chain selectors to select elements within a certain context. The descendant selector uses a space between selectors. Example:

```
div.container .item {
  /* CSS for elements with class "item" inside divs with class
"container" */
}
```

This selector targets all elements with the class `item` within `<div>` elements that have the class `container`.

- **Using Child Selectors:** The child selector > selects direct children of an element. Example:

```
ul > li {
```

```
    /* CSS for direct children "li" within "ul" */
}
```

This selector targets all direct `<li>` children within a `<ul>`.

- **Using in Selenium WebDriver:** In Selenium, these selector combinations allow you to retrieve elements within specific structures. Examples:

```
List<WebElement> itemsInContainer =
driver.findElements(By.cssSelector("div.container .item"));
List<WebElement> listItems = driver.findElements(By.cssSelector("ul >
li"));
```

Combining selectors for precise element retrieval is a powerful technique that enhances your ability to work with complex web pages. By understanding how to combine tag, class, and attribute selectors, and how to chain selectors to navigate structures, you can improve the accuracy and stability of your Selenium WebDriver automation scripts.

Using Child and Descendant Selectors

Child and descendant selectors in CSS are powerful tools for navigating through complex web structures to retrieve elements based on their hierarchical relationships. When working with Selenium WebDriver, understanding these selectors is crucial for precise element retrieval. This section will cover the difference between child and descendant selectors, provide examples, and demonstrate their use in real-world scenarios.

Understanding the Difference Between Child and Descendant Selectors

- **Child Selectors:** The child selector (>) selects only the direct children of a parent element. This ensures you are interacting with elements that are one level deep in the hierarchy. This is useful when you need to avoid selecting nested elements within deeper levels.
- **Descendant Selectors:** The descendant selector (a space) selects all elements that are descendants of a parent, regardless of their depth in the hierarchy. This is helpful when you're interested in all levels within a specific container.

Child Selectors

The child selector targets only the direct children of a parent element. This can help reduce ambiguity when multiple levels of nested elements exist. Let's explore some use cases and examples:

- **Selecting Direct Child Elements:** If you have a list and want to target only the immediate children, you can use the child selector. Example:

```
ul > li {
    /* CSS for direct "li" children within "ul" */
}
```

This selector targets all immediate `<li>` children within a `<ul>`.

- **Using in Selenium WebDriver:** To retrieve direct children in Selenium WebDriver, you can use the `By.cssSelector` method with the child selector. Example in Java:

```
List<WebElement> directChildren = driver.findElements(By.cssSelector("ul
> li"));
```

Descendant Selectors

The descendant selector allows you to select all elements within a parent, regardless of depth. This is useful for targeting elements within nested structures.

- **Selecting All Descendants:** If you want to select all descendants within a specific parent, you can use the descendant selector. Example:

```
div.container span {
  /* CSS for all "span" descendants within "div.container" */
}
```

  This selector targets all `<span>` elements that are descendants of a `<div>` with the class `container`, no matter how deep they are nested.

- **Using in Selenium WebDriver:** To retrieve all descendants within a specific parent in Selenium WebDriver, use `By.cssSelector` with the descendant selector. Example in Java:

```
List<WebElement> spanDescendants =
driver.findElements(By.cssSelector("div.container span"));
```

Practical Scenarios for Child and Descendant Selectors

Let's consider a few scenarios where child and descendant selectors are particularly useful:

- **Navigating Forms:** If you have a form with multiple input fields, child selectors can help you target only the direct input elements without affecting nested structures. For example, selecting direct inputs within a form:

```
form > input {
  /* CSS for direct input fields within a form */
}
```

- **Navigating Nested Lists:** If you're dealing with nested lists, descendant selectors can be useful. For example, if you have a navigation menu with multiple levels, you might use a descendant selector to select all items within a main menu:

```
nav.main-menu li {
  /* CSS for all "li" descendants within "nav.main-menu" */
}
```

Child and descendant selectors offer flexibility when selecting elements based on hierarchical relationships. Understanding when to use child selectors versus descendant selectors is key to precise element retrieval, avoiding unintended matches, and ensuring that your Selenium WebDriver scripts are robust and maintainable. By mastering these selectors, you can confidently navigate complex web structures and retrieve elements as needed for automation and testing.

Working with Sibling Selectors

Sibling selectors in CSS enable you to select elements that share the same parent and are adjacent or general siblings. These selectors are useful when you need to retrieve elements that are positioned relative to each other within the same hierarchy. This section covers the different types of sibling selectors, provides examples of their use, and demonstrates how they can be applied in Selenium WebDriver.

Understanding Sibling Selectors

Sibling selectors allow you to select elements based on their position relative to one another under the same parent. There are two main types of sibling selectors:

- **Adjacent Sibling Selector (+):** This selector targets an element that immediately follows another element, i.e., they are direct siblings.
- **General Sibling Selector (~):** This selector targets all elements that follow a specific element within the same parent, not just the immediate next one.

Adjacent Sibling Selector (+)

The adjacent sibling selector allows you to select an element that directly follows another element. This is useful when you need to target an element that is always placed next to another specific element.

- **Example Usage:** If you want to select the next paragraph following a heading, you can use the adjacent sibling selector. Example:

```
h1 + p {
  /* CSS for the first paragraph after each "h1" */
}
```

  This selector targets the first <p> that follows each <h1>.

- **Using in Selenium WebDriver:** To retrieve adjacent siblings in Selenium WebDriver, you can use `By.cssSelector`. Here's an example in Java:

```
WebElement firstParagraph = driver.findElement(By.cssSelector("h1 + p"));
```

General Sibling Selector (~)

The general sibling selector allows you to select all elements that follow a specific element within the same parent, regardless of whether they are directly adjacent. This selector is useful for targeting multiple related elements that might not be immediately next to each other.

- **Example Usage:** To select all paragraphs that follow a heading within the same parent, you can use the general sibling selector. Example:

```
h1 ~ p {
  /* CSS for all paragraphs following each "h1" */
}
```

  This selector targets all <p> elements that follow each <h1> within the same parent.

- **Using in Selenium WebDriver:** To retrieve all general siblings in Selenium WebDriver, you can use `By.cssSelector` with the general sibling selector. Example in Java:

```
List<WebElement> followingParagraphs =
driver.findElements(By.cssSelector("h1 ~ p"));
```

Practical Scenarios for Sibling Selectors

Sibling selectors are useful in various scenarios, such as:

- **Navigating Lists with Headers:** If you have a list where each section starts with a header, you can use sibling selectors to retrieve all related elements within that section.

- **Handling Forms:** When dealing with forms where a label is followed by an input field, adjacent sibling selectors can help target the correct input based on its preceding label.
- **Working with Table Rows:** If you need to select specific rows or cells within a table based on their relative position to other rows or cells, sibling selectors can be effective.

Sibling selectors, including adjacent and general sibling selectors, offer a flexible approach to selecting elements that share a common parent. They allow you to navigate elements that are positioned relative to each other, providing more precise control over element retrieval. By understanding how to use these selectors, you can enhance your Selenium WebDriver scripts to accurately interact with elements based on their sibling relationships. This knowledge is essential for complex automation scenarios where element hierarchy plays a significant role.

Locating Multiple Elements Within a Specific Context

Locating multiple elements within a specific context on a web page is crucial when using Selenium WebDriver for automation and testing. This section explores various techniques to restrict the search scope to a particular section of the page, allowing you to avoid unwanted matches and retrieve only the relevant elements.

The Need for Contextual Searches

When automating interactions with a complex web page, you might encounter multiple elements with similar characteristics spread across different sections. Contextual searches are useful to:

- **Reduce Ambiguity:** By limiting the scope, you avoid retrieving elements from unintended sections.
- **Improve Performance:** Searching within a smaller scope can improve script efficiency.
- **Enhance Test Stability:** Narrowing the search context reduces the risk of unintended interactions.

Identifying the Context

To locate elements within a specific context, you need a clear understanding of the web page structure. Key elements to consider include:

- **Container Elements:** Identify unique parent elements (like `<div>`, `<section>`, or `<form>`) that define the desired context.
- **Attributes:** Use attributes (like `id`, `class`, or custom data attributes) to select the specific container.
- **Hierarchy:** Understand the parent-child and sibling relationships within the context.

Using CSS Selectors to Define the Context

CSS selectors provide flexible options to define the search context. Common techniques include:

1. Context with Unique Parent Element

You can start by identifying a unique parent element that defines the context. This element can be targeted by `id`, `class`, or other attributes.

- **Using ID Selector:** If the context has a unique ID, you can use the # symbol to locate it. Example:

    ```
    #main-content {
      /* CSS styles for the context with ID "main-content" */
    }
    ```

    This selector targets the element with ID `main-content`.

- **Using in Selenium WebDriver:** To retrieve elements within a specific context by ID in Selenium WebDriver, use By.cssSelector. Example in Java:

```
WebElement mainContent =
driver.findElement(By.cssSelector("#main-content"));
List<WebElement> elementsInContext =
mainContent.findElements(By.cssSelector("p"));
```

2. Context with Class-Based Selectors

If the context is defined by a unique class, you can use the . symbol to select the specific context.

- **Using Class Selector:** If the context is defined by a unique class, you can use the class selector to identify it. Example:

```
.container {
  /* CSS for the context with class "container" */
}
```

This selector targets all elements with the class container.

- **Using in Selenium WebDriver:** To retrieve elements within a specific context defined by a class, use By.cssSelector. Example in Java:

```
WebElement container = driver.findElement(By.cssSelector(".container"));
List<WebElement> elementsInContainer =
container.findElements(By.cssSelector("a"));
```

3. Context with Nested Structures

If the context involves nested structures, you can use descendant selectors to narrow the scope to a specific section.

- **Using Descendant Selectors:** If the context involves nested structures, descendant selectors help target the correct section. Example:

```
div.main-section .sub-section {
  /* CSS for all elements with class "sub-section" within "main-section"
*/
}
```

This selector targets all elements with class sub-section within main-section.

- **Using in Selenium WebDriver:** To retrieve elements within nested contexts in Selenium WebDriver, you can use By.cssSelector. Example in Java:

```
WebElement mainSection =
driver.findElement(By.cssSelector("div.main-section"));
List<WebElement> subSections =
mainSection.findElements(By.cssSelector(".sub-section"));
```

Locating multiple elements within a specific context is a key technique when working with Selenium WebDriver. By using CSS selectors to define the search context, you can reduce ambiguity, improve performance, and enhance test stability. Understanding how to identify unique container elements, use class-based selectors, and work with nested structures is essential for effective web automation. With these techniques, you can confidently locate elements in complex web pages, ensuring your Selenium scripts are reliable and efficient.

Iterating and Manipulating Collections in Selenium WebDriver

When working with Selenium WebDriver, iterating over collections of web elements and manipulating them is a common task. Whether you're interacting with a list of elements, processing rows in a table, or performing bulk operations, understanding how to iterate over and manipulate collections is crucial for efficient automation. This section provides a comprehensive guide to handling collections in Selenium WebDriver, including retrieving multiple elements, iterating through them, and manipulating them to achieve your automation goals.

Retrieving Collections of WebElements

Before you can iterate and manipulate collections, you need to retrieve multiple elements from a web page. Here's how to do that in Selenium WebDriver:

- **Using findElements:** To retrieve a collection of WebElements, use findElements with a specific locator. This returns a list of elements matching your CSS or XPath selector. Example in Java:

```java
List<WebElement> buttons = driver.findElements(By.cssSelector("button"));
```

- **Validating Collections:** After retrieving a collection, it's essential to check if the collection is empty or has elements before iterating through it. Example:

```java
if (buttons.isEmpty()) {
  System.out.println("No buttons found.");
} else {
  System.out.println("Found " + buttons.size() + " buttons.");
}
```

Iterating Through Collections

Once you have a collection of elements, you can iterate through them to perform specific operations. Common approaches include using loops, such as for or foreach, to process each element in the collection.

- **Using a for Loop:** A for loop allows you to iterate through the collection and perform operations on each element. Example:

```java
for (int i = 0; i < buttons.size(); i++) {
  WebElement button = buttons.get(i);
  System.out.println("Button " + i + ": " + button.getText());
}
```

- **Using a foreach Loop:** A foreach loop (enhanced for) provides a more concise syntax for iterating through a collection. Example:

```java
for (WebElement button : buttons) {
  System.out.println("Button: " + button.getText());
}
```

Manipulating Collections of WebElements

Manipulating collections involves performing actions on each element, such as clicking, entering text, or extracting information. Here are some common manipulation tasks:

- **Clicking Elements in a Collection:** To click each element in a collection, you can use a loop to iterate through the collection and perform the click action. Example:

```
for (WebElement button : buttons) {
  button.click();
}
```

- **Extracting Text from a Collection:** If you need to retrieve text from each element, you can use a loop to extract and process the text. Example:

```
List<String> buttonTexts = new ArrayList<>();
for (WebElement button : buttons) {
  buttonTexts.add(button.getText());
}

System.out.println("Button texts: " + String.join(", ", buttonTexts));
```

- **Entering Text into a Collection of Inputs:** If you have a collection of input fields, you can use a loop to enter text into each one. Example:

```
List<WebElement> inputFields =
driver.findElements(By.cssSelector("input[type='text']"));
for (WebElement inputField : inputFields) {
  inputField.sendKeys("Sample text");
}
```

Handling Exceptions and Errors

When iterating through and manipulating collections, it's important to handle exceptions and errors to ensure the stability of your automation scripts.

- **Try-Catch Blocks:** Using try-catch blocks allows you to gracefully handle exceptions that might occur during iteration or manipulation. Example:

```
for (WebElement button : buttons) {
  try {
    button.click();
  } catch (Exception e) {
    System.out.println("Error clicking button: " + e.getMessage());
  }
}
```

Iterating and manipulating collections of WebElements in Selenium WebDriver is a fundamental skill for web automation. By understanding how to retrieve collections, iterate through them, and perform various manipulation tasks, you can build robust automation scripts that handle complex scenarios. Remember to validate collections before processing them and use proper exception handling to ensure script stability. With these techniques, you can confidently automate interactions with multiple elements on a web page.

Common Challenges and Troubleshooting

Working with Selenium WebDriver to automate interactions with web pages can be complex, especially when it involves locating and manipulating web elements. This section discusses some of the common challenges faced when using Selenium and provides troubleshooting techniques to resolve them. Whether it's difficulty in locating elements, handling dynamic content, or managing browser-specific issues, understanding these challenges and how to overcome them is key to building robust automation scripts.

Challenges in Locating Web Elements

One of the most frequent challenges in Selenium WebDriver is locating elements. Here are some common issues and solutions:

- **Element Not Found:** This occurs when Selenium cannot find an element with the specified locator. Common reasons include incorrect locators, timing issues, or dynamic content.
  - **Troubleshooting Tips:**
    - Double-check the locator for typos or syntax errors.
    - Verify the element's existence using browser developer tools.
    - Add explicit waits to ensure the element has loaded.
    - Try different locator strategies (CSS, XPath, etc.).
- **Multiple Matching Elements:** When multiple elements match the locator, Selenium might select the wrong one or throw an error.
  - **Troubleshooting Tips:**
    - Use more specific locators to narrow down the results.
    - If needed, select elements by index or iterate over them to find the correct one.
    - Check the parent-child structure to confirm you're in the right context.

Challenges with Dynamic Content

Web pages with dynamic content, such as AJAX-based elements or client-side rendering, can cause timing issues. Here's how to address these challenges:

- **Elements Not Immediately Available:** If elements are loaded asynchronously, Selenium might try to interact with them before they are ready.
  - **Troubleshooting Tips:**
    - Use explicit waits (like `WebDriverWait`) to wait for elements to become visible or interactable.
    - Use conditions like `visibilityOfElementLocated`, `elementToBeClickable`, or `presenceOfElementLocated`.
    - Implement retries or loop-based checks to handle sporadic delays.
- **Elements Disappearing or Changing:** Dynamic content might cause elements to disappear or change unexpectedly.
  - **Troubleshooting Tips:**
    - Check if elements are being replaced, updated, or removed, and adjust your locators accordingly.
    - Use stable attributes or consistent patterns for your locators.
    - Implement error handling to manage unexpected changes.

Challenges with Browser-Specific Issues

Different browsers can behave differently, leading to cross-browser compatibility issues. Here's how to address common browser-specific challenges:

- **Inconsistent Behavior Across Browsers:** Some scripts might work in one browser but not in another.
  - **Troubleshooting Tips:**
    - Test your scripts across multiple browsers (Chrome, Firefox, Edge, etc.) to identify inconsistencies.

- Use browser-specific options to mitigate differences (e.g., browser-specific capabilities).
- Update browser drivers to ensure compatibility with the latest browser versions.
- **Pop-Ups and Alerts:** Pop-ups and alerts can interrupt automation scripts, causing failures or unexpected behavior.
  - **Troubleshooting Tips:**
    - Use Selenium's `Alert` class to handle pop-ups and alerts.
    - Implement exception handling to catch and close unexpected pop-ups.
    - Use browser options to disable certain pop-ups if necessary.

Challenges with Test Flakiness

Test flakiness can occur when scripts produce inconsistent results, often due to timing issues or unstable locators. Here's how to reduce test flakiness:

- **Flaky Tests Due to Timing Issues:** Timing issues are a common cause of flaky tests.
  - **Troubleshooting Tips:**
    - Use explicit waits to ensure elements are ready before interacting with them.
    - Avoid hard-coded delays; use condition-based waits instead.
    - Implement retries or conditional checks to improve script reliability.
- **Flaky Tests Due to Unstable Locators:** If locators are unstable, it can lead to inconsistent test outcomes.
  - **Troubleshooting Tips:**
    - Use stable attributes like `id` or `class` rather than position-based locators.
    - Regularly review and update locators as the web page evolves.
    - Implement fallbacks or alternative locators to improve robustness.

Common challenges in Selenium WebDriver include issues with locating elements, dynamic content, browser-specific problems, and test flakiness. By understanding these challenges and employing the troubleshooting techniques outlined in this section, you can build more reliable and robust automation scripts. Remember to use explicit waits, ensure consistent locators, and test across multiple browsers to minimize issues and improve the stability of your Selenium-based automation projects.

Chapter Summary

This chapter provided an in-depth exploration of how to retrieve multiple WebElements with CSS selectors in Selenium WebDriver. CSS selectors offer a flexible and powerful way to target elements on a web page, allowing you to interact with collections of elements such as lists, tables, and other repeated structures. Here's a summary of the key points discussed in the chapter:

Overview of CSS Selectors for Multiple Elements

- CSS selectors can be used to locate multiple WebElements on a web page, offering a variety of techniques to accomplish this task.
- Common use cases for retrieving multiple elements include interacting with lists, tables, and navigation menus.

Basic Techniques for Retrieving Multiple Elements

- **Tag-Based Selectors:** Selecting elements based on their tag (e.g., `div`, `span`, `li`).
- **Class-Based Selectors:** Selecting elements with a specific class (e.g., `.item`, `.row`).
- **Attribute-Based Selectors:** Selecting elements based on specific attributes (e.g., `input[type='text']`).

Combining Selectors for Precise Element Retrieval

- Combining different types of selectors can achieve more precise element retrieval.
- **Combining Tag and Class Selectors:** This provides specificity by targeting elements with a specific combination of tag and class.
- **Combining Class Selectors:** Useful when elements have multiple classes.
- **Combining Tag, Class, and Attribute Selectors:** Allows for more complex element retrieval.
- **Chaining Selectors:** Enables navigation through complex structures using descendant () and child (>) relationships.

Using Child and Descendant Selectors

- **Child Selectors:** Targeting only the direct children of a parent element.
- **Descendant Selectors:** Selecting all descendants of a parent, regardless of depth.
- These selectors help narrow down the context and improve specificity.

Working with Sibling Selectors

- **Adjacent Sibling Selector (+):** Selects an element that directly follows another element.
- **General Sibling Selector (~):** Selects all elements that follow a specific element within the same parent.
- Sibling selectors are useful for targeting elements that share a common parent but have relative positions.

Locating Multiple Elements Within a Specific Context

- Defining a specific context helps reduce ambiguity and improves script stability.
- **Using Unique Parent Elements:** Identify a unique parent (by `id`, `class`, or other attributes) to define the context.
- **Nested Structures:** Using descendant selectors to locate elements within specific contexts.
- This approach helps ensure you're interacting with the correct elements within a complex web structure.

Iterating and Manipulating Collections in Selenium WebDriver

- Once you retrieve multiple elements, you can iterate through them and manipulate them to perform specific operations.
- **Using `findElements`:** Retrieve a collection of WebElements to iterate and manipulate.
- **Iterating Through Collections:** Using loops (`for` or `foreach`) to process each element.
- **Manipulating Collections:** Clicking elements, entering text, or extracting information from collections.
- Proper exception handling is essential to ensure stability when manipulating collections.

Common Challenges and Troubleshooting

- Common challenges include locating elements, handling dynamic content, managing browser-specific issues, and test flakiness.
- Troubleshooting techniques include using explicit waits, ensuring consistent locators, handling exceptions, and validating collections.
- By addressing these challenges, you can build more reliable and robust Selenium WebDriver automation scripts.

Conclusion

Retrieving multiple WebElements with CSS is a fundamental skill in Selenium WebDriver. By mastering the techniques outlined in this chapter, you can interact with collections of elements effectively, navigate complex web structures, and handle common challenges with confidence. The knowledge gained from this chapter provides a solid foundation for building robust web automation scripts that are both reliable and efficient.

Managing Collections of WebElements

Outline

1. Introduction to WebElement Collections
2. Identifying Collections with CSS Selectors
3. Iterating Through WebElement Collections
4. Common Pitfalls and Challenges
5. Real-World Scenarios for WebElement Collections
6. Best Practices for Managing Collections
7. Chapter Summary

Introduction to WebElement Collections

When automating web applications with Selenium WebDriver, you'll often encounter scenarios where multiple elements share common characteristics, such as a list of items, a collection of buttons, or rows in a table. These groups of elements are referred to as "collections," and handling them efficiently is crucial for robust automation scripts.

Managing collections of WebElements allows you to interact with multiple elements simultaneously, loop through them, apply certain actions, or retrieve specific data. In this chapter, we'll cover techniques for identifying, accessing, and manipulating collections of WebElements, focusing on CSS selectors. You'll learn about common use cases, like selecting all options in a dropdown menu or processing all rows in a table, and how to avoid common pitfalls.

Understanding how to work with collections empowers you to write flexible, maintainable automation scripts that can handle complex web page structures. Whether you're automating form submissions, data extraction, or navigating complex page layouts, mastering WebElement collections is an essential skill for any Selenium WebDriver practitioner.

Identifying Collections with CSS Selectors

CSS (Cascading Style Sheets) selectors are a powerful tool for identifying collections of WebElements on a web page. They allow you to define patterns that match one or more elements, which is particularly useful when dealing with groups of similar elements like lists, tables, or other structured content. In this section, we'll explore several techniques to help you identify collections using CSS selectors.

Basic CSS Selectors for Collections

- **Class-Based Selectors**: You can select elements with the same class name, making it easy to retrieve collections. For example, `.product-item` selects all elements with the class "product-item".
- **Tag-Based Selectors**: If you want all elements of a certain type, such as all `<li>` elements, you can use tag-based selectors. This is helpful for retrieving lists or collections based on their HTML tag.
- **ID-Based Selectors**: While typically used to select single elements, sometimes an ID can represent a container for a collection. For instance, `#menu > li` selects all `<li>` elements within the element with the ID "menu".

Attribute-Based CSS Selectors

- **Attributes and Attribute Values**: You can use attribute-based selectors to find collections of elements with specific attributes or attribute values. For example, `input[type='checkbox']` retrieves all checkboxes on a page, while `[data-type='user']` selects all elements with a "data-type" attribute equal to "user".
- **Partial Attribute Matching**: CSS provides ways to match partial attribute values, useful for identifying collections with similar characteristics. For instance, `[class*='button']` matches all elements with "button" in their class name.

Hierarchical CSS Selectors

- **Child Selectors**: Child selectors help you retrieve collections of elements within a specific parent. For example, `ul > li` selects all direct child `<li>` elements within a `<ul>`.
- **Descendant Selectors**: These are similar to child selectors but work with any nested level. For instance, `div .highlight` selects all elements with the class "highlight" that are descendants of any `<div>`.
- **Nth-Child and Nth-Of-Type Selectors**: These selectors allow you to access elements based on their order. `ul > li:nth-child(2)` selects the second child within an unordered list, while `tr:nth-of-type(odd)` selects all odd rows in a table.

Special CSS Selectors for Collections

- **Sibling Selectors**: Use sibling selectors to select elements that share a common parent but aren't direct children. For example, `h2 + p` selects a `<p>` that immediately follows an `<h2>`.
- **General Sibling Selectors**: To select all siblings, you can use the tilde (~). For example, `h2 ~ p` selects all `<p>` elements that follow an `<h2>` with the same parent.
- **Combining Selectors**: You can combine different selectors to create complex patterns. For instance, `div > ul > li[data-status='active']` selects all `<li>` elements with "data-status" equal to "active" within a nested structure.

These CSS selector techniques give you a wide range of options for identifying collections of WebElements on a web page. By mastering these methods, you can efficiently locate, interact with, and manipulate groups of elements in your Selenium WebDriver automation scripts.

Iterating Through WebElement Collections

When automating web interactions with Selenium WebDriver, you'll often need to interact with multiple WebElements at once. This might involve checking all checkboxes in a form, extracting all rows from a table, or verifying the contents of a list. To do this, you need techniques for iterating through WebElement collections, allowing you to perform operations on each element in a collection efficiently. In this section, we'll cover different methods for iterating through WebElement collections and provide best practices for smooth automation.

Retrieving Collections of WebElements

Before you can iterate through a collection, you must first retrieve it using CSS selectors or XPath expressions. The `driver.findElements()` method is key for this, as it returns a list of WebElements matching the specified selector. For example:

```
List<WebElement> checkboxes =
driver.findElements(By.cssSelector("input[type='checkbox']"));
```

This retrieves a list of all checkboxes on the page, allowing you to iterate through them.

Iterating with Loops

The most common way to iterate through a collection of WebElements is with loops. Here are some common loop structures used in Selenium automation:

For Loop

A basic `for` loop is useful for iterating through a collection with a known number of elements. This structure allows you to access elements by index, which can be helpful for certain operations.

```java
List<WebElement> items = driver.findElements(By.cssSelector("ul > li"));
for (int i = 0; i < items.size(); i++) {
    System.out.println(items.get(i).getText());
}
```

Enhanced For Loop (For-Each)

An enhanced `for` loop, also known as a "for-each" loop, is a simplified way to iterate through collections. This loop automatically iterates through all elements without needing an index.

```java
List<WebElement> buttons = driver.findElements(By.cssSelector(".button"));
for (WebElement button : buttons) {
    button.click();
}
```

Using Streams (Java 8 and Beyond)

For more advanced manipulation of collections, you can use Java Streams. This approach allows you to perform operations like filtering, mapping, and collecting in a more functional style.

```java
List<String> names = driver.findElements(By.cssSelector(".name"))
                           .stream()
                           .map(WebElement::getText)
                           .collect(Collectors.toList());
```

Handling Stale Elements and Other Pitfalls

Iterating through collections can lead to issues like stale element references, especially in dynamic environments where the DOM changes. To mitigate this, consider:

- **Re-fetching Collections**: If the DOM changes, you may need to re-fetch the collection during iteration.
- **Using Try-Catch**: To handle unexpected exceptions or stale element errors, wrap your loop in a try-catch block.
- **Implementing Delays**: For pages with AJAX or dynamic content, adding implicit or explicit waits can help ensure elements are ready before interacting with them.

Best Practices for Iterating Through Collections

- **Check Collection Size**: Before iterating, check if the collection is empty or has the expected number of elements.
- **Minimize DOM Interactions**: Store information from WebElements in variables to avoid excessive DOM queries during iteration.
- **Use Descriptive Variable Names**: This improves readability and maintainability of your code.

By using these techniques, you can iterate through WebElement collections with confidence, enabling robust and efficient automation scripts for Selenium WebDriver.

Common Pitfalls and Challenges

When dealing with collections of WebElements in Selenium WebDriver, you may encounter several challenges that can affect the robustness and reliability of your automation scripts. Understanding these common pitfalls and learning how to address them will help ensure smoother execution and fewer unexpected issues. In this section, we'll explore some of the typical problems and discuss how to overcome them.

Stale Element References

A "stale element reference" occurs when the WebElement becomes invalid, usually because the DOM has changed since the element was originally retrieved. This can happen in dynamic web applications where elements are frequently updated or removed.

How to Avoid Stale Element References:

- **Re-fetch the Collection**: If you expect DOM changes, re-fetch the WebElement collection before each operation.
- **Use Explicit Waits**: Use WebDriver's `WebDriverWait` with conditions like `ExpectedConditions.refreshed()` to wait for elements to stabilize.
- **Catch StaleElementReferenceException**: Implement try-catch blocks to handle this exception and retry the operation when necessary.

Timing Issues and Asynchronous Content

Dynamic web pages often load content asynchronously, leading to timing issues where elements may not be available when needed. This can cause tests to fail or behave inconsistently.

How to Address Timing Issues:

- **Explicit Waits**: Use `WebDriverWait` with conditions like `ExpectedConditions.visibilityOfAllElementsLocatedBy()` to ensure elements are ready.
- **Implicit Waits**: Set a default waiting time for all element retrievals with `driver.manage().timeouts().implicitlyWait()`.
- **Polling and Re-checking**: Implement custom logic to poll for elements or re-check if an operation fails due to timing issues.

Incorrect or Ambiguous CSS Selectors

Poorly constructed CSS selectors can lead to incorrect collections or unexpected elements. This can happen when selectors are ambiguous, too broad, or don't account for dynamic page structures.

How to Create Accurate CSS Selectors:

- **Use Unique Identifiers**: Select elements by unique attributes like ID or specific class names.
- **Leverage Hierarchies**: Use parent-child relationships to narrow down selections.
- **Test Selectors**: Use browser developer tools to test CSS selectors before implementing them in automation scripts.

Handling Dynamic WebElement Collections

When working with collections that change dynamically, you may face challenges like varying collection sizes or elements appearing/disappearing.

Strategies for Dynamic Collections:

- **Conditional Checks**: Before iterating through a collection, check if it's empty or if the expected number of elements is present.
- **Graceful Handling of Missing Elements**: Implement error handling to manage cases where elements are removed or missing.
- **Dynamic Re-fetching**: Re-fetch collections as needed to ensure you're working with the latest set of elements.

Performance Concerns

Working with large collections or frequently re-fetching elements can lead to performance issues, slowing down your automation scripts.

How to Improve Performance:

- **Minimize DOM Queries**: Reduce the number of interactions with the DOM by storing element data in variables or caching collections.
- **Optimize Selectors**: Use efficient CSS selectors that minimize unnecessary processing.
- **Use Efficient Loops**: Consider using enhanced for loops or streams to iterate through collections.

By understanding and addressing these common pitfalls and challenges, you'll be better equipped to handle collections of WebElements effectively, ensuring your Selenium WebDriver scripts are robust, reliable, and performant.

Real-World Scenarios for WebElement Collections

Managing collections of WebElements is a critical skill in Selenium WebDriver automation, especially when automating complex or dynamic web applications. Real-world scenarios often involve working with lists, tables, forms, or other structures containing multiple elements. In this section, we'll explore common use cases where managing collections is essential, along with examples and best practices for handling them effectively.

Processing Data in Tables

One of the most common real-world scenarios involves interacting with table-based data. Whether it's a dashboard with statistics, an inventory list, or a report, tables often contain valuable information.

Example Scenario: Extracting Table Data

Consider a table with product information, including product name, price, and stock status. To extract this data, you would first locate the table and then retrieve collections of rows or cells:

```
WebElement table = driver.findElement(By.id("product-table"));
List<WebElement> rows = table.findElements(By.tagName("tr"));

for (WebElement row : rows) {
    List<WebElement> cells = row.findElements(By.tagName("td"));
    String productName = cells.get(0).getText();
    String price = cells.get(1).getText();
    String stockStatus = cells.get(2).getText();
    System.out.println(productName + ": " + price + " - " + stockStatus);
}
```

Handling Forms and User Input

Forms are a fundamental part of many web applications. They often consist of collections of input fields, checkboxes, radio buttons, and dropdowns.

Example Scenario: Completing a Form

Suppose you need to fill out a registration form with multiple fields. You can use a collection of WebElements to locate and interact with each input field:

```java
List<WebElement> inputs = driver.findElements(By.tagName("input"));

for (WebElement input : inputs) {
    String inputType = input.getAttribute("type");
    if ("text".equals(inputType)) {
        input.sendKeys("Sample Text");
    } else if ("checkbox".equals(inputType)) {
        if (!input.isSelected()) {
            input.click();
        }
    } else if ("radio".equals(inputType)) {
        input.click();
    }
}
```

Navigating Multi-Page Structures

Some web applications use pagination to display data across multiple pages. Managing collections is essential to navigate between pages and interact with elements across them.

Example Scenario: Handling Pagination

Imagine a scenario where you need to navigate a multi-page list to find a specific item:

```java
while (true) {
    List<WebElement> items = driver.findElements(By.cssSelector(".item"));

    // Search for a specific item
    boolean found = false;
    for (WebElement item : items) {
        if (item.getText().contains("Desired Item")) {
            found = true;
            item.click(); // or perform another action
            break;
        }
    }

    if (found) break; // Exit loop if item is found

    // Move to the next page if available
    WebElement nextPage = driver.findElement(By.cssSelector(".pagination
.next"));
    if (nextPage.isEnabled()) {
        nextPage.click();
    } else {
        break; // Exit loop if no more pages
    }
}
```

Managing Complex UI Components

Complex UI components, like dropdown menus, carousels, or tabs, often involve collections of WebElements to represent their structure and functionality.

Example Scenario: Interacting with Dropdown Menus

Dropdowns can contain collections of selectable options. Here's how you might interact with a dropdown to select an option by text:

```java
WebElement dropdown = driver.findElement(By.id("dropdown-menu"));
dropdown.click(); // Open the dropdown

List<WebElement> options = dropdown.findElements(By.tagName("li"));
for (WebElement option : options) {
    if (option.getText().equals("Desired Option")) {
        option.click();
        break;
    }
}
```

Best Practices for Real-World Scenarios

- **Validate Collections**: Before iterating, ensure the collection has the expected number of elements to avoid errors.
- **Use Explicit Waits**: When dealing with dynamic content or AJAX, use explicit waits to ensure elements are ready before interacting.
- **Implement Robust Error Handling**: Use try-catch blocks and appropriate logging to handle unexpected situations during collection management.
- **Optimize Performance**: Minimize unnecessary DOM interactions and use efficient iteration techniques to improve performance.

These real-world scenarios demonstrate how managing collections of WebElements is crucial in various contexts. By applying the right techniques and best practices, you can create robust and efficient automation scripts that handle complex web applications with ease.

Best Practices for Managing Collections

Successfully managing collections of WebElements is a critical skill for Selenium WebDriver automation. By adhering to best practices, you can ensure that your automation scripts are reliable, maintainable, and efficient. In this section, we'll discuss the key best practices for working with WebElement collections, focusing on structure, robustness, performance, and maintainability.

Validate Collections Before Iteration

- **Check for Null or Empty Collections**: Always confirm that a collection contains elements before iterating over it. This prevents `NullPointerException` and avoids errors due to empty collections.
- **Assert Collection Size**: If you expect a specific number of elements, use assertions or condition checks to ensure the collection meets your expectations.

  ```java
  List<WebElement> items = driver.findElements(By.cssSelector("ul > li"));
  assert !items.isEmpty() : "The collection is empty";
  ```

Implement Robust Error Handling

- **Use Try-Catch Blocks**: Implement error handling to manage exceptions that might occur during collection operations, like `StaleElementReferenceException`.
- **Log Errors for Debugging**: When catching exceptions, ensure errors are logged with meaningful information to facilitate troubleshooting.

```
try {
    for (WebElement item : items) {
        item.click(); // Example operation
    }
} catch (StaleElementReferenceException e) {
    System.err.println("Stale element reference encountered: " +
e.getMessage());
    // Optionally, re-fetch the collection and retry
}
```

Use Explicit Waits for Dynamic Content

- **Explicit Waits**: Use explicit waits to handle asynchronous content or AJAX-based changes. This ensures that elements are ready before you interact with them.
- **Common Wait Conditions**: Conditions like `visibilityOfAllElementsLocatedBy()` or `presenceOfAllElementsLocatedBy()` help ensure collections are stable.

```
WebDriverWait wait = new WebDriverWait(driver, 10);
List<WebElement> items =
wait.until(ExpectedConditions.visibilityOfAllElementsLocatedBy(By.cssSele
ctor("ul > li")));
```

Optimize Performance and Minimize DOM Interactions

- **Reduce DOM Queries**: Minimize the number of times you interact with the DOM by storing information in variables or caching collections.
- **Use Efficient Loops**: Prefer enhanced `for` loops or streams to reduce overhead during iteration.
- **Batch Operations**: When performing multiple actions, try to group them to reduce interaction with the browser.

```
List<String> texts = items.stream()
                        .map(WebElement::getText)
                        .collect(Collectors.toList());
```

Use Descriptive Variable Names

- **Meaningful Names**: Use descriptive variable names to improve code readability and maintainability. This helps others understand the purpose of each collection.
- **Avoid Ambiguity**: Ensure variable names are unique and do not conflict with other names in the same scope.

```
List<WebElement> productItems =
driver.findElements(By.cssSelector(".product-item"));
```

Ensure Collection Stability

- **Re-fetch Collections as Needed**: If the DOM is dynamic, consider re-fetching the collection to ensure you're working with the latest data.
- **Avoid Hard-Coded Indexes**: Instead of relying on specific indexes, use conditions or loop through collections to find elements dynamically.

```
WebElement dynamicButton = null;
for (WebElement button :
driver.findElements(By.cssSelector(".dynamic-buttons > button"))) {
    if (button.getText().equals("Click Me")) {
        dynamicButton = button;
        break;
    }
}
```

Leverage Tools for Selector Testing

- **Use Browser Developer Tools**: Test CSS selectors in the browser's developer tools before using them in automation scripts. This helps ensure selectors are accurate and effective.
- **SelectorsHub or Other Tools**: Tools like SelectorsHub can assist in building and verifying XPath and CSS selectors.

By following these best practices for managing collections of WebElements, you can create more reliable and maintainable Selenium WebDriver automation scripts. These practices help you avoid common pitfalls, improve performance, and ensure robust error handling, leading to better automation outcomes in real-world scenarios.

Chapter Summary

In this chapter, we explored the critical topic of managing collections of WebElements in Selenium WebDriver automation. We discussed the various aspects of working with collections, from identifying them with CSS selectors to iterating through them and addressing common challenges. Here's a summary of the key points covered in this chapter:

Identifying Collections with CSS Selectors

- CSS selectors provide a versatile and efficient way to identify collections of WebElements.
- We discussed basic selectors, attribute-based selectors, hierarchical selectors, and special selectors for collections.
- Leveraging these selectors, you can locate groups of elements such as lists, tables, or dropdown options with ease.

Iterating Through WebElement Collections

- Iterating through collections requires efficient loops and careful handling of potential issues like stale element references.
- We covered common iteration techniques, including basic `for` loops, enhanced `for` loops, and Java Streams.
- Best practices include validating collections before iteration, using explicit waits for dynamic content, and implementing robust error handling.

Common Pitfalls and Challenges

- Managing collections in dynamic environments introduces risks like stale element references, timing issues, and performance concerns.
- We discussed strategies to mitigate these challenges, including re-fetching collections, implementing try-catch blocks, and optimizing CSS selectors.
- Other pitfalls to avoid include incorrect or ambiguous CSS selectors and handling dynamic WebElement collections effectively.

Real-World Scenarios for WebElement Collections

- Real-world scenarios demonstrate the importance of managing collections in practical contexts like processing data in tables, handling forms and user input, and navigating multi-page structures.
- These scenarios require robust iteration techniques, careful handling of dynamic elements, and best practices to ensure reliable automation.
- We provided examples to illustrate common use cases and how to address them with collections.

Best Practices for Managing Collections

- To ensure robustness and reliability, best practices include checking collection size, minimizing DOM interactions, and optimizing performance.
- Using descriptive variable names, leveraging tools for selector testing, and ensuring collection stability are crucial for maintainable scripts.
- These practices help prevent common pitfalls and ensure smooth automation across different scenarios.

By understanding and applying these concepts and best practices, you can manage collections of WebElements effectively in your Selenium WebDriver automation scripts. This chapter provides a comprehensive guide for handling collections, offering techniques, examples, and recommendations to help you create robust and efficient automation workflows.

Identifying Visible and Hidden WebElements

Outline

1. Understanding the Need to Identify Visible and Hidden WebElements
2. Exploring Visibility Attributes in CSS
3. Identifying Hidden Elements in Web Pages
4. Handling Dynamic Visibility Changes
5. Techniques for Locating Visible and Hidden Elements
6. Best Practices for Testing with Hidden Elements
7. Examples and Case Studies
8. Chapter Summary

Understanding the Need to Identify Visible and Hidden WebElements

Web applications often include elements that are not immediately visible to the user but play a crucial role in the overall functionality of the application. These hidden elements can be dynamically displayed when certain conditions are met, such as user interactions or automated processes. Understanding the distinction between visible and hidden WebElements is vital for test automation engineers, QA testers, and developers to create robust and reliable tests.

Why It's Important to Identify Visible and Hidden WebElements

- **Ensuring Test Accuracy:** Automated tests need to interact with elements on a web page. If an element is hidden, the test may fail because it can't locate the intended element, leading to inaccurate test results.
- **Simulating User Behavior:** Hidden elements can affect user interaction, such as dropdowns that appear on click or modals that open on certain triggers. Identifying these elements allows you to simulate real-world user scenarios accurately.
- **Managing Dynamic Content:** Modern web applications often change elements' visibility based on user actions or asynchronous events. Tests must accommodate these dynamic changes to ensure they are reliable and robust.
- **Avoiding False Positives and Negatives:** Hidden elements can lead to false-positive test results if tests assume they are visible when they are not. Similarly, hidden elements appearing unexpectedly can cause false negatives. Proper identification helps prevent these issues.

Common Scenarios Involving Hidden WebElements

- **Dropdown Menus:** Dropdowns and similar elements are typically hidden until a user interaction occurs. Tests must be aware of these dynamics to ensure proper functionality.
- **Modals and Dialogs:** Pop-up modals and dialogs often start hidden and become visible when triggered. Identifying these elements is crucial for ensuring they function correctly in various scenarios.
- **Collapsible Sections:** Sections of a web page that can be expanded or collapsed depending on user input. Tests must account for the state of these sections when interacting with elements within them.
- **Loading Spinners and Overlays:** Temporary elements that indicate loading or processing. Proper test scripts ensure these elements are hidden before interacting with other parts of the page.

Challenges in Identifying Hidden WebElements

- **Dynamic Visibility Changes:** Elements may change their visibility state due to animations, AJAX calls, or user interactions. Test scripts need to detect these changes accurately.
- **CSS Techniques for Hiding Elements:** Developers use various CSS properties to hide elements, such as `display`, `visibility`, `opacity`, and others. Understanding these properties helps testers locate hidden elements.
- **XPath and CSS Selectors Limitations:** Both XPath and CSS Selectors have specific limitations when dealing with hidden elements. Testers must understand these limitations and work around them to create reliable test scripts.

By identifying visible and hidden WebElements, test automation engineers can build robust and reliable test scripts that effectively simulate user behavior and ensure the accuracy of web application testing. Understanding the scenarios and challenges involved is the first step in creating effective automation tests that work in dynamic web environments.

Exploring Visibility Attributes in CSS

In web development, CSS (Cascading Style Sheets) is used to control the visual presentation of web elements, including their visibility. Understanding how different CSS properties affect an element's visibility is crucial for automated testing and web development in general. This section explores key CSS attributes that determine whether an element is visible or hidden, and discusses how these attributes can be manipulated to achieve desired effects on a webpage.

Key CSS Properties for Visibility

- `display`: Determines how an element is rendered and whether it occupies space on the page.
  - `display: none`: The element is not displayed and doesn't occupy any space. It's effectively removed from the rendering flow.
  - `display: block`, `display: inline`, etc.: These values indicate that the element is visible and takes up space in the layout.
- `visibility`: Controls whether an element is visible without affecting the layout.
  - `visibility: hidden`: The element is invisible, but it still occupies space on the page.
  - `visibility: visible`: The element is visible and occupies its designated space.
- `opacity`: Represents the transparency level of an element.
  - `opacity: 0`: The element is completely transparent, making it effectively invisible, but it still occupies space in the layout.
  - `opacity: 1`: The element is fully opaque and visible.
- `z-index`: Affects the stacking order of elements.
  - Higher `z-index` values make elements appear on top of others, which can affect visibility if elements overlap.
- **Other Positioning Attributes**: Certain positioning techniques can also affect visibility.
  - Using absolute or fixed positioning with negative coordinates can effectively hide elements from view.
  - Setting a height or width of 0 can make an element visually disappear.

Combining CSS Properties to Hide Elements

Developers often use a combination of CSS properties to control an element's visibility. For example:

- An element with `display: none` is completely removed from the layout, making it invisible and unclickable.
- An element with `visibility: hidden` is invisible but still occupies space, useful for maintaining layout integrity.

- An element with `opacity: 0` is invisible but can still be interacted with, which can be used for hidden form inputs or accessibility features.

Common Scenarios Involving Visibility Changes

- **Dropdown Menus and Collapsible Sections**: These often change their `display` or `visibility` property based on user interaction.
- **Modals and Pop-ups**: Typically have `display: none` until they are activated, then switch to `display: block`.
- **Loading Indicators**: Often controlled by `opacity`, allowing them to fade in and out smoothly.

Challenges with CSS Visibility Attributes

- **Dynamic Changes**: Automated tests must handle elements that change visibility dynamically during execution.
- **Timing and Synchronization**: Because elements may become visible at different times, tests must include mechanisms to wait until they are visible or hidden before proceeding.
- **Selector Limitations**: Some CSS selectors may not account for visibility attributes, leading to unreliable test results.

Understanding these CSS visibility attributes is essential for both web development and automated testing. When writing tests with Selenium WebDriver or similar frameworks, being aware of how these attributes impact visibility helps ensure accurate and reliable automation scripts.

Identifying Hidden Elements in Web Pages

In modern web development, hidden elements are often used to manage user interfaces, data storage, and other purposes. Identifying hidden elements is crucial for test automation, debugging, and ensuring a smooth user experience. Hidden elements can affect both automated testing outcomes and user interactions, so understanding how to detect and work with them is a key skill for Selenium WebDriver users and web developers.

Why Elements are Hidden

- **User Interface Control**: Hidden elements can be used to create dropdown menus, pop-up modals, or collapsible sections. They may remain hidden until triggered by user interaction.
- **Data Management**: Hidden form fields can store data or unique identifiers that don't need to be visible to users.
- **Loading and Overlays**: Elements like loading spinners or overlay screens are often hidden until specific events occur, like AJAX requests or background processes.

Common Methods for Hiding Elements

- **CSS Attributes**: Using `display: none`, `visibility: hidden`, or `opacity: 0` to hide elements from view.
- **Positioning and Layout**: Moving elements off-screen with `position: absolute` or setting zero width and height to make them invisible.
- **JavaScript Manipulation**: JavaScript can dynamically change an element's visibility based on user interaction or system events.

Techniques for Identifying Hidden Elements

- **Using Browser Developer Tools**: Modern browsers offer developer tools that let you inspect the structure and styles of a webpage.

- Open the browser's developer tools (e.g., in Chrome, right-click and select "Inspect").
- Examine the CSS properties to identify elements that are hidden due to specific attributes like `display`, `visibility`, or `opacity`.
- Check for JavaScript events that manipulate the DOM to hide or show elements.
- **Writing Automated Tests**: Automated test scripts can detect hidden elements.
  - Use Selenium WebDriver to check the visibility of elements before interacting with them.
  - Use conditions like `is_displayed()` to determine if an element is visible.
  - Employ explicit waits to ensure elements become visible or hidden before proceeding with a test.
- **XPath and CSS Selectors**: XPath and CSS selectors can help identify hidden elements based on their attributes or position.
  - Create XPath expressions to find elements with specific visibility attributes (e.g., `@style='display:none'`).
  - Use CSS selectors to locate elements with specific classes or IDs commonly used for hidden elements.

Handling Hidden Elements in Automation

- **Waiting for Visibility Changes**: Automated tests often require waiting for elements to become visible or hidden. Use Selenium's WebDriverWait and ExpectedConditions to implement these waits.
- **Asserting Visibility State**: Test scripts should include assertions to check if an element is hidden or visible at expected times.
- **Dealing with Intermittent Visibility**: Some elements may change visibility based on asynchronous events, leading to test flakiness. Use robust waits and retry logic to mitigate this issue.

Best Practices for Working with Hidden Elements

- **Consistency in CSS Practices**: Use consistent CSS practices across a project to make it easier to predict and detect hidden elements.
- **Modular Test Design**: Design automated tests to handle hidden elements in a modular fashion, allowing for easier updates when UI changes occur.
- **Regular Maintenance and Debugging**: As web applications evolve, the visibility of elements may change. Regularly update test scripts and use browser developer tools to understand these changes.

By effectively identifying and managing hidden elements in web pages, you can create robust and reliable test automation scripts, ensuring that your web applications deliver a seamless user experience and consistent functionality.

Handling Dynamic Visibility Changes

Dynamic visibility changes refer to scenarios where elements on a webpage appear or disappear in response to user interactions or background processes. This is common in modern web applications where dynamic content and animations play a crucial role in enhancing user experience. As a result, automated tests must be able to handle these dynamic visibility changes effectively. Here's how you can address these challenges:

Common Causes of Dynamic Visibility Changes

- **User Interactions**: Actions like clicks, hovers, or text input can trigger elements to appear or disappear. Examples include dropdowns, modals, and collapsible sections.
- **JavaScript Events**: Elements might change visibility due to asynchronous operations, such as AJAX calls, which load new content without reloading the page.

- **Animations and Transitions**: CSS animations or JavaScript-based transitions can gradually change an element's visibility over time.

Techniques to Handle Dynamic Visibility Changes

- **Explicit Waits**: Explicit waits allow you to wait for a specific condition before proceeding with an operation. This is useful when elements might become visible or hidden after a delay.
  - Use Selenium's `WebDriverWait` with `ExpectedConditions` to wait for elements to become visible or hidden.
  - Common conditions include `visibilityOf`, `invisibilityOf`, `elementToBeClickable`, and others.
- **Polling and Retry Logic**: When elements appear or disappear intermittently, use polling mechanisms to periodically check the element's state.
  - This is especially useful when handling AJAX-based elements, where content might load asynchronously.
- **Handling Timeouts**: Set appropriate timeouts for explicit waits to avoid excessive waiting times. This ensures your tests don't hang indefinitely if elements don't become visible or hidden within a reasonable timeframe.
- **Conditional Logic**: Write test scripts with conditional logic to handle different visibility states.
  - For example, if an element is visible, interact with it; if not, handle the alternate scenario.
- **Handling CSS Animations**: When animations affect visibility, consider waiting for a specific duration or until the animation completes before proceeding.
  - Use techniques like `Thread.sleep()` with caution and only when necessary to account for animation delays.
- **Using Hidden Attributes**: Elements might have hidden attributes, like `aria-hidden`, to indicate their visibility state. Check for these attributes to confirm an element's visibility status.

Best Practices for Dealing with Dynamic Visibility Changes

- **Understand the Web Page Structure**: Familiarize yourself with the structure and behavior of the web page you're testing. This includes understanding when and why elements change visibility.
- **Use Clear Element Locators**: Use clear and stable locators for identifying elements that might change visibility. This minimizes test flakiness due to incorrect element identification.
- **Implement Robust Test Frameworks**: Design your test framework to handle dynamic visibility changes with minimal impact on test stability. This includes implementing reusable wait logic and consistent test structure.
- **Consistent Test Data**: Ensure test data remains consistent across test runs to avoid unexpected visibility changes due to varying data.
- **Regular Test Maintenance**: As web applications evolve, elements might change their behavior. Regularly update and maintain your tests to ensure they reflect the latest state of the application.

Common Challenges and Solutions

- **Flaky Tests**: Dynamic visibility changes can lead to flaky tests. Use explicit waits and retry logic to reduce flakiness.
- **Timing Issues**: Elements may change visibility at unpredictable times. Implement flexible waiting mechanisms to accommodate varying response times.
- **Unexpected Visibility States**: Tests might fail if elements aren't in the expected visibility state. Include assertions and error handling to manage unexpected outcomes.

By incorporating these techniques and best practices, you can create robust automated tests that effectively handle dynamic visibility changes, ensuring reliable test results and a smooth user experience.

Techniques for Locating Visible and Hidden Elements

Locating visible and hidden elements on a webpage is a critical task for web development and automated testing. Selenium WebDriver, along with XPath and CSS selectors, provides a powerful set of tools for this purpose. This section explores various techniques for identifying elements, whether they are currently visible or hidden, and discusses the best practices for interacting with them.

1. Understanding Visibility in Web Elements

- Web elements can be visible, hidden, or conditionally displayed based on user interactions or JavaScript events. Understanding their visibility status is key to writing effective automated tests.
- Visibility can be influenced by CSS properties like display, visibility, opacity, position, and others. JavaScript can also change an element's visibility dynamically.

2. Locating Visible Elements

- Visible elements are those currently displayed on a webpage and are generally interactable.
- **CSS Selectors**: Use CSS selectors to locate elements based on attributes, class names, or ID.
  - Examples:
    - #elementID: Locate by ID.
    - .className: Locate by class name.
    - [attribute="value"]: Locate by attribute-value pairs.
  - Use combinational selectors to locate elements within specific parent-child structures.
- **XPath Expressions**: Use XPath to locate elements with more complex relationships.
  - Examples:
    - //div[@id='elementID']: Locate a div with a specific ID.
    - //button[contains(text(), 'Submit')]: Locate a button with specific text.
  - XPath is useful for more complex queries, like finding elements by partial attributes or relative to other elements.
- **Selenium Methods**: Selenium WebDriver provides methods to check if an element is displayed.
  - isDisplayed(): Returns true if an element is visible on the page.
  - findElement and findElements: To locate single or multiple elements using various selectors.

3. Locating Hidden Elements

- Hidden elements are those that are not currently displayed but may still be in the DOM.
- **Detecting Hidden Status**: Use CSS properties or JavaScript events to determine why an element is hidden.
  - display: none, visibility: hidden, opacity: 0: Common indicators of hidden elements.
- **Using CSS Selectors**: Locate hidden elements by specific attributes or structure.
  - Example: div[style='display:none']: Find elements that have display:none.
- **Using XPath**: Find hidden elements based on their relationship with other elements or specific attributes.
  - Example: //div[contains(@style, 'display:none')]: Locate hidden elements with certain styles.
- **JavaScript Interaction**: For advanced cases, you might need to execute JavaScript to determine if an element is hidden or to interact with hidden elements.
  - executeScript: Allows executing custom JavaScript code to interact with hidden elements or check their state.

4. Techniques for Handling Visibility Changes

- **Explicit Waits**: Use explicit waits to ensure an element becomes visible or hidden before interacting with it.
    - WebDriverWait: Use with ExpectedConditions to wait for specific conditions, like visibility or invisibility.
- **Polling and Retry Logic**: When visibility changes are dynamic, implement retry logic to check for the expected state periodically.
- **Handling Dynamic Content**: Implement test logic that accounts for elements appearing or disappearing based on user interactions or AJAX events.
- **Robust Locators**: Design locators to be resilient to changes in element structure or CSS attributes.

5. Best Practices for Locating Visible and Hidden Elements

- **Consistent Locators**: Use consistent and clear locators to minimize test flakiness.
- **Handle Exceptions Gracefully**: Implement exception handling for scenarios where elements are not found or behave unexpectedly.
- **Design for Modularity**: Create modular test scripts that allow easy adaptation when element structure changes.
- **Use Explicit Waits**: Ensure visibility changes are handled properly with explicit waits to avoid race conditions in automated tests.

By using these techniques, you can effectively locate and interact with both visible and hidden elements, creating more reliable and robust automated test scripts.

Best Practices for Testing with Hidden Elements

Testing web applications often involves interacting with hidden elements, which may be used to control complex UI components or as placeholders for data. Proper handling of hidden elements is crucial to ensure reliable and robust automated tests. This section covers best practices for testing with hidden elements, ensuring accuracy, stability, and maintainability in your test scripts.

1. Understand Why Elements Are Hidden

- Hidden elements might be used to create dynamic UIs, manage user interactions, or maintain data without displaying it to users.
- Common reasons for hiding elements include dropdown menus, modals, AJAX-based components, and collapsible sections.

2. Identify Hidden Elements in the DOM

- **Developer Tools**: Use browser developer tools to inspect the DOM and understand why elements are hidden.
    - Look for common CSS properties that indicate hidden status, such as display: none, visibility: hidden, or opacity: 0.
- **Hidden Attributes**: Some elements have attributes indicating hidden status, like aria-hidden or style="display:none".
- **XPath and CSS Selectors**: Use XPath expressions or CSS selectors to locate hidden elements based on their attributes or relationships.

3. Design Test Scenarios for Hidden Elements

- Consider scenarios where hidden elements become visible or vice versa.

- Implement test cases that interact with hidden elements in various states, ensuring your tests can handle dynamic changes.

4. Use Explicit Waits for Visibility Changes

- **Explicit Waits**: Use Selenium WebDriver's `WebDriverWait` and `ExpectedConditions` to wait for specific visibility conditions.
  - Examples include `visibilityOf`, `invisibilityOf`, and `elementToBeClickable`.
- **Poll for Visibility Changes**: When elements change visibility based on events or animations, implement polling mechanisms to periodically check their state.

5. Ensure Robustness in Test Scripts

- **Conditional Logic**: Write test scripts with conditional logic to handle hidden elements effectively. This ensures your tests are flexible when dealing with varying visibility states.
- **Graceful Error Handling**: Implement error handling to manage scenarios where hidden elements do not behave as expected.
- **Assertions for Hidden Elements**: Include assertions to confirm if an element is hidden or visible at appropriate times, ensuring test stability.

6. Implement Test Data Consistency

- **Consistent Test Data**: Ensure test data remains consistent across test runs. This avoids unexpected visibility changes due to varying input.
- **Manage State Transitions**: Design your tests to account for hidden elements that transition between visible and hidden states during interactions.

7. Use JavaScript for Advanced Interactions

- **Executing JavaScript**: In complex scenarios, use Selenium's `executeScript` to interact with hidden elements or to change their visibility dynamically.
  - This can be useful for triggering JavaScript events or handling elements not easily accessible through standard WebDriver methods.
- **Handling Animations and Transitions**: If elements change visibility with animations, use JavaScript to determine when these animations are complete before interacting with other elements.

8. Regularly Maintain and Update Tests

- **Adapt to UI Changes**: As web applications evolve, the behavior of hidden elements may change. Regularly update your test scripts to reflect these changes.
- **Monitor for Flaky Tests**: Hidden elements can lead to test flakiness due to dynamic visibility changes. Monitor and adjust your tests to improve stability.

9. Use Modular Test Design

- **Encapsulation and Reusability**: Design test scripts with modular components that handle specific scenarios involving hidden elements. This makes it easier to update tests when UI structures change.
- **Centralize Wait Logic**: Create reusable wait logic for handling hidden elements, reducing redundancy and ensuring consistency across test scripts.

By following these best practices, you can create robust and reliable automated tests that effectively handle hidden elements in various scenarios, ensuring consistent test results and a stable testing process.

Examples and Case Studies

To understand how best practices can be applied to real-world scenarios, let's examine a few examples and case studies that involve interacting with hidden elements in web automation testing. These examples demonstrate various techniques for locating hidden elements, handling visibility changes, and ensuring test stability.

Example 1: Testing a Dropdown Menu

A common scenario involves testing dropdown menus that are hidden until a user interaction, such as a button click.

- **Problem**: You want to verify the content of a dropdown menu, but it's initially hidden. Simply attempting to find the elements inside the dropdown won't work, as they're not visible at first.
- **Solution**: Use explicit waits to wait for the dropdown to become visible before attempting to interact with it.
  - Use Selenium's `WebDriverWait` and `ExpectedConditions` to wait for the menu to be visible.
  - Click on the button or element that triggers the dropdown to appear.
  - Once visible, interact with the dropdown's contents and validate the expected behavior.

```
WebDriverWait wait = new WebDriverWait(driver, 10);
WebElement dropdownButton = driver.findElement(By.id("dropdown-button"));
dropdownButton.click();

WebElement dropdownMenu =
wait.until(ExpectedConditions.visibilityOfElementLocated(By.id("dropdown-
menu")));
List<WebElement> menuItems = dropdownMenu.findElements(By.tagName("li"));

assertEquals(menuItems.size(), 5); // Verify the number of menu items
```

Example 2: Testing a Collapsible Section

Collapsible sections often start expanded or collapsed, changing their state upon user interaction.

- **Problem**: You want to test interactions within a collapsible section that starts hidden and becomes visible when expanded.
- **Solution**: Use explicit waits to ensure the section is visible before interacting with its contents.
  - Click the toggle button to expand the section.
  - Wait for the section to become visible using `WebDriverWait`.
  - Interact with the section's elements and verify expected behavior.

```
WebElement toggleButton = driver.findElement(By.id("collapse-toggle"));
toggleButton.click();

WebElement collapsibleSection =
wait.until(ExpectedConditions.visibilityOfElementLocated(By.id("collapsib
le-section")));
WebElement sectionContent =
collapsibleSection.findElement(By.className("content"));
```

```
assertTrue(sectionContent.isDisplayed()); // Confirm the content is
visible
```

Case Study: Handling AJAX-based Elements

AJAX-based elements can be challenging to test because they load asynchronously, and their visibility may change based on background events.

- **Scenario**: You want to test an application that uses AJAX to load content after a form submission.
- **Problem**: The test must wait for the AJAX call to complete and ensure the newly loaded content is visible.
- **Solution**: Implement explicit waits to detect when AJAX-based elements become visible. Use Selenium's `WebDriverWait` to wait for specific conditions, like visibility or text content.
  - Submit the form to trigger the AJAX request.
  - Use a wait condition to detect when the new content is loaded.
  - Validate the expected behavior, like checking text content or element visibility.

```
WebElement submitButton = driver.findElement(By.id("submit-button"));
submitButton.click();

WebDriverWait wait = new WebDriverWait(driver, 10);
WebElement ajaxContent =
wait.until(ExpectedConditions.visibilityOfElementLocated(By.id("ajax-cont
ent")));

String expectedText = "Content Loaded";
assertEquals(ajaxContent.getText(), expectedText); // Validate the loaded
content
```

These examples and case studies demonstrate how to apply best practices when dealing with hidden elements in web automation testing. By using explicit waits, conditional logic, and handling dynamic visibility changes, you can create robust and reliable automated tests that interact with elements effectively, regardless of their visibility status.

Chapter Summary

In this chapter, we explored the concept of identifying visible and hidden WebElements within the context of automated testing and web development. Here's a summary of the key points discussed:

Understanding Visibility and Hidden Elements

- WebElements can be visible, hidden, or conditionally displayed based on user interactions or JavaScript events. Hidden elements are often used to control complex UI components or to store data that doesn't need to be displayed to the user.

Techniques for Locating Visible Elements

- **CSS Selectors**: Locate visible elements based on attributes, class names, or IDs. These are useful for straightforward visibility scenarios.
- **XPath Expressions**: XPath offers more complex queries, allowing you to find elements by relative relationships or specific properties.

- **Selenium Methods**: Use Selenium's `isDisplayed()` to check if an element is visible before interacting with it.

Techniques for Locating Hidden Elements

- **CSS Properties**: Hidden elements often use `display: none`, `visibility: hidden`, or `opacity: 0`.
- **XPath and CSS Selectors**: Locate hidden elements by specific attributes or based on their position in the DOM.
- **JavaScript Interaction**: Use Selenium's `executeScript` to handle advanced cases where elements are hidden or need specific interactions.

Handling Dynamic Visibility Changes

- **Explicit Waits**: Use `WebDriverWait` and `ExpectedConditions` to wait for elements to become visible or hidden.
- **Polling and Retry Logic**: Implement polling mechanisms to account for intermittent visibility changes, common with AJAX-based content.
- **Handling Timeouts**: Set appropriate timeouts for waits to ensure tests do not hang indefinitely.

Best Practices for Testing with Hidden Elements

- **Conditional Logic**: Design test scripts with logic to handle both visible and hidden elements effectively.
- **Graceful Error Handling**: Implement robust error handling for unexpected visibility scenarios.
- **Use Modular Test Design**: Create reusable and modular test components to ensure flexibility as web applications evolve.
- **Regular Test Maintenance**: As elements may change visibility behavior, regularly maintain and update your test scripts.

Examples and Case Studies

- We examined real-world examples where hidden elements are used, such as dropdown menus, collapsible sections, and AJAX-based content.
- These examples demonstrated best practices in handling hidden elements, including using explicit waits, interacting with hidden elements, and implementing stable test scripts to reduce flakiness.

By understanding these techniques and best practices, you can create robust automated tests that effectively handle visible and hidden WebElements. Whether you're using CSS selectors, XPath expressions, or JavaScript interactions, these skills will help ensure your test scripts are reliable and can adapt to dynamic web environments.

Locating Elements Within Other Elements

Outline

1. Introduction to Nested Element Structures
2. Understanding Contextual CSS Selectors
3. Techniques for Locating Elements Within Containers
4. Using CSS Parent-Child Selectors
5. Advanced CSS Combinators for Nested Structures
6. Practical Examples and Case Studies
7. Chapter Summary

Introduction to Nested Element Structures

Web elements often have complex relationships due to nested structures. Understanding how these elements are organized is crucial for efficiently locating them. In this chapter, we will explore nested element structures and discuss various techniques for finding elements within other elements.

Web pages commonly contain elements nested within other elements, creating a hierarchy. For example, in a typical HTML document, you might find a div with multiple p tags inside, or a ul with various li elements. This nesting allows for complex layouts and organization but can complicate the task of locating specific elements.

In this introduction, we will cover:

1. **Why Nested Structures Matter**: Explore why web developers use nested structures and how they impact automation and testing.
2. **Common Nested Structures**: Identify some common scenarios where elements are nested, such as navigation menus, forms, and tables.
3. **Challenges of Nested Structures**: Discuss the challenges associated with locating elements within nested structures, including specificity, ambiguity, and performance.
4. **Overview of CSS Selectors for Nested Structures**: Briefly introduce the CSS selectors and combinators that are useful for navigating nested elements.

Why Nested Structures Matter

Nested structures allow web developers to create complex and responsive web pages. These structures help organize content logically, create stylized layouts, and maintain clear relationships between elements. Understanding these nested structures is critical for tasks like web scraping, automated testing, and browser automation, where finding specific elements is key.

Common Nested Structures

To identify nested structures, you should be familiar with common HTML patterns. Examples include:

- **Forms**: Often contain nested inputs, labels, and buttons.
- **Tables**: Contain rows (tr) with cells (td or th), forming a grid-like structure.
- **Lists**: ul and ol contain multiple li elements.
- **Navigation Menus**: Often consist of nested div, ul, and li elements, representing different levels of the menu hierarchy.

Challenges of Nested Structures

Locating elements within nested structures presents several challenges:

- **Specificity**: The deeper the nesting, the more specific the selectors need to be.
- **Ambiguity**: With similar structures, it can be challenging to determine the correct element.
- **Performance**: Searching through deeply nested structures can be computationally expensive.

Overview of CSS Selectors for Nested Structures

To navigate nested structures, CSS provides a variety of selectors and combinators:

- **Child Selector (>)**: Selects direct children of an element.
- **Descendant Selector (space)**: Selects all descendants of an element.
- **Adjacent Sibling Selector (+)**: Selects an element immediately following another.
- **General Sibling Selector (~)**: Selects all elements following a specified element within the same parent.

In this chapter, we will explore these selectors and their applications in depth to help you effectively locate elements within nested structures.

Understanding Contextual CSS Selectors

Contextual CSS selectors are powerful tools for precisely locating and interacting with web elements based on their context within the structure of a web page. This concept is crucial when working with nested elements, where you might need to target specific elements within a complex hierarchy. This section will explain contextual CSS selectors, discuss various types, and provide examples to demonstrate their utility in locating elements within a given context.

What Are Contextual CSS Selectors?

A contextual CSS selector is a selector that identifies an element based on its position relative to other elements. Unlike simple attribute-based selectors, contextual selectors consider the relationships between elements, allowing you to target elements with greater specificity. Contextual selectors are commonly used in web automation, testing, and web development to locate elements in complex document object models (DOMs).

Types of Contextual CSS Selectors

Here are some of the most common contextual CSS selectors and how they are used to locate elements within different contexts:

1. **Descendant Selector (Whitespace)**: This selector allows you to select all descendants of a given element, regardless of their depth in the hierarchy. It uses a space to indicate the relationship.
   - Example: `div p` selects all `<p>` elements that are descendants of a `<div>`.
2. **Child Selector (>)**: This selector targets direct children of an element. It is more specific than the descendant selector because it does not include deeper nested descendants.
   - Example: `ul > li` selects only the immediate `<li>` children of a `<ul>`.
3. **Adjacent Sibling Selector (+)**: This selector locates an element that immediately follows another element within the same parent.
   - Example: `h1 + p` selects the first `<p>` that directly follows an `<h1>`.
4. **General Sibling Selector (~)**: This selector targets all sibling elements that follow a specific element, not just the immediate one.
   - Example: `h2 ~ p` selects all `<p>` elements that follow an `<h2>`, even if other elements are in between.

5. **Parent Selector (:):** Although not as widely implemented as other contextual selectors, parent selectors can target elements based on the presence of children.
   - Example: `div:has(p)` selects `<div>` elements that contain at least one `<p>`.

Examples of Contextual CSS Selectors in Practice

Here are some practical examples demonstrating how contextual CSS selectors are used to locate elements in common scenarios:

- **Navigating Nested Structures:**
  - To find a specific item within a nested list, you might use `ul > li > a` to select all links (`<a>`) that are direct children of list items (`<li>`) within an unordered list (`<ul>`).
- **Handling Forms:**
  - To select the label for a particular input field in a form, you could use `label + input` to get the input field that directly follows a label.
- **Selecting Specific Sections:**
  - If you have sections with different elements, you can use `div.section > h2` to select all `<h2>` headings that are direct children of a section (`<div class="section">`).

Understanding contextual CSS selectors is critical for effective web element location. By using these selectors, you can navigate complex nested structures, locate elements with precision, and build robust automated tests. This knowledge is valuable for Selenium WebDriver automation, web scraping, and more.

Techniques for Locating Elements Within Containers

When working with nested web elements, it's crucial to understand how to locate elements within specific containers accurately. These techniques allow you to interact with deeply nested elements, ensuring that you are selecting the correct targets for web automation or testing. This section discusses various techniques for locating elements within containers using CSS selectors, focusing on both basic and advanced methods.

1. Overview of Containers in Web Development

Containers are elements that hold other elements within them. Common examples include:

- **Divs:** Often used to create sections or blocks of content.
- **Forms:** Used to gather user input and contain various form fields.
- **Tables:** Composed of rows and cells, each a container of sorts.
- **Lists:** Structures like unordered (`ul`) and ordered (`ol`) lists contain list items (`li`).

These containers are the building blocks of many web pages, and understanding how to navigate them is key to locating elements efficiently.

2. Basic Techniques for Locating Elements in Containers

The following basic techniques are often sufficient for most scenarios involving nested elements:

- **Descendant Selectors:** This technique selects all descendants within a given container.
  - Example: `div.container p` selects all `<p>` elements within a `<div class="container">`.
- **Child Selectors:** Useful for targeting direct children within a container.
  - Example: `ul > li` selects immediate `<li>` children within a `<ul>`, avoiding deeper nested items.

- **Combining Selectors with Attributes**:
  - This approach combines contextual selectors with attributes to increase specificity.
  - Example: `div.form > input[name='username']` selects an `<input>` with the name "username" that is a direct child of a `<div class="form">`.

3. Advanced Techniques for Locating Elements in Containers

In more complex scenarios, you may need to employ advanced techniques to locate elements:

- **Adjacent Sibling Selector (+)**:
  - This allows you to find elements that are immediate siblings within the same container.
  - Example: `label + input` selects the `<input>` immediately following a `<label>`.
- **General Sibling Selector (~)**:
  - This selects all siblings following a specified element within the same container.
  - Example: `div.header ~ div.content` selects all `<div class="content">` following a `<div class="header">`.
- **Combining Multiple Selectors**:
  - This technique allows for more complex targeting within a container.
  - Example: `div.wrapper > div.content > p` selects all `<p>` elements within a `<div class="content">` that's inside a `<div class="wrapper">`.

4. Practical Examples of Locating Elements in Containers

- **Selecting Form Fields in a Container**:
  - To select all input fields in a specific form, you could use `form#loginForm > input`.
  - To select a specific field by label, you might use `label[for='email'] + input`.
- **Navigating Nested Lists**:
  - To locate specific items within a nested list, consider `ul > li > ul > li` to select the second level of list items.
- **Finding Elements in Tables**:
  - To find all cells in the second row, you might use `table tr:nth-child(2) > td`.

Locating elements within containers requires a solid understanding of CSS selectors and their relationships. By mastering both basic and advanced techniques, you can navigate complex nested structures and interact with specific elements within any container. This skill is invaluable for web automation, Selenium WebDriver scripts, and other testing frameworks.

Using CSS Parent-Child Selectors

Parent-child relationships are fundamental in web development, representing the structure of a document's elements. CSS parent-child selectors allow you to precisely target elements based on these direct relationships, providing a reliable way to navigate nested structures. This section focuses on using CSS parent-child selectors to locate and interact with elements in various scenarios, with a particular emphasis on selecting direct children in nested containers.

1. Understanding Parent-Child Selectors

A parent-child selector in CSS targets elements that are direct children of a specified parent. This selector is indicated by the ">" symbol and only considers immediate children, not deeper descendants. By using this selector, you can reduce ambiguity when working with complex nested structures.

- **Parent-Child Selector (>)**:
  - This selector targets direct children within a parent container.

○ Example: `ul > li` selects immediate `<li>` children within a `<ul>`, excluding deeper nested `li` elements.

2. Benefits of Using Parent-Child Selectors

Parent-child selectors offer several benefits in web automation and testing:

- **Precision**: By targeting only direct children, you can avoid unintentional selection of nested elements that may share similar attributes.
- **Performance**: Because this selector doesn't scan deeply, it can be more efficient in large, complex documents.
- **Clarity**: It clearly represents the structural relationship between elements, aiding in code readability and maintainability.

3. Common Use Cases for Parent-Child Selectors

Parent-child selectors are useful in a variety of scenarios, including:

- **Navigating Lists**:
  ○ To locate list items in a navigation menu, you might use `nav > ul > li` to target only the top-level items.
- **Interacting with Forms**:
  ○ To select input fields within a form, use `form > input` to avoid nested elements within the form.
  ○ Example: `form#login > input[type='text']` selects text inputs that are direct children of the form with ID "login."
- **Finding Table Data**:
  ○ To select all cells in a specific row, use `table > tbody > tr > td`. This approach avoids selecting nested tables or other elements within the table structure.

4. Practical Examples of Parent-Child Selectors

Here are some examples demonstrating the use of parent-child selectors in real-world contexts:

- **Selecting Top-Level List Items**:
  ○ To select all top-level list items in a sidebar menu, use `aside > ul > li`.
- **Working with Forms and User Input**:
  ○ To find all immediate button elements in a form, use `form > button`.
  ○ To locate labels that are direct children of a form, use `form > label`.
- **Targeting Elements in a Specific Context**:
  ○ To select headings within a specific container, use `div.content > h2`.
  ○ For images within a specific section, use `section.gallery > img`.

5. Limitations and Considerations

While parent-child selectors are powerful, they have some limitations:

- **No Deep Nesting**:
  ○ They do not select elements beyond direct children, which may require additional selectors for deeper elements.
- **Requires Specific Structure**:
  ○ If the document structure changes, these selectors may break, necessitating updates to the automation script.

CSS parent-child selectors are invaluable for targeting direct relationships between elements in web pages. Understanding how to use them effectively allows for precise and efficient element location, essential for web automation, testing, and Selenium WebDriver scripts. By mastering this selector, you can confidently navigate complex nested structures and create robust automation scenarios.

Advanced CSS Combinators for Nested Structures

Advanced CSS combinators offer a powerful way to locate and interact with elements within complex nested structures. Combinators establish relationships between elements based on their position in the Document Object Model (DOM). This section will explore these advanced combinators and demonstrate their practical applications for efficiently navigating nested elements in web automation and testing scenarios.

1. Understanding Combinators in CSS

Combinators in CSS define the relationships between elements. The most common combinators used for nested structures are:

- **Descendant Selector (Whitespace)**:
    - Selects any descendant of a given element, regardless of depth.
    - Example: `div.container p` selects all `<p>` elements within a `<div class="container">`.
- **Child Selector (>)**:
    - Targets direct children of an element.
    - Example: `ul > li` selects immediate `<li>` children within a `<ul>`.
- **Adjacent Sibling Selector (+)**:
    - Selects the element immediately following another element within the same parent.
    - Example: `h1 + p` selects the `<p>` that follows an `<h1>`.
- **General Sibling Selector (~)**:
    - Targets all siblings following a specific element within the same parent.
    - Example: `div.header ~ div.content` selects all `<div class="content">` that follow a `<div class="header">`.

2. Using Combinators to Navigate Nested Structures

Let's explore how to use these combinators effectively in complex nested structures.

Descendant Selector (Whitespace)

The descendant selector allows you to select any element within a parent, regardless of depth. It's useful for targeting elements deeply nested within a container, but can be less precise if multiple similar elements exist.

- **Example**: `div.content p` selects all `<p>` elements within a container `<div class="content">`. This approach is useful when you're unsure of the exact structure or depth.

Child Selector (>)

The child selector targets only direct children, making it more precise than the descendant selector. It's ideal when you want to avoid selecting deeper nested elements.

- **Example**: `ul > li` selects only the immediate list items, ignoring any further nesting. This is useful for targeting top-level navigation items or direct children in forms.

Adjacent Sibling Selector (+)

The adjacent sibling selector is helpful for selecting an element immediately following another, within the same parent. It is precise and useful for accessing elements in a specific order.

- **Example**: h1 + p selects the first <p> that follows an <h1>. This is useful in structured content like articles or blog posts where certain elements follow a defined order.

General Sibling Selector (~)

The general sibling selector targets all elements that follow a specific element within the same parent, offering broader coverage than the adjacent sibling selector.

- **Example**: div.note ~ p selects all paragraphs following a <div class="note">. This can be useful when you need to select a range of elements that share a common parent.

3. Practical Applications of Advanced Combinators

Let's examine how these combinators are used in practical scenarios.

- **Navigation Menus**:
  - To locate all direct child links in a navigation menu, use nav > ul > li > a.
- **Forms and User Input**:
  - To select a label and the immediate input it describes, use label + input.
- **Table Structures**:
  - To select all cells in a specific row, use table > tbody > tr > td.
- **Content Layouts**:
  - To locate all sections that follow a specific header, use h2 ~ div.section.

4. Considerations and Best Practices

When using advanced combinators, keep in mind:

- **Performance**: Descendant selectors can be less performant due to deep scanning. Use child selectors where possible for more efficient scripts.
- **Precision**: Ensure combinators align with the desired structure to avoid selecting unintended elements.
- **Readability**: Use clear and descriptive combinators to maintain readability in automation scripts and test cases.

Advanced CSS combinators offer a flexible and precise way to navigate nested structures in web pages. Understanding how to use descendant selectors, child selectors, adjacent sibling selectors, and general sibling selectors will enable you to create robust and efficient automation scripts. These skills are essential for web automation with tools like Selenium WebDriver, ensuring accurate element location in complex nested environments.

Practical Examples and Case Studies

Locating elements within nested structures is a critical skill in web automation and testing. This section provides practical examples and case studies demonstrating how to use CSS selectors to navigate complex structures, emphasizing scenarios where elements are deeply nested. By exploring these examples, you will gain insights into effective strategies for locating and interacting with specific elements in a web page.

1. Example: Navigating a Nested Navigation Menu

Navigation menus often contain nested elements, such as dropdowns or submenus. Here's an example of locating specific links within a multi-level navigation menu.

HTML Structure:

```
<nav class="main-nav">
  <ul>
    <li><a href="/home">Home</a></li>
    <li><a href="/products">Products</a>
      <ul>
        <li><a href="/products/electronics">Electronics</a></li>
        <li><a href="/products/clothing">Clothing</a></li>
      </ul>
    </li>
    <li><a href="/contact">Contact</a></li>
  </ul>
</nav>
```

Selectors to Locate Nested Elements:

- To select the first level of navigation items, you can use:

```
.main-nav > ul > li > a
```

- To locate links within a specific submenu, such as "Products," you can use:

```
.main-nav > ul > li:nth-child(2) > ul > li > a
```

These selectors help you precisely navigate the nested structure of a multi-level navigation menu.

2. Case Study: Locating Form Fields Within a Complex Form

In complex forms, elements are often nested within containers, making it essential to use specific selectors to locate fields and buttons.

HTML Structure:

```
<form id="registrationForm">
  <div class="form-group">
    <label for="username">Username</label>
    <input type="text" id="username" name="username">
  </div>
  <div class="form-group">
    <label for="password">Password</label>
    <input type="password" id="password" name="password">
  </div>
  <button type="submit">Register</button>
</form>
```

Selectors to Locate Form Fields:

- To select the "Username" input, you can use:

```
#registrationForm > .form-group > input[name='username']
```

- To locate the "Register" button, the selector might be:

```
#registrationForm > button[type='submit']
```

These selectors ensure you interact with the correct elements in a complex form structure.

3. Example: Extracting Data from a Table with Nested Elements

Tables often contain nested rows and cells, requiring specific selectors to locate relevant data.

HTML Structure:

```html
<table class="data-table">
  <thead>
    <tr>
      <th>Product</th>
      <th>Price</th>
    </tr>
  </thead>
  <tbody>
    <tr>
      <td>Laptop</td>
      <td>$1200</td>
    </tr>
    <tr>
      <td>Smartphone</td>
      <td>$800</td>
    </tr>
  </tbody>
</table>
```

Selectors for Extracting Table Data:

- To locate all rows in the table body, you can use:

  ```
  .data-table > tbody > tr
  ```

- To extract the second cell (price) from each row, the selector might be:

  ```
  .data-table > tbody > tr > td:nth-child(2)
  ```

These selectors enable you to extract specific data from a table, even when rows contain nested structures.

4. Case Study: Navigating Content Sections in a Blog Post

Blog posts often have structured content with headings and paragraphs. Navigating these sections accurately requires understanding parent-child and sibling relationships.

HTML Structure:

```html
<article class="blog-post">
  <h1>Understanding XPath</h1>
  <p>XPath is a language used to navigate XML documents.</p>
  <h2>Basic Syntax</h2>
  <p>XPath uses various syntax elements to select nodes.</p>
  <h2>Advanced Concepts</h2>
  <p>Advanced XPath concepts include predicates and axes.</p>
```

```
</article>
```

Selectors for Navigating Content:

- To locate all headings in the blog post, use:

```
.blog-post > h2
```

- To select all paragraphs following a specific heading, such as "Advanced Concepts," you can use:

```
.blog-post > h2:nth-child(3) ~ p
```

These selectors demonstrate how to navigate content sections within a blog post structure, focusing on parent-child and sibling relationships.

These practical examples and case studies illustrate how CSS selectors can be used to locate elements within nested structures. By understanding the relationships between elements, you can create precise selectors that allow for accurate interaction with specific elements, enabling effective web automation, Selenium WebDriver scripts, and other testing scenarios.

Chapter Summary

Locating elements within nested structures is a critical skill in web automation, testing, and development. This chapter focused on techniques and best practices for identifying and interacting with elements within other elements. Here's a summary of the key points covered:

Understanding Nested Structures

Web pages often have elements nested within other elements, forming complex hierarchies. These nested structures can include common scenarios like multi-level navigation menus, complex forms, and nested tables. Understanding the structure of the web page is the first step in accurately locating elements.

Techniques for Locating Elements Within Containers

Several CSS selectors can be used to navigate nested structures, including:

- **Descendant Selector (Whitespace)**: Selects any descendant within a parent element, allowing for deep nesting.
- **Child Selector (>)**: Targets direct children within a parent, providing more precision.
- **Adjacent Sibling Selector (+)**: Selects elements immediately following another within the same parent.
- **General Sibling Selector (~)**: Targets all siblings following a specified element within the same parent.

These selectors can be combined with other criteria, such as class names and attributes, to locate specific elements within containers.

Using CSS Parent-Child Selectors

Parent-child selectors are crucial for locating direct relationships between elements. The child selector (>) allows you to focus on immediate children within a parent container, reducing ambiguity and improving precision. This is particularly useful in scenarios like navigation menus, forms, and table rows.

Advanced CSS Combinators for Nested Structures

Advanced CSS combinators provide more flexibility when working with complex nested structures. The descendant selector, child selector, adjacent sibling selector, and general sibling selector offer different levels of specificity, allowing you to navigate nested elements efficiently. Understanding when to use each combinator is key to successful element location.

Practical Examples and Case Studies

The chapter provided practical examples and case studies to illustrate how to locate elements within other elements in real-world scenarios. Examples included:

- Navigating multi-level navigation menus.
- Locating specific form fields within complex forms.
- Extracting data from tables with nested rows and cells.
- Navigating content sections within structured blog posts.

These examples demonstrated the application of various CSS selectors and combinators to solve common challenges in web automation and testing.

Conclusion

Locating elements within other elements requires a deep understanding of CSS selectors and the relationships between elements in a web page. By mastering these techniques, you can create robust automation scripts, interact with complex nested structures, and ensure precise element location in various scenarios. This knowledge is crucial for successful web automation with tools like Selenium WebDriver and for building efficient automated tests.

Section 6:
XPath and CSS in Real-World Scenarios

Best Practices for Complex Web Page Structures

Outline

1. Overview of Complex Web Page Structures
2. Strategies for Simplifying Element Location
3. Using XPath and CSS Selectors for Nested Elements
4. Handling Repeated Structures with Unique Identifiers
5. Managing Element Location in Responsive Designs
6. Dealing with Dynamic Content and AJAX Requests
7. Optimizing Performance in Complex Structures
8. Tips for Testing Complex Web Page Structures
9. Chapter Summary

Overview of Complex Web Page Structures

Complex web page structures are increasingly common in modern web development, especially as user interfaces become more dynamic and feature-rich. This complexity arises from a variety of factors, each contributing to the intricacy of locating web elements for testing and automation. Let's examine the primary reasons behind complex web page structures, the common challenges they pose, and why mastering XPath and CSS selectors is crucial for tackling them.

What Makes a Web Page Structure Complex?

- **Nested Elements**: A common feature in complex web pages is a deeply nested DOM (Document Object Model) structure, where elements are contained within layers of parent and child relationships. This depth can make it challenging to find and interact with specific elements.
- **Dynamic Content**: Web applications often rely on JavaScript frameworks to load content asynchronously, leading to dynamic and ever-changing page structures. AJAX requests and dynamic loading can affect the visibility and position of elements.
- **Responsive Design**: Modern websites are designed to adapt to various screen sizes and orientations, resulting in a layout that can change depending on the device. This fluidity introduces variability in element location and visibility.
- **Repeated Structures**: Many complex web pages feature repeating elements, such as tables, lists, or grid-based components. Identifying unique elements within these repeated sections requires advanced techniques.
- **Component-Based Frameworks**: Frameworks like React, Angular, and Vue often create complex, component-based structures. These frameworks may generate dynamic IDs or use virtual DOM, adding complexity to locating specific elements.

Challenges in Locating Elements on Complex Pages

- **Ambiguity**: With multiple elements sharing similar attributes, it can be unclear which one to target. This ambiguity often leads to incorrect element identification.

- **Element Instability**: Dynamic content can cause elements to shift or disappear, requiring strategies to manage these changes.
- **Performance**: Deeply nested or complex XPath and CSS selectors can impact performance, leading to slower test execution.
- **Responsive Layout Changes**: The same page might look and behave differently on mobile, tablet, and desktop, complicating the element locating process.
- **Hidden Elements**: Some elements might be hidden until triggered by user interaction, requiring specialized techniques to locate and interact with them.

Why XPath and CSS Selectors Matter

XPath and CSS selectors are powerful tools for navigating complex web page structures. They allow testers and automation engineers to:

- Define precise paths to locate specific elements, even within nested structures.
- Utilize attributes, text, and other patterns to identify unique elements.
- Adapt to changing web page structures by employing flexible and robust strategies.

By understanding the sources of complexity and the challenges associated with complex web page structures, you can better appreciate the importance of mastering XPath and CSS selectors. This chapter will guide you through best practices for dealing with these complexities, ensuring you are well-equipped to tackle even the most intricate web pages.

Strategies for Simplifying Element Location

Finding elements on complex web pages can be challenging, especially when dealing with deeply nested structures, dynamic content, and responsive design. This section discusses practical strategies to simplify element location, helping you create more efficient and reliable XPath and CSS selectors.

1. Start with a Clear Understanding of the Page Structure

- **Analyze the DOM**: Use browser developer tools (like Chrome DevTools or Firefox Inspector) to examine the Document Object Model (DOM). Understand the hierarchy of elements and identify key structures.
- **Identify Key Elements**: Determine which elements are crucial for your tests or automation tasks. Focus on these to avoid unnecessary complexity.

2. Leverage Unique Identifiers

- **Use IDs and Unique Attributes**: If elements have unique IDs or attributes, use them in your XPath or CSS selectors. These are often the most reliable and straightforward methods for locating elements.
- **Create Consistent Naming Conventions**: If you're involved in development, encourage the use of consistent and descriptive naming for elements to simplify identification.

3. Simplify Complex Selectors

- **Avoid Overly Complex Selectors**: Deeply nested or complex XPath expressions can slow down your tests and increase the likelihood of errors. Aim for simplicity where possible.
- **Break Down Selectors into Smaller Parts**: If you must use complex selectors, consider breaking them into smaller, manageable parts and combining them to create more readable and maintainable selectors.

4. Use Parent-Child Relationships

- **Navigate with Direct Parent-Child Relationships**: When locating nested elements, use direct relationships (like `/child::node()` in XPath) to avoid excessive traversal of the DOM.
- **Use Relative Paths**: Relative paths (`//element[@attribute='value']`) are often more flexible and easier to maintain than absolute paths.

5. Implement Effective Use of Attributes

- **Utilize Descriptive Attributes**: Besides IDs, use other unique attributes like `data-*`, name, or `aria-label`. These can offer simple ways to locate elements.
- **Combine Multiple Attributes**: When a single attribute isn't sufficient, combine multiple attributes to create more robust selectors.

6. Handle Dynamic Content and Timing Issues

- **Implement Wait Strategies**: Use explicit waits to ensure that elements are loaded before attempting to interact with them. This reduces the chance of errors caused by timing issues.
- **Check for Dynamic Content**: Be aware of AJAX and JavaScript-based content that may not be immediately available. Use waits and retry logic to handle such cases.

7. Utilize Browser Developer Tools

- **Inspect Elements for Quick Insights**: Use browser developer tools to quickly inspect and locate elements. This can help you understand the structure and create effective selectors.
- **Test XPath and CSS Selectors**: Most developer tools allow you to test XPath and CSS selectors, enabling you to validate your selectors before implementing them in code.

8. Optimize for Responsive Design

- **Adjust for Different Screen Sizes**: Consider how your selectors will perform across different screen sizes and orientations. Test your selectors in various responsive scenarios to ensure reliability.
- **Use Conditional Logic for Dynamic Layouts**: Implement conditional logic to adjust selectors based on the page layout, ensuring that your automation scripts work in diverse environments.

By following these strategies, you can significantly simplify the process of locating elements on complex web pages. This simplification will lead to more robust and maintainable automation scripts, reducing the risk of errors and improving overall efficiency.

Using XPath and CSS Selectors for Nested Elements

When dealing with nested elements on web pages, choosing the right approach is key to successful automation and testing. This section explores the nuances of using XPath and CSS selectors to locate elements within complex, multi-level structures.

Understanding Nested Elements

Nested elements occur when HTML elements are placed within other elements, creating a hierarchy or "tree" structure. This nesting can happen for various reasons, such as creating tables, forms, navigation menus, or grid layouts. Here's how to navigate these complex structures with XPath and CSS selectors.

1. Navigating Nested Structures with XPath

- **Direct Parent-Child Relationships**: In XPath, you can use a single `/` to refer to a direct child element. This is helpful when you know the exact parent-child relationship.

- Example: /html/body/div locates the first div within body.
- **Using Descendant Relationships**: The // operator is used to find elements at any level within a given context. This is useful when dealing with deep nesting.
  - Example: //div[@class='content'] finds any div with a class of 'content', regardless of its position in the hierarchy.
- **Navigating by Relative Relationships**: XPath allows you to reference elements based on their relationships, like ancestors, siblings, or following nodes.
  - Example: //div[@id='main']//a locates all a tags within the div with id='main'.
- **Combining Conditions**: XPath supports combining multiple conditions to create more specific selectors.
  - Example: //ul/li[@class='active' and @data-value='123'] finds li elements with a specific class and data attribute.

2. Navigating Nested Structures with CSS Selectors

- **Direct Child Selectors**: In CSS, the > symbol indicates a direct parent-child relationship.
  - Example: body > div selects only direct children div within body.
- **Descendant Selectors**: A space between elements in CSS signifies a descendant relationship, allowing you to find elements at any level of nesting.
  - Example: div.content p selects all p elements within any div with class 'content'.
- **Combining Selectors**: CSS allows you to chain multiple selectors to create more specific patterns.
  - Example: div.content > ul > li.active finds li elements that are direct children of an ul, which is a direct child of a div with class 'content'.
- **Sibling Selectors**: CSS provides sibling selectors (+ for adjacent siblings and ~ for general siblings), enabling you to locate elements relative to others.
  - Example: input + label selects label that immediately follows an input.
  - Example: div ~ p selects all p elements that are siblings of a div.

3. Tips for Working with Nested Elements

- **Use Descriptive Attributes**: When dealing with deeply nested structures, unique attributes like id, name, or data-* can significantly simplify selectors.
- **Limit Deep Nesting**: Although XPath and CSS allow for extensive traversal, try to avoid excessive depth, which can lead to brittle selectors.
- **Use Parent Elements for Context**: To ensure flexibility, start your XPath or CSS selector from a known parent or context element, rather than using absolute paths.
- **Validate Selectors with Browser Tools**: Always test your XPath and CSS selectors using browser developer tools to ensure they work correctly in the current context.

By mastering these techniques for working with nested elements, you'll be better equipped to locate web elements efficiently, regardless of the complexity of the web page structure.

Handling Repeated Structures with Unique Identifiers

Repeated structures are common on web pages, especially in applications with tables, lists, grids, or sections that contain similar elements. Locating specific elements within these repeated structures can be challenging without a clear strategy. This section outlines techniques for handling repeated structures and ensuring accurate identification of unique elements.

Understanding Repeated Structures

Repeated structures can take various forms, such as:

- **Tables**: Rows and columns with similar or identical structure.
- **Lists**: Ordered (`<ol>`) and unordered (`<ul>`) lists with multiple list items.
- **Grid Layouts**: Components with similar layout or design patterns.
- **Forms**: Multiple fields with similar attributes or structure.

These structures often share common elements, making it crucial to identify unique attributes or patterns for accurate element location.

Strategies for Identifying Unique Elements in Repeated Structures

1. **Use Unique Identifiers**
   - **ID Attributes**: If each repeated structure has a unique ID, this can be the simplest way to locate specific elements.
     - Example: `//*[@id='row1']` locates the structure with the specified ID.
   - **Custom Data Attributes**: Attributes like `data-*` can provide unique information to distinguish repeated elements.
     - Example: `//div[@data-row='1']` finds a div with a specific data attribute.
2. **Combine Multiple Attributes**
   - **Use Attribute Combinations**: Combine multiple attributes to uniquely identify elements within repeated structures.
     - Example: `//div[@class='row' and @data-id='123']` combines a class and a data attribute.
   - **Leverage Text Content**: Use text-based conditions to locate specific elements.
     - Example: `//td[text()='John Doe']` finds a table cell containing the specified text.
3. **Utilize Indexing**
   - **XPath Indexing**: XPath allows for indexing based on position, which can be useful in repeated structures.
     - Example: `//tr[1]` selects the first row in a table.
   - **CSS nth-child and nth-of-type**: CSS offers similar indexing capabilities.
     - Example: `ul > li:nth-child(3)` selects the third list item in an unordered list.
4. **Identify Context and Ancestor Elements**
   - **Context-Based Selectors**: Define a broader context and then locate unique elements within that context.
     - Example: `//div[@class='container']//span[@data-value='456']` locates a span within a specific container.
   - **Use Ancestor Relationships**: Identify elements based on their position within a specific ancestor structure.
     - Example: `//table[@id='userTable']//tr[3]` selects the third row in a specific table.
5. **Find Unique Patterns**
   - **Locate Unique Sequences**: Identify unique sequences or patterns in repeated structures to create robust selectors.
     - Example: `//ul/li[contains(@class, 'highlighted')]` finds list items with a specific class pattern.
   - **Use Sibling Relationships**: Select elements based on their position relative to other similar elements.
     - Example: `//div[@id='section1']//p[preceding-sibling::h2]` selects a paragraph that follows an h2 tag.

Tips for Working with Repeated Structures

- **Avoid Hard-Coded Indices**: While indexing is useful, avoid relying solely on fixed indices, as these can change if the structure is altered.
- **Validate Selectors with Browser Tools**: Use browser developer tools to test and validate your XPath and CSS selectors to ensure they correctly locate elements in repeated structures.
- **Implement Resilient Strategies**: Consider various scenarios where repeated structures may change, and design your selectors to be flexible and resilient to such changes.

By applying these strategies, you can effectively navigate repeated structures and locate unique elements, ensuring your automation scripts remain robust and reliable.

Managing Element Location in Responsive Designs

Responsive design has become the norm in modern web development, allowing web pages to adapt to different devices and screen sizes. While this flexibility is great for users, it can create challenges for automation testers who need to locate elements that might change position, size, or visibility depending on the device. This section explores strategies for managing element location in responsive designs.

Understanding Responsive Design

Responsive design involves creating web pages that adjust their layout and content to provide an optimal viewing experience across a range of devices, from desktops to tablets and mobile phones. This flexibility is achieved through techniques like:

- **CSS Media Queries**: Defining different styles for various screen sizes and orientations.
- **Flexible Layouts**: Using grid systems and flexible units like percentages to allow for dynamic resizing.
- **Conditional Rendering**: Displaying or hiding elements based on device characteristics.

Challenges in Responsive Design for Element Location

- **Changing Layouts**: As screen sizes change, the structure and order of elements can vary, affecting element location.
- **Dynamic Visibility**: Certain elements might be visible on some devices but hidden on others.
- **Conditional Rendering**: Content that appears on one type of device might be absent on another.
- **Performance Concerns**: Responsive designs might require additional JavaScript, potentially affecting page load times and element interaction timing.

Strategies for Managing Element Location

1. **Use Flexible and Relative XPath/CSS Selectors**
   - **Avoid Absolute Paths**: Absolute XPath selectors can break if the layout changes. Use relative paths to ensure flexibility.
     - Example: `//div[contains(@class, 'container')]//button[text()='Submit']` finds a button with specific text within a container, regardless of its exact position.
   - **Use Descendant and Child Relationships**: This allows for more flexible traversal of the DOM.
     - Example: `//nav//a` selects all links within a navigation structure, regardless of depth.
2. **Implement Conditional Logic for Different Layouts**
   - **Check Device Type or Orientation**: Use logic in your automation framework to determine the current device or screen orientation, and adjust element location accordingly.
   - **Use CSS Media Queries for Testing**: If your application uses CSS media queries, consider implementing similar logic in your tests to adjust based on screen size.

3. Handle Dynamic Visibility
   - **Use Explicit Waits for Element Visibility**: Implement explicit waits to ensure that elements are visible before interacting with them.
   - **Check Element Display Properties**: Determine if an element is visible by examining its CSS properties, like `display` and `visibility`.
   - **Use "isDisplayed" Methods**: Many automation frameworks offer methods to check if an element is displayed on the page.
4. Account for Conditional Rendering
   - **Implement Logic to Handle Missing Elements**: If certain elements are conditionally rendered, ensure your automation logic can handle cases where these elements are absent.
   - **Use "Optional" Element Locators**: Write XPath/CSS selectors that can work even if some parts of the structure are missing.
     - Example: `//div[@id='optional-section']`? (using a framework that supports optional selectors).
5. Optimize for Performance and Responsiveness
   - **Test Across Multiple Devices and Screen Sizes**: Ensure your automation scripts work on various devices, from mobile to desktop.
   - **Leverage Browser-Specific Features**: Some browsers offer tools to emulate different devices and screen sizes, allowing you to test responsive designs without needing multiple physical devices.
   - **Use Efficient XPath/CSS Selectors**: Avoid overly complex selectors that could slow down your tests.

Tips for Managing Element Location in Responsive Designs

- **Stay Up to Date with Responsive Design Trends**: Responsive design is an evolving field. Stay informed about the latest techniques and best practices to ensure your element location strategies remain relevant.
- **Use Frameworks and Tools that Support Responsive Design**: Choose automation frameworks and tools that offer robust support for responsive design testing.
- **Collaborate with Development Teams**: Work closely with developers to understand the responsive design strategy for your application and ensure your automation scripts align with it.

By implementing these strategies, you can effectively manage element location in responsive designs, ensuring your automation scripts are robust and adaptable to different devices and screen sizes.

Dealing with Dynamic Content and AJAX Requests

Modern web applications increasingly rely on dynamic content and AJAX (Asynchronous JavaScript and XML) requests to provide seamless, real-time user experiences. While this enhances usability, it creates challenges for automation testers who need to locate elements that may change or load asynchronously. This section explores strategies for dealing with dynamic content and AJAX requests, ensuring robust and reliable element location.

Understanding Dynamic Content and AJAX Requests

Dynamic content refers to web elements that are generated or modified at runtime, often through JavaScript interactions. AJAX requests allow web applications to fetch data from the server without reloading the entire page, enabling smoother user experiences but introducing variability in content and timing.

Challenges with Dynamic Content and AJAX Requests

- **Asynchronous Loading**: Elements may not be present when the page initially loads, appearing only after an AJAX request completes.
- **Changing DOM Structure**: Dynamic content can alter the DOM, causing element location to shift or change.
- **Unpredictable Timing**: The time it takes for AJAX requests to complete can vary, requiring explicit waits or synchronization strategies.
- **Invisible or Hidden Elements**: Some elements might be hidden or not displayed until certain user interactions occur.

Strategies for Handling Dynamic Content and AJAX Requests

1. **Implement Explicit Waits**
   - **Wait for Element Visibility**: Use explicit waits to ensure elements are visible before interacting with them.
   - **Wait for AJAX Requests to Complete**: If possible, wait for specific network activity or events indicating that an AJAX request has finished.
   - **Framework-Specific Wait Strategies**: Many automation frameworks offer built-in waiting mechanisms to handle asynchronous content.
     - Example: Selenium's `WebDriverWait` allows you to wait until specific conditions are met, like element visibility or AJAX completion.
2. **Use Dynamic XPath and CSS Selectors**
   - **Select Elements Based on Content**: Use selectors that adapt to changing content.
     - Example: `//div[contains(text(), 'Welcome')]` selects a div containing specific text, regardless of its position.
   - **Use Ancestor or Parent References**: If the structure changes, use a known parent element to maintain relative stability.
     - Example: `//div[@id='container']//a[contains(@href, 'profile')]` finds a link within a specific container.
3. **Leverage JavaScript for Element Interaction**
   - **Execute JavaScript to Interact with Elements**: If elements are hidden or not directly accessible, consider using JavaScript to trigger interactions.
   - **Use JavaScript to Wait for Conditions**: You can execute JavaScript to wait for specific conditions, like AJAX completion or DOM changes.
     - Example: `driver.execute_script("return document.readyState") == 'complete'` checks if the page has fully loaded.
4. **Monitor AJAX Requests and Network Activity**
   - **Use Browser Tools to Monitor Network**: Browser developer tools offer network monitoring features, allowing you to track AJAX requests and their completion times.
   - **Wait for Specific Network Events**: Some frameworks allow you to wait for network activity, ensuring AJAX requests are complete before proceeding.
5. **Use Conditional Logic for Dynamic Content**
   - **Handle Optional or Conditional Elements**: If elements are conditionally rendered, ensure your automation logic can adapt to their presence or absence.
   - **Implement Retry Logic**: If an element is expected but not found, implement retry logic to attempt interaction after a brief delay.

Tips for Dealing with Dynamic Content and AJAX Requests

- **Identify Key Elements for Synchronization**: Determine which elements or events indicate that dynamic content has fully loaded, and use these as synchronization points.
- **Validate Selectors in Real-Time**: Test XPath and CSS selectors in real-time scenarios to ensure they work as expected with dynamic content.

- **Stay Informed on Framework-Specific Features**: Different automation frameworks offer various features for handling dynamic content and AJAX requests. Stay updated on these to make the most of your automation tools.
- **Collaborate with Developers on AJAX Logic**: Work with your development team to understand how AJAX requests are implemented and what triggers them, allowing you to create more effective automation strategies.

By implementing these strategies, you can effectively handle dynamic content and AJAX requests, ensuring your automation scripts remain robust and adaptable to asynchronous changes in web applications.

Optimizing Performance in Complex Structures

When working with complex web page structures, performance can become a significant concern. XPath and CSS selectors that are too complex or inefficient can slow down test execution and affect the reliability of automated tests. This section discusses techniques for optimizing performance when dealing with complex structures in web automation.

Understanding Performance Challenges in Complex Structures

Complex web structures often consist of deeply nested elements, dynamic content, and conditional rendering, all of which can impact performance. Common performance-related issues include:

- **Slow Element Location**: Complex XPath or CSS selectors can take longer to locate elements, impacting test speed.
- **Inconsistent Results**: Inefficient selectors may not consistently find the correct elements, leading to flaky tests.
- **Resource-Intensive Operations**: Deep traversal of the DOM can increase memory usage and processing time.

Strategies for Optimizing Performance

1. **Use Efficient XPath and CSS Selectors**
   - **Keep Selectors Simple and Direct**: Avoid overly complex selectors that require deep traversal of the DOM. Use direct paths or relative selectors where possible.
   - **Leverage Unique Identifiers**: Use unique IDs, names, or other attributes to locate elements quickly.
     - Example: `//*[@id='main-content']` locates an element by ID, providing a fast and reliable selector.
   - **Use CSS Selectors for Simplicity**: CSS selectors are often faster than XPath. Use them where applicable.
     - Example: `div.content > ul > li.active` is a straightforward CSS selector.
2. **Minimize DOM Traversal**
   - **Start from a Known Context**: Begin your selector from a known parent or context element to reduce unnecessary traversal.
     - Example: `//div[@class='container']//button[text()='Submit']` starts from a specific container, reducing search space.
   - **Use Direct Relationships**: Opt for parent-child relationships instead of ancestor-descendant when possible.
     - Example: `//div[@id='main-content']/button` is more efficient than `//div[@id='main-content']//button`.
3. **Implement Explicit Waits and Synchronization**

- o **Wait for Elements to Be Ready**: Implement explicit waits to ensure elements are visible and interactive before attempting to locate them. This reduces the need for retries due to timing issues.
- o **Synchronize with AJAX Requests**: Use waits or synchronization logic to ensure AJAX requests have completed before locating elements.
  - Example: `WebDriverWait(driver, 10).until(EC.visibility_of_element_located((By.ID, 'dynamic-content')))`

4. **Optimize Locator Strategies for Different Structures**
   - o **Adapt to Responsive Designs**: Consider different screen sizes and orientations when creating selectors. Test across multiple devices to ensure consistent performance.
   - o **Use Indexing Sparingly**: While indexing can be useful, avoid overreliance on hard-coded indices, as they can be fragile.
     - Example: `//tr[1]` may change if the table structure is altered. Use relative references where possible.

5. **Utilize Framework-Specific Features**
   - o **Leverage Framework Optimizations**: Some automation frameworks offer features for optimizing performance, such as lazy loading or caching. Use these features to reduce resource usage.
   - o **Use Parallel Testing**: If possible, implement parallel testing to reduce overall test execution time.
   - o **Optimize Browser Settings**: Adjust browser settings for better performance during automation, such as disabling unnecessary plugins or extensions.

Tips for Optimizing Performance

- **Test and Measure Performance**: Regularly test and measure the performance of your automation scripts to identify bottlenecks and areas for improvement.
- **Avoid Repetitive Operations**: Minimize repetitive operations in your test scripts, such as re-fetching the same element multiple times.
- **Collaborate with Development Teams**: Work with developers to understand the structure and behavior of the application, enabling you to create more efficient locator strategies.
- **Stay Informed on Framework Updates**: Automation frameworks often release updates with performance improvements. Stay updated to ensure you're using the latest optimizations.

By following these strategies, you can optimize performance when dealing with complex web structures, ensuring your automation scripts are efficient, reliable, and robust.

Tips for Testing Complex Web Page Structures

Testing complex web page structures poses unique challenges due to nested elements, dynamic content, responsive design, and AJAX interactions. Effective strategies can help you navigate these complexities and ensure reliable, maintainable, and robust test automation. This section provides practical tips for testing complex web page structures.

Understand the Structure of the Web Page

- **Analyze the DOM with Developer Tools**: Use browser-based tools like Chrome DevTools or Firefox Inspector to inspect the Document Object Model (DOM). This helps you understand the layout and identify key elements.
- **Identify Key Elements and Patterns**: Determine which elements are critical for your tests, and look for patterns in the structure to guide your locator strategies.

- **Note Changes in Layout for Responsive Design**: Be aware of how the page layout changes across different devices and screen sizes. Identify elements that vary with the design.

Use Effective XPath and CSS Selectors

- **Opt for Unique Identifiers**: Use unique attributes such as `id`, `name`, or `data-*` to quickly locate elements. This is typically the most straightforward and reliable approach.
- **Use Relative Paths Over Absolute Paths**: Relative XPath or CSS selectors are more flexible and resilient to changes in the DOM structure.
- **Simplify Complex Selectors**: Avoid overly complex or deeply nested XPath expressions, as they can impact test performance and reliability.

Implement Robust Synchronization Strategies

- **Use Explicit Waits for Dynamic Content**: Implement explicit waits to ensure elements are ready before interacting with them. This helps deal with AJAX and asynchronous loading.
- **Synchronize with AJAX Requests**: Wait for AJAX activity to complete before proceeding with test steps. Some frameworks offer built-in synchronization features for AJAX.
- **Handle Element Visibility**: Use waits to ensure elements are visible and interactive before attempting to locate or interact with them.

Optimize for Performance and Maintainability

- **Reduce DOM Traversal**: Start from a known context or parent element to minimize unnecessary traversal of the DOM.
- **Minimize Repetitive Operations**: Avoid fetching the same element multiple times in different test steps. Store frequently accessed elements in variables or use caching mechanisms.
- **Use Parallel Testing**: If your framework supports it, consider running tests in parallel to reduce overall execution time.

Test Across Multiple Environments

- **Account for Responsive Design**: Test on various devices and screen sizes to ensure your automation scripts work in different environments.
- **Use Browser Emulation Tools**: Many browsers offer tools to emulate different devices, allowing you to test responsive design without needing multiple physical devices.
- **Consider Cross-Browser Testing**: Ensure your tests work across different browsers, as they might render complex structures differently.

Collaborate with Development Teams

- **Work with Developers to Understand the Structure**: Collaborate with developers to understand the design and structure of the application. This helps you create more effective test strategies.
- **Coordinate on Changes and Updates**: Stay informed about changes to the application's structure or design that might affect your test automation.

Tips for Managing Complex Test Scenarios

- **Implement Retry Logic**: If elements might change or load asynchronously, implement retry logic to handle cases where the first attempt fails.
- **Use Framework-Specific Features**: Different automation frameworks offer various features to handle complex structures. Familiarize yourself with these features to make the most of your automation tools.
- **Stay Informed on Industry Trends**: Keep up to date with the latest trends and best practices in test automation for complex web applications.

By following these tips, you can create effective test automation scripts that are resilient, maintainable, and adaptable to the complexities of modern web page structures.

Chapter Summary

Testing and automating complex web page structures requires a thorough understanding of their intricacies and the right strategies to navigate them. This chapter focused on best practices for handling complex web structures, providing insights into effective element location, synchronization, and performance optimization. Here are the key takeaways:

Overview of Complex Web Page Structures

- Complex structures are common in modern web applications, characterized by deeply nested elements, dynamic content, responsive design, and AJAX-based interactions.
- Challenges include changing layouts, dynamic visibility, conditional rendering, and varying timing due to asynchronous content.

Strategies for Simplifying Element Location

- Start by analyzing the DOM with browser developer tools to understand the page structure.
- Use unique identifiers (like id, name, or data-*) to locate elements quickly.
- Prefer relative XPath or CSS selectors over absolute paths for flexibility and resilience to structure changes.
- Implement explicit waits and synchronization strategies to deal with asynchronous content and dynamic elements.

Using XPath and CSS Selectors for Nested Elements

- Navigate complex structures using direct parent-child relationships in XPath and CSS selectors.
- Combine attributes to create robust and efficient selectors.
- Avoid deeply nested or overly complex selectors to ensure performance and reliability.

Handling Repeated Structures with Unique Identifiers

- Repeated structures, like tables, lists, and grids, require unique strategies for element location.
- Use indexing, parent-child relationships, and unique attributes to differentiate among repeated elements.
- Implement retry logic to manage cases where elements are missing or change due to dynamic content.

Managing Element Location in Responsive Designs

- Responsive design requires a flexible approach to element location, as layouts can change across different devices and screen sizes.
- Use conditional logic to adapt selectors based on the context.
- Implement explicit waits to ensure elements are visible and interactive before attempting to interact with them.

Dealing with Dynamic Content and AJAX Requests

- Dynamic content and AJAX requests introduce timing and synchronization challenges.
- Use explicit waits and synchronization strategies to handle asynchronous content.
- Implement retry logic and framework-specific features to ensure robust test automation in dynamic environments.

Optimizing Performance in Complex Structures

- Optimize XPath and CSS selectors to reduce DOM traversal and improve performance.
- Use relative selectors and unique identifiers to simplify element location.
- Leverage parallel testing and framework-specific optimizations to enhance performance.

Tips for Testing Complex Web Page Structures

- Test across multiple devices and screen sizes to ensure compatibility with responsive designs.
- Use browser emulation tools and cross-browser testing to validate your automation scripts.
- Collaborate with development teams to understand the structure and behavior of the application.

By following these best practices, you can create robust and reliable automation scripts that effectively navigate complex web page structures. This ensures your test automation is adaptable to changing environments and delivers consistent results, regardless of the intricacies of the web application.

Working with Forms and User Input

Outline

Understanding Web Forms

Web forms are integral to user interaction on the internet. They serve as a bridge between users and applications, allowing users to submit information, make selections, and trigger various processes. In this section, we'll explore the structure and components of web forms, laying the groundwork for later discussions on locating, interacting with, and automating form-based tasks.

1. Basics of Web Forms

Web forms typically consist of an HTML `<form>` element that encapsulates various input fields and other interactive components. The form's structure provides context for where data is collected and how it's submitted. Here's an example of a simple HTML form:

```html
<form action="/submit" method="post">
  <label for="name">Name:</label>
  <input type="text" id="name" name="name">
  <button type="submit">Submit</button>
</form>
```

In this example, the form has an action attribute specifying where the data will be sent upon submission, and a method attribute indicating whether the data will be sent using HTTP GET or POST.

2. Common Form Elements

Forms contain various input elements, each serving a specific purpose. These include:

- **Text Fields**: Used for user text input. Attributes like `id`, `name`, `placeholder`, and `value` help identify and pre-fill these fields.
- **Radio Buttons and Checkboxes**: Allow users to select single or multiple options. These elements are identified by `name` and `value`.
- **Dropdowns (Select)**: Offer users a list of predefined options to choose from. Dropdowns use `<select>` tags with nested `<option>` tags.
- **Buttons**: Can trigger form submission or other actions. Common types include `submit`, `reset`, and `button`.
- **Other Elements**: Additional elements like file inputs, sliders, and date pickers provide more specialized interactions.

3. Form Attributes and Configuration

Forms can be configured with various attributes to define their behavior. Key attributes include:

- **Action**: Specifies where the form data should be submitted.
- **Method**: Defines the HTTP method used for submission (typically GET or POST).
- **Target**: Determines where the response will be displayed (e.g., a new window or the same window).
- **Enctype**: Specifies how form data is encoded when sent to the server (e.g., `multipart/form-data` for file uploads).

4. Client-Side Form Validation

Modern forms often include client-side validation to ensure user input is valid before submission. This can involve HTML attributes like `required`, `minlength`, and `pattern`, as well as JavaScript-based validation logic.

5. Server-Side Form Handling

After form submission, server-side logic processes the data and takes appropriate actions. Understanding this flow helps in designing robust automation scripts that interact with web forms in a real-world context.

With this foundational knowledge of web forms, we can proceed to discuss more advanced topics like locating elements with XPath and CSS selectors, automating form interactions with Selenium, and handling common challenges in form-based automation scenarios.

Common Form Elements and Their Attributes

Web forms are composed of various elements that users interact with to submit information. Understanding these elements and their key attributes is crucial for effective automation with Selenium and other web automation frameworks. This section explores the common form elements you'll encounter, along with the attributes used to identify and interact with them.

1. Text Fields

Text fields are the most common form elements for user input. They can be used for names, addresses, email addresses, and more.

- **Input Types**: The default is `text`, but there are specialized types like `email`, `password`, `number`, `date`, etc.
- **Attributes**:
  - `id`: A unique identifier for the field.
  - `name`: Often used for server-side processing.
  - `placeholder`: A hint to the user about what to enter.
  - `value`: The pre-filled value in the field.
- **Common Usage**: These fields are used to enter various forms of textual data.

2. Radio Buttons and Checkboxes

These elements are used for selecting options. Radio buttons allow a single choice within a group, while checkboxes allow multiple selections.

- **Attributes**:
  - `name`: Identifies the group (important for radio buttons).
  - `value`: The value submitted when selected.
  - `checked`: Indicates if the option is selected by default.

- **Common Usage**: Radio buttons are often used for mutually exclusive choices, while checkboxes are used for multiple selections.

3. Dropdowns (Select)

Dropdowns, represented by the `<select>` element, allow users to choose from a list of options. They contain nested `<option>` elements for each choice.

- **Attributes**:
  - `name`: Identifier for the dropdown.
  - `multiple`: Allows multiple selections.
  - `size`: Specifies the number of visible options.
- **Option Attributes**:
  - `value`: The value submitted when the option is selected.
  - `selected`: Indicates if an option is selected by default.
- **Common Usage**: Dropdowns are used for predefined lists of options, such as selecting a country or state.

4. Buttons

Buttons can trigger form submissions or other actions within a form.

- **Button Types**:
  - `submit`: Submits the form.
  - `reset`: Resets form fields to default values.
  - `button`: Custom button for JavaScript actions.
- **Attributes**:
  - `id`: Unique identifier for the button.
  - `name`: Used for server-side processing.
  - `value`: The text displayed on the button.
- **Common Usage**: Submit buttons send form data, while custom buttons trigger JavaScript-based actions.

5. File Uploads

File input fields allow users to upload files.

- **Attributes**:
  - `accept`: Specifies accepted file types (e.g., `.jpg`, `.pdf`).
  - `multiple`: Allows multiple file uploads.
  - `id` and `name`: Standard identifiers.
- **Common Usage**: File inputs are used for attaching documents, images, or other files.

6. Other Common Elements

- **Textareas**: Multi-line text fields with attributes like `rows` and `cols` for size control.
- **Sliders and Ranges**: Input elements for numerical values within a specified range.
- **Date Pickers**: Elements for selecting dates, often with built-in calendars.

Each of these form elements has unique attributes that can be used to locate, interact with, and manipulate them in Selenium scripts. Understanding these common elements and their attributes is the first step in mastering web form automation.

Locating Form Fields with XPath and CSS

Locating form fields accurately is critical for successful web automation. XPath and CSS selectors are two powerful methods to pinpoint elements on a web page. This section will explain how to use both techniques to find form fields in various scenarios, providing examples to demonstrate different strategies.

1. Using XPath to Locate Form Fields

XPath is a flexible language for selecting elements in an XML-like structure, such as HTML. Here are some common ways to locate form fields with XPath:

- **Locating by ID**: If the field has a unique id, it's the most straightforward way to find it.

  ```
  //*[@id='username']
  ```

- **Locating by Attribute**: You can locate elements by any attribute, such as name, type, or placeholder.

  ```
  //*[@name='email']   <!-- by name -->
  //input[@type='password']   <!-- by type -->
  //*[@placeholder='Enter your name']   <!-- by placeholder →
  ```

- **Locating by Text**: For fields with associated labels, you can locate by text content.

  ```
  //label[text()='Password']/following-sibling::input   <!-- label to field
  →
  ```

- **Locating by Position or Relationships**: XPath provides the ability to locate elements based on their position or relation to other elements.

  ```
  //form[1]//input[2]   <!-- second input in the first form -->
  //input[@name='username']/ancestor::form   <!-- find form containing
  'username' →
  ```

2. Using CSS Selectors to Locate Form Fields

CSS selectors are generally shorter and faster than XPath, with a syntax resembling CSS styling. Here are some common strategies for locating form fields with CSS:

- **Locating by ID**: Using the # symbol, you can quickly find elements by id.

  ```
  #username
  ```

- **Locating by Class**: The . symbol is used to locate elements by class name.

  ```
  .form-control   <!-- elements with class 'form-control' →
  ```

- **Locating by Attribute**: CSS selectors can locate elements based on any attribute.

  ```
  [name='email']   <!-- locate by 'name' -->
  input[type='password']   <!-- locate by 'type' →
  ```

- **Combining Selectors**: CSS allows combining multiple conditions to create more specific selectors.

```
form#login-form input[type='text']    <!-- input field in a specific form
→
```

- **Navigating Relationships**: CSS selectors can also navigate parent-child and sibling relationships.

```
form > input   <!-- direct child of form -->
label + input  <!-- sibling input following a label -->
```

3. Handling Dynamic Form Fields

Web forms can contain dynamic elements that change based on user interaction or other factors. Using XPath and CSS, you can account for these variations:

- **Using Wildcards in XPath**: You can use * as a wildcard for attributes.

```
//*[@id*='dynamic']   <!-- any id containing 'dynamic' →
```

- **Partial Matching with CSS**: CSS allows partial attribute matching.

```
[name^='user']   <!-- name starts with 'user' -->
[id$='-field']   <!-- id ends with '-field' →
```

- **Index-Based Locating**: Sometimes, indexing is needed to find specific elements within dynamic content.

```
//form[1]//input[2]   <!-- second input field in the first form -->
```

Using XPath and CSS selectors, you can locate form fields with precision. Whether dealing with static or dynamic forms, understanding how to use these techniques allows you to build robust automation scripts that can adapt to changing web page structures.

Handling User Input and Validations

Interacting with form fields and validating user input are key aspects of web automation. This section explores techniques for entering data into various types of form fields, managing user input validations, and handling errors or dynamic changes in forms.

1. Entering Text into Form Fields

To interact with text-based form fields, you can use Selenium WebDriver's sendKeys method, which sends keystrokes to the specified element. This is useful for fields like text boxes, textareas, and email fields.

- **Sending Text to a Field**:

```
WebElement usernameField = driver.findElement(By.id("username"));
usernameField.sendKeys("myUsername");
```

- **Clearing Existing Text**: To clear existing text before entering new data, you can use the clear method.

```
WebElement searchField = driver.findElement(By.name("search"));
searchField.clear();
```

```
searchField.sendKeys("Selenium");
```

2. Selecting Options in Radio Buttons and Checkboxes

Radio buttons and checkboxes require specific interactions to toggle their state.

- **Selecting a Radio Button**: Radio buttons are mutually exclusive within a group, so selecting one typically deselects others.

```
WebElement maleRadio =
driver.findElement(By.xpath("//input[@name='gender' and
@value='male']"));
maleRadio.click();
```

- **Selecting/Deselecting a Checkbox**: Checkboxes can be toggled on or off.

```
WebElement newsletterCheckbox = driver.findElement(By.id("subscribe"));
if (!newsletterCheckbox.isSelected()) {
  newsletterCheckbox.click();  // Selects if not already selected
}
```

3. Choosing Options in Dropdowns

Dropdowns (select elements) often require selecting specific options.

- **Selecting by Visible Text**: Use Selenium's Select class to select dropdown options by visible text.

```
Select countryDropdown = new
Select(driver.findElement(By.id("country")));
countryDropdown.selectByVisibleText("United States");
```

- **Selecting by Index or Value**: Dropdown options can also be selected by their index or value attribute.

```
countryDropdown.selectByIndex(1);  // Selects the first option
countryDropdown.selectByValue("US");  // Selects by value attribute
```

4. Handling Client-Side Validations

Client-side validations ensure that user input meets certain criteria before form submission. Selenium allows you to interact with these validations to ensure proper behavior.

- **Checking Required Fields**: If a field is required, you can simulate invalid input to test validation.

```
WebElement emailField = driver.findElement(By.id("email"));
emailField.clear();  // Clear the field to trigger validation
```

- **Using JavaScript for Advanced Interactions**: If a form has complex validations or behaviors, you can use Selenium's JavaScript executor to interact with it.

```
JavascriptExecutor js = (JavascriptExecutor) driver;
js.executeScript("document.getElementById('email').value =
'invalid-email';");
```

5. Submitting Forms

After entering data, you need to submit the form. You can do this by interacting with the submit button or triggering form submission directly.

- **Clicking the Submit Button**:

```
WebElement submitButton =
driver.findElement(By.cssSelector("button[type='submit']"));
submitButton.click();
```

- **Submitting the Form Programmatically**: You can submit a form directly without clicking the submit button.

```
WebElement form = driver.findElement(By.tagName("form"));
form.submit();
```

6. Handling Validation Errors and Dynamic Changes

Web forms may display validation errors or change dynamically based on user input. Selenium can help manage these scenarios.

- **Checking for Error Messages**: If a form displays validation errors, you can locate and assert their content.

```
WebElement errorMessage = driver.findElement(By.className("error"));
assert(errorMessage.getText().contains("Invalid email"));
```

- **Handling Dynamic Elements**: If form elements change or load dynamically, use Selenium's explicit waits to ensure they are ready.

```
WebDriverWait wait = new WebDriverWait(driver, 10);
WebElement dynamicField =
wait.until(ExpectedConditions.visibilityOfElementLocated(By.id("dynamic-f
ield")));
dynamicField.sendKeys("dynamicValue");
```

Handling user input and validations is a core aspect of interacting with web forms. Using Selenium WebDriver, you can enter data, validate input, manage errors, and submit forms in an automated manner. This section covered various techniques to ensure robust form automation and discussed how to tackle client-side validations, form submissions, and dynamic changes.

Automating Form Submission with Selenium

Automating form submission is a common use case for Selenium. It involves interacting with various form elements, ensuring all required fields are completed, and finally submitting the form. This section guides you through different techniques to automate form submissions with Selenium, highlighting best practices and addressing common challenges.

1. Identifying the Form for Submission

Before automating form submission, you need to locate the form and understand its structure.

- **Locating the Form**: You can locate forms by their tag, ID, or other unique identifiers.

```
WebElement form = driver.findElement(By.tagName("form"));  // First form
on the page
WebElement loginForm = driver.findElement(By.id("login-form"));  // Form
with specific ID
```

- **Understanding the Form Structure**: Identify all the required fields and any additional elements needed for form submission, such as buttons, checkboxes, or radio buttons.

2. Completing Form Fields

To submit a form, ensure all necessary fields are filled out correctly.

- **Filling Out Text Fields**: Use the sendKeys method to enter text into fields.

```
WebElement usernameField = driver.findElement(By.id("username"));
usernameField.sendKeys("testuser");

WebElement passwordField = driver.findElement(By.id("password"));
passwordField.sendKeys("password123");
```

- **Selecting Radio Buttons and Checkboxes**: Click on the desired radio button or checkbox to set its state.

```
WebElement genderRadio =
driver.findElement(By.xpath("//input[@name='gender' and
@value='male']"));
genderRadio.click();

WebElement termsCheckbox = driver.findElement(By.id("agree-terms"));
if (!termsCheckbox.isSelected()) {
  termsCheckbox.click();
}
```

- **Choosing Options from Dropdowns**: Use the Select class to interact with dropdowns.

```
Select countryDropdown = new
Select(driver.findElement(By.name("country")));
countryDropdown.selectByVisibleText("United States");
```

3. Submitting the Form

There are various ways to submit a form with Selenium, depending on the form's structure and your requirements.

- **Clicking the Submit Button**: The most common method is to locate and click the submit button.

```
WebElement submitButton =
driver.findElement(By.cssSelector("button[type='submit']"));
submitButton.click();
```

- **Submitting Directly**: You can also use the submit method on a form element.

```
WebElement form = driver.findElement(By.tagName("form"));
form.submit();  // Submits the form directly
```

4. Verifying Form Submission

After submitting the form, it's important to verify that the submission was successful.

- **Checking for Successful Submission**: You can use assertions to ensure the expected outcome, such as a success message or redirect to a new page.

```
WebElement successMessage = driver.findElement(By.className("success"));
assert(successMessage.getText().contains("Form submitted successfully"));
```

- **Handling Redirects**: If the form submission triggers a redirect, use Selenium's wait mechanisms to ensure the new page has loaded.

```
WebDriverWait wait = new WebDriverWait(driver, 10);
wait.until(ExpectedConditions.urlContains("submission-success"));
```

5. Handling Form Submission Errors

Sometimes, form submission may fail due to validation errors or other issues.

- **Checking for Error Messages**: Locate and inspect error messages to determine the cause of failure.

```
WebElement errorMessage =
driver.findElement(By.className("error-message"));
assert(errorMessage.isDisplayed());
```

- **Debugging Form Submission Failures**: If form submission fails, consider potential reasons such as incorrect input, missing required fields, or JavaScript-based validation. Use Selenium's JavaScript executor to investigate further if needed.

6. Automating Complex Form Submissions

For complex forms with dynamic content or AJAX-based elements, additional techniques may be required.

- **Handling Dynamic Content**: Use explicit waits to ensure elements are ready before interacting with them.

```
WebDriverWait wait = new WebDriverWait(driver, 10);
WebElement dynamicField =
wait.until(ExpectedConditions.visibilityOfElementLocated(By.id("dynamic-field")));
dynamicField.sendKeys("dynamicValue");
```

- **Handling AJAX and Asynchronous Operations**: If form submission involves AJAX or asynchronous operations, consider using JavaScript-based waits or polling to ensure all necessary processes are complete.

```
JavascriptExecutor js = (JavascriptExecutor) driver;
js.executeScript("return $.active == 0");  // Waits until all AJAX calls
are complete
```

Automating form submission with Selenium involves multiple steps, from identifying and filling out form fields to handling various types of form interactions and validations. This section provided a comprehensive overview of automating form submissions, including best practices and techniques to ensure smooth and reliable automation. With these skills, you can effectively automate a wide range of form-based tasks and ensure robust test coverage in your web automation projects.

Debugging Form-Related Issues

When automating form-related tasks with Selenium, you might encounter various issues ranging from incorrect form submissions to failures in validation. Debugging these issues requires a systematic approach to identify and resolve the underlying problems. This section provides strategies for troubleshooting form-related issues and suggests best practices for effective debugging.

1. Identifying Common Form-Related Issues

Form-related issues can manifest in several ways. Here are some common scenarios:

- **Form Submission Failures**: The form does not submit as expected, or the submission leads to an error.
- **Validation Errors**: Form fields fail client-side or server-side validation.
- **Dynamic Content**: Fields or elements that change or load asynchronously, causing timing issues.
- **Invisible or Hidden Elements**: Some form elements may be hidden or not interactable.
- **JavaScript-Driven Forms**: Forms with extensive JavaScript logic that can affect automation.

2. Debugging Techniques for Form-Related Issues

To resolve form-related issues, consider the following techniques:

- **Check the Form's Structure**: Examine the form's HTML structure to ensure you're targeting the correct elements.

```
WebElement form = driver.findElement(By.tagName("form"));
System.out.println(form.getAttribute("innerHTML"));  // Print the form's
contents
```

- **Use Explicit Waits**: If form elements are dynamic or load asynchronously, use explicit waits to ensure they are ready before interaction.

```
WebDriverWait wait = new WebDriverWait(driver, 10);
WebElement submitButton =
wait.until(ExpectedConditions.elementToBeClickable(By.id("submit-button")
));
```

- **Check for Validation Errors**: If a form has validation, inspect error messages or other indicators to understand why validation failed.

```
WebElement errorMessage =
driver.findElement(By.className("error-message"));
System.out.println(errorMessage.getText());  // Check the error message
```

- **Inspect JavaScript Console Logs**: Errors in JavaScript can affect form interactions. You can retrieve console logs to identify issues.

```
LogEntries logs = driver.manage().logs().get(LogType.BROWSER);
for (LogEntry entry : logs) {
  System.out.println(entry.getMessage());  // Output console logs
}
```

- **Debug with Screenshots**: Screenshots can help visualize the state of the form and identify issues.

```
File screenshot = ((TakesScreenshot)
driver).getScreenshotAs(OutputType.FILE);
FileUtils.copyFile(screenshot, new File("form_debug.png"));
```

3. Resolving Common Form-Related Issues

Once you've identified the source of the issue, apply the appropriate resolution:

- **Incorrect Element Locators**: If locators are incorrect, update them to ensure they point to the correct elements.

```
WebElement correctField =
driver.findElement(By.xpath("//input[@name='correctName']"));
correctField.sendKeys("correctInput");
```

- **Handling Dynamic Content**: Use explicit waits or JavaScript-based checks to ensure elements are available for interaction.

```
JavascriptExecutor js = (JavascriptExecutor) driver;
js.executeScript("return document.readyState").equals("complete");
```

- **Addressing Validation Issues**: Modify input data to meet validation criteria. If the validation logic is complex, consider adding additional waits or re-evaluating the automation approach.

```
WebElement emailField = driver.findElement(By.id("email"));
emailField.clear();
emailField.sendKeys("valid.email@example.com");  // Ensure valid email
format
```

- **Handling JavaScript-Driven Forms**: For forms with extensive JavaScript, consider using Selenium's JavaScript executor for more direct interaction.

```
JavascriptExecutor js = (JavascriptExecutor) driver;
js.executeScript("document.getElementById('submit-button').click();");
```

4. Best Practices for Debugging Form-Related Issues

Following best practices can help reduce form-related issues and improve debugging efficiency:

- **Use Descriptive Element Locators**: Ensure locators are specific and descriptive to avoid ambiguity.
- **Implement Explicit Waits**: Avoid implicit waits and use explicit waits to manage dynamic content and asynchronous behavior.
- **Test in Different Browsers**: Some issues might be browser-specific, so ensure your automation works across different environments.
- **Regularly Check for Errors and Warnings**: Monitoring browser console logs and other indicators can help detect issues early.
- **Maintain Detailed Logs and Screenshots**: Keeping detailed logs and screenshots can provide valuable insights during debugging.

Debugging form-related issues in Selenium requires a thorough understanding of the form's structure, behavior, and validation logic. By employing a systematic approach, using effective debugging techniques, and following best practices, you can identify and resolve most form-related issues, ensuring robust and reliable web automation.

Chapter Summary

Forms are central to web automation tasks, allowing users to interact with web applications by providing inputs and triggering actions. This chapter covered various aspects of working with forms and user input, focusing on techniques and best practices for automating interactions with Selenium WebDriver.

1. Understanding Web Forms We began by exploring the structure and common elements of web forms. From text fields to radio buttons, checkboxes, dropdowns, and buttons, we examined the different form components and their attributes. Understanding these fundamentals laid the groundwork for automating form interactions.

2. Locating Form Fields with XPath and CSS Next, we delved into using XPath and CSS selectors to locate form fields. Various strategies were discussed, including finding elements by ID, name, attribute, or relationship. This section also explored techniques for handling dynamic content, crucial for robust form automation.

3. Handling User Input and Validations Handling user input involves sending data to form fields and managing validation. We discussed common interactions like entering text, selecting options, and dealing with client-side validations. Techniques for submitting forms, either through buttons or programmatically, were also covered. Additionally, we examined ways to handle validation errors and dynamic changes in form elements.

4. Automating Form Submission with Selenium Automating form submission is a key aspect of web automation. This section covered how to interact with different form elements and successfully submit forms. We also discussed verifying form submissions, managing redirects, and handling form submission errors.

5. Debugging Form-Related Issues In this section, we explored common form-related issues and effective debugging techniques. Strategies for resolving problems such as incorrect element locators, validation errors, and JavaScript-driven forms were outlined. Best practices for debugging were also highlighted, including using explicit waits, inspecting JavaScript console logs, and taking screenshots to aid in troubleshooting.

By the end of this chapter, readers should have a solid understanding of how to work with forms and user input in web automation. This knowledge is essential for building reliable and effective Selenium scripts, allowing you to automate complex interactions, handle validation and dynamic content, and troubleshoot common issues in web forms.

Finding and Handling AJAX-based Elements

Outline

1. Overview of AJAX Technology
2. Challenges in Locating AJAX-based Elements
3. Strategies for Locating AJAX-based Elements
4. Using Waits with AJAX in Selenium WebDriver
5. Implementing Explicit and Implicit Waits
6. Handling Common AJAX Issues in Automation
7. Best Practices for Reliable AJAX-based Automation
8. Chapter Summary

Overview of AJAX Technology

AJAX, short for Asynchronous JavaScript and XML, is a web development technique that allows websites to send and receive data asynchronously without reloading the entire web page. This technology has become a cornerstone for building interactive and dynamic websites, enabling features like auto-updates, live searches, and real-time content refreshing. Here's a breakdown of key concepts that explain why AJAX is significant in modern web applications:

The Basics of AJAX

- **Asynchronous Communication**: Unlike traditional web requests, which reload the entire page when sending or receiving data, AJAX allows the browser to communicate with the server in the background. This asynchronous nature provides a smoother user experience, as it reduces page reloads and interruptions.
- **Technologies Involved**: While AJAX includes "XML" in its name, it actually encompasses a variety of technologies and data formats. The core components are JavaScript for client-side logic, XML or JSON for data transfer, and HTTP/HTTPS for communication. JSON has become more popular than XML due to its simplicity and compatibility with JavaScript.
- **XMLHttpRequest and Fetch API**: AJAX requests are typically made using the XMLHttpRequest object or the more modern Fetch API. These APIs enable developers to send HTTP requests from the browser to a server and handle the responses without affecting the entire page.

How AJAX Works in Web Applications

AJAX operates through a few key steps:

1. **Initiate Request**: JavaScript triggers an AJAX request when certain conditions are met, such as a button click or a form submission.
2. **Send Data to Server**: The AJAX request carries data to the server, which processes it and responds with the appropriate information.
3. **Receive Response**: The client-side JavaScript handles the server's response. This response could contain updated data, validation results, or error messages.
4. **Update Web Page**: The JavaScript logic processes the received data and updates the DOM (Document Object Model) to reflect the changes without reloading the page.

Benefits of AJAX

- **Enhanced User Experience**: Since AJAX allows asynchronous data exchange, users experience smoother interactions with web applications, leading to higher satisfaction and engagement.

- **Reduced Server Load**: AJAX can reduce server load by updating only parts of a page instead of reloading the entire page, optimizing bandwidth and server resources.
- **Dynamic Content**: AJAX is perfect for applications that require real-time updates, such as news feeds, social media platforms, or online gaming.

Challenges and Considerations

Despite its advantages, AJAX poses certain challenges for automation, testing, and accessibility:

- **Timing Issues**: Because AJAX elements can load at unpredictable times, automating interactions with them can be challenging, requiring special strategies to ensure proper synchronization.
- **Complexity**: AJAX can complicate the web development process, as developers need to manage asynchronous operations, error handling, and user experience consistency.
- **SEO and Accessibility**: Search engine optimization (SEO) and accessibility can be affected by AJAX, as dynamic content may not be indexed properly by search engines, and screen readers might not fully understand asynchronous changes.

In summary, AJAX technology has revolutionized how web applications work, allowing for more dynamic, responsive, and user-friendly experiences. However, its asynchronous nature presents unique challenges, especially for automation and testing. Understanding these challenges is critical for those working with web automation tools like Selenium WebDriver.

Challenges in Locating AJAX-based Elements

AJAX-based elements present unique challenges when automating web tests or scraping content due to their asynchronous and dynamic nature. This section explores these challenges and offers insights into overcoming them with reliable strategies.

1. Asynchronous Loading

One of the primary challenges in locating AJAX-based elements is that they may not be immediately available after a page loads or an action occurs. This asynchronous behavior can cause automation scripts to attempt to interact with elements that haven't yet rendered, leading to errors or unexpected behavior.

- **Example Scenario**: You click a button to trigger an AJAX request, expecting a modal window to appear with a form. If your script tries to interact with the form before it's fully loaded, it will fail.

2. Unpredictable Load Times

The load times for AJAX-based content can vary greatly depending on network conditions, server response times, and the complexity of the data being processed. This variability makes it difficult to predict when elements will be ready for interaction.

- **Example Scenario**: An AJAX-based search result might take a variable amount of time to return results. If the automation script doesn't account for this, it might result in test failures.

3. Stale Elements

When AJAX updates the DOM, it can change the structure of the page, causing elements to become "stale." Stale elements occur when a reference to an element becomes invalid due to a DOM update, leading to a StaleElementReferenceException in Selenium.

- **Example Scenario**: Your script selects a table row and then clicks a button that triggers an AJAX update. If you try to interact with the same row after the update, it may throw a `StaleElementReferenceException`.

4. Hidden or Collapsed Elements

AJAX-based elements might be hidden or collapsed by default, becoming visible only after certain user interactions. This can pose a challenge when locating and interacting with them.

- **Example Scenario**: A sidebar menu is collapsed by default and only expands when you hover over it. Automating this interaction requires additional logic to simulate user behavior.

5. Complex DOM Structures

AJAX can create highly dynamic and complex DOM structures, making it difficult to create stable XPath or CSS selectors. The use of dynamic IDs, multiple nested elements, and changing attributes complicates locating elements reliably.

- **Example Scenario**: A dynamic form where input fields are generated based on user choices. Locating specific inputs can be challenging if their identifiers change or if they are nested within other elements.

6. Timeout Issues

Given the asynchronous nature of AJAX, it's common to encounter timeout issues when automating interactions. Scripts may fail if they don't wait long enough for elements to load or if they wait too long without proper synchronization mechanisms.

- **Example Scenario**: A timeout occurs when an automation script expects an AJAX-based element to load within a specific timeframe, but it takes longer due to server latency or other factors.

7. Element Fluctuations

AJAX-based elements might change their position or attributes based on user interactions or other asynchronous events, leading to unstable locators.

- **Example Scenario**: A list of items that can be sorted by various criteria. Automating interactions with these items becomes challenging if their positions shift based on sorting order.

Addressing these challenges requires a combination of effective synchronization techniques, robust selectors, and dynamic handling strategies. The following sections will explore practical approaches to overcome these challenges and ensure reliable interaction with AJAX-based elements in automation scripts.

Strategies for Locating AJAX-based Elements

Locating AJAX-based elements in automated testing requires a unique approach due to their asynchronous and dynamic nature. This section explores various strategies to effectively locate and interact with these elements, ensuring your Selenium WebDriver scripts run smoothly.

1. Using Explicit Waits with ExpectedConditions

The most reliable strategy for locating AJAX-based elements is using explicit waits. Selenium WebDriver's `WebDriverWait` and `ExpectedConditions` provide robust mechanisms to wait until an element is in the desired state before interacting with it. This strategy helps avoid timing issues and reduces the risk of errors due to asynchronous loading.

- **Common ExpectedConditions**: `elementToBeClickable`, `visibilityOfElementLocated`, and `presenceOfElementLocated` are examples of explicit waits that can be used to synchronize your script with AJAX-based content.

2. Implementing Custom Waits

Sometimes, default explicit waits may not cover specific scenarios encountered with AJAX-based elements. Implementing custom wait conditions tailored to your application's behavior can be an effective strategy.

- **Example Custom Waits**: A custom wait that checks for the presence of specific text within an element or waits for a particular attribute to change, indicating the AJAX process is complete.

3. Relative XPath and CSS Selectors

To locate AJAX-based elements, use relative XPath or CSS selectors rather than absolute paths. Relative selectors are more adaptable to dynamic changes in the DOM structure, allowing for more reliable element identification.

- **Benefits of Relative Selectors**: They provide flexibility and resilience against DOM changes caused by AJAX updates. This strategy reduces the likelihood of encountering `NoSuchElementException` or `StaleElementReferenceException`.

4. Handling Stale Elements

AJAX can cause elements to become stale as the DOM updates. To handle this, implement retry logic or check for element stability before interacting with it.

- **Stale Element Handling**: A simple try-catch block can retry locating the element if it becomes stale. Alternatively, wait until the element's attributes stabilize before interacting with it.

5. Utilizing Page Load Strategies

Selenium offers page load strategies that control when the WebDriver considers the page "loaded." Adjusting these strategies can help with AJAX-based applications.

- **Page Load Strategies**: The `eager` strategy allows scripts to proceed when the DOM content is ready but before AJAX is fully completed, while `complete` waits until everything, including AJAX requests, has finished.

6. Synchronizing with AJAX Events

To ensure accurate synchronization, consider using browser developer tools to monitor AJAX requests. This approach allows you to identify key events or signals indicating that AJAX-based elements are ready for interaction.

- **Network Monitoring**: Tools like Chrome DevTools can track AJAX requests, enabling you to determine when specific elements are loaded based on network activity. This information can inform your explicit waits or custom wait conditions.

7. Using JavaScript for Advanced Synchronization

In some cases, direct interaction with JavaScript may be necessary to locate AJAX-based elements. This approach allows you to execute custom JavaScript to check conditions or trigger events to ensure elements are available.

- **JavaScript Execution**: Selenium's executeScript method can be used to run JavaScript snippets that check for specific conditions, trigger AJAX processes, or verify element states before proceeding with further automation steps.

These strategies provide a comprehensive approach to locating AJAX-based elements, addressing common challenges such as asynchronous loading, stale elements, and dynamic DOM structures.

Using Waits with AJAX in Selenium WebDriver

Automation with Selenium WebDriver often requires interacting with elements that load asynchronously due to AJAX (Asynchronous JavaScript and XML). The use of waits is crucial to ensure your scripts work reliably with AJAX-based elements. This section will explore different types of waits in Selenium, how to use them effectively, and best practices for handling AJAX-related delays.

Understanding Implicit and Explicit Waits

Selenium WebDriver provides two types of waits to handle asynchronous loading: implicit waits and explicit waits. Each has its specific use cases and can be leveraged to interact with AJAX-based elements.

Implicit Waits

An implicit wait tells Selenium to wait for a certain amount of time before throwing an exception if it can't find an element. This approach applies a global delay to all element-finding operations, making it useful for dealing with general timing issues.

- **Setting Implicit Waits**: To set an implicit wait, use the manage().timeouts().implicitlyWait() method, specifying the duration and time unit (e.g., seconds). This wait applies to all subsequent element searches.
- **Advantages of Implicit Waits**: They are simple to implement and can be useful for minor delays where elements eventually become available without specific conditions.
- **Disadvantages of Implicit Waits**: They can lead to longer test runtimes if the wait duration is high, and they don't allow for fine-tuning based on specific scenarios.

Explicit Waits

Explicit waits are more versatile and recommended for handling AJAX-based elements. With explicit waits, you define a condition that must be met before Selenium proceeds. This flexibility allows you to wait for specific events or states, making it ideal for asynchronous scenarios.

- **Using Explicit Waits**: Explicit waits require creating a WebDriverWait object with a specified timeout duration. You then define the conditions under which the wait ends using ExpectedConditions.
- **Common ExpectedConditions**: Some useful conditions for handling AJAX include elementToBeClickable, visibilityOfElementLocated, presenceOfElementLocated, and textToBePresentInElement.
- **Custom Conditions**: You can create custom expected conditions to wait for unique situations, such as a specific attribute change, network request completion, or a JavaScript variable reaching a certain value.

Implementing Explicit Waits

Explicit waits are implemented as follows:

1. **Create a WebDriverWait Object**: Define a `WebDriverWait` with the desired timeout and polling interval (if needed).
2. **Define an Expected Condition**: Use predefined `ExpectedConditions` or create custom conditions based on your application's AJAX behavior.
3. **Apply the Explicit Wait**: Use the `WebDriverWait` object to wait until the expected condition is met, allowing the script to proceed with reliable synchronization.
4. **Example of Explicit Wait**:

```
WebDriverWait wait = new WebDriverWait(driver, 10); // 10-second timeout
WebElement element =
wait.until(ExpectedConditions.visibilityOfElementLocated(By.id("ajax-elem
ent")));
```

Best Practices for Using Waits with AJAX

To effectively use waits with AJAX in Selenium WebDriver, consider these best practices:

- **Use Explicit Waits for Specific Conditions**: Explicit waits are better suited for AJAX-based elements, as they allow for tailored synchronization with specific conditions.
- **Avoid Excessive Implicit Waits**: Implicit waits can lead to longer test runtimes and are less flexible in handling AJAX delays.
- **Monitor Network Activity**: Use browser developer tools to understand AJAX timing and set your waits accordingly.
- **Handle Stale Elements**: When using explicit waits, be prepared for `StaleElementReferenceException` and implement retry logic if necessary.
- **Utilize Polling Intervals**: Explicit waits can be configured with custom polling intervals, allowing for more frequent checks during the wait period.
- **Set Appropriate Timeouts**: Ensure timeouts are neither too short (leading to false failures) nor too long (causing excessive delays). Adjust based on your application's AJAX behavior and typical network response times.

These strategies and best practices help ensure that your Selenium WebDriver scripts effectively handle AJAX-based elements, reducing the likelihood of timing-related errors and improving test reliability.

Implementing Explicit and Implicit Waits

Implementing waits in Selenium WebDriver is crucial for ensuring scripts interact reliably with elements on dynamic web pages, especially those that use AJAX. This chapter discusses the implementation of explicit and implicit waits, with examples and best practices for their use in real-world scenarios.

Implicit Waits

Implicit waits are simple to set up and apply globally to all element searches. They instruct Selenium WebDriver to wait for a specified time before raising an exception if an element is not found. However, they don't allow for condition-specific waits.

- **Setting Implicit Waits**: To set an implicit wait, you use `driver.manage().timeouts().implicitlyWait()`. This tells WebDriver to wait for a certain period for an element to become available before failing.

```
driver.manage().timeouts().implicitlyWait(10, TimeUnit.SECONDS); // 10
seconds
```

- **Pros of Implicit Waits**:

- ○ Easy to implement.
  - ○ Works as a general-purpose delay to handle minor timing issues.
- **Cons of Implicit Waits**:
  - ○ Applies globally, potentially causing longer test runtimes.
  - ○ Doesn't offer precise control over specific conditions or elements.

Explicit Waits

Explicit waits are more flexible, allowing you to define specific conditions that must be met before continuing. They are recommended for handling AJAX-based elements due to their precision.

- **Creating Explicit Waits**: Explicit waits involve creating a `WebDriverWait` object with a timeout duration. You then define conditions that trigger the end of the wait.

```
WebDriverWait wait = new WebDriverWait(driver, 10); // 10-second timeout
WebElement element =
wait.until(ExpectedConditions.visibilityOfElementLocated(By.id("element-i
d")));
```

- **Common ExpectedConditions**: Selenium provides several predefined expected conditions, including:
  - ○ `visibilityOfElementLocated`: Waits until an element is visible.
  - ○ `elementToBeClickable`: Waits until an element is clickable (visible and enabled).
  - ○ `presenceOfElementLocated`: Waits until an element is present in the DOM, regardless of visibility.
  - ○ `textToBePresentInElement`: Waits until a specified text appears in an element.

Custom Explicit Waits

In some cases, you may need custom explicit waits to handle specific scenarios. This can be useful when interacting with AJAX-based elements that require more complex conditions.

- **Creating Custom Waits**: You can create custom expected conditions using lambda functions or other logical expressions.

```
WebDriverWait wait = new WebDriverWait(driver, 15); // 15-second timeout
WebElement element = wait.until(driver ->
driver.findElement(By.id("dynamic-element")).isDisplayed());
```

Implementing Explicit and Implicit Waits in Selenium WebDriver

To effectively implement explicit and implicit waits, consider the following guidelines:

- **Choose Explicit Waits for Specific Scenarios**: Use explicit waits to handle specific conditions, particularly when dealing with AJAX-based elements that may take time to load or change state.
- **Set Reasonable Timeouts**: Avoid excessive timeouts, as they can lead to slow test execution. Consider typical load times and adjust as needed.
- **Combine Implicit and Explicit Waits**: While explicit waits are preferred for precise control, you can use implicit waits as a baseline to ensure that all element searches have a minimum wait time.
- **Use Polling for Frequent Checks**: Explicit waits allow you to set polling intervals, enabling frequent checks during the wait period. This can be useful for scenarios with varying load times.
- **Handle Stale Element Issues**: Stale elements can occur in AJAX-heavy applications. Implement retry logic or additional explicit waits to address this issue.

Example: Using Explicit and Implicit Waits Together

Here's an example of using both implicit and explicit waits to handle AJAX-based elements:

```
// Set an implicit wait for general element searches
driver.manage().timeouts().implicitlyWait(5, TimeUnit.SECONDS); // 5
seconds

// Explicit wait to ensure an AJAX-based element is visible
WebDriverWait explicitWait = new WebDriverWait(driver, 15); // 15-second
explicit wait
WebElement element =
explicitWait.until(ExpectedConditions.visibilityOfElementLocated(By.id("a
jax-element")));
```

By combining implicit and explicit waits, you can create a robust framework for interacting with AJAX-based elements in Selenium WebDriver, ensuring your scripts are reliable and resilient against timing issues.

Handling Common AJAX Issues in Automation

Working with AJAX-based elements in automation scripts can be challenging due to the asynchronous and dynamic nature of AJAX. This section addresses common issues that arise when dealing with AJAX in automated testing and provides solutions to tackle them.

1. Stale Element Reference

A common problem in AJAX-heavy environments is the "stale element" issue, which occurs when the DOM updates after a reference to an element has been stored. This leads to StaleElementReferenceException, indicating that the referenced element is no longer valid.

- **Causes**: AJAX can cause elements to be removed or replaced after an interaction, leading to stale references.
- **Solution**: Implement retry logic or use explicit waits to ensure the element is still present before interacting with it.

```
WebDriverWait wait = new WebDriverWait(driver, 10);
WebElement element;

try {
  element =
wait.until(ExpectedConditions.visibilityOfElementLocated(By.id("ajax-elem
ent")));
} catch (StaleElementReferenceException e) {
  // Retry to get a fresh reference
  element =
wait.until(ExpectedConditions.visibilityOfElementLocated(By.id("ajax-elem
ent")));
}
```

2. NoSuchElementException

This exception occurs when Selenium cannot find the specified element, often due to asynchronous loading delays. In AJAX contexts, this can happen when elements take longer to load or are hidden until triggered by specific interactions.

- **Causes**: The element is not yet present in the DOM or has been removed by AJAX operations.

- **Solution**: Use explicit waits to ensure the element is present before interacting with it.

```
WebDriverWait wait = new WebDriverWait(driver, 10);
WebElement element =
wait.until(ExpectedConditions.presenceOfElementLocated(By.id("ajax-elemen
t")));
```

3. TimeoutException

A `TimeoutException` indicates that an expected condition wasn't met within a specified timeframe. This can happen in AJAX-heavy applications if the script doesn't wait long enough for elements to load or AJAX requests to complete.

- **Causes**: Delays in AJAX operations, network latency, or insufficient wait times.
- **Solution**: Increase explicit wait time or use polling intervals to check for conditions regularly.

```
WebDriverWait wait = new WebDriverWait(driver, 20); // 20 seconds
wait.pollingEvery(Duration.ofSeconds(2)); // Poll every 2 seconds
WebElement element =
wait.until(ExpectedConditions.elementToBeClickable(By.id("ajax-element"))
);
```

4. Dynamic Element Identifiers

AJAX-based elements often have dynamically generated identifiers, making it challenging to create stable locators. This can lead to inconsistent test results if the locator strategy is not flexible enough.

- **Causes**: AJAX-generated IDs, changing attributes, or dynamic DOM structures.
- **Solution**: Use relative XPath or CSS selectors to locate elements based on structure or attributes, rather than fixed IDs.

```
// Locate an element based on its relative position in the DOM
WebElement element =
driver.findElement(By.xpath("//div[@class='ajax-container']//button[text(
)='Submit']"));
```

5. Element Visibility Issues

AJAX-based elements might be hidden or have delayed visibility, causing errors if the script tries to interact with them before they are visible.

- **Causes**: AJAX updates might hide elements or require specific interactions to make them visible.
- **Solution**: Use explicit waits for element visibility or implement custom logic to ensure the element is visible before interacting.

```
WebDriverWait wait = new WebDriverWait(driver, 10);
WebElement element =
wait.until(ExpectedConditions.visibilityOfElementLocated(By.id("ajax-elem
ent")));
```

6. AJAX Timing Variability

AJAX operations can vary in timing, making it difficult to predict when elements will be ready for interaction. This can lead to inconsistent test results and unreliable automation scripts.

- **Causes**: Network latency, server processing time, or complex AJAX operations.

- **Solution**: Monitor AJAX requests using browser developer tools to understand typical timing patterns and adjust waits accordingly.

```
// Example of using a JavaScript snippet to check AJAX completion
JavascriptExecutor js = (JavascriptExecutor) driver;
Boolean ajaxComplete = (Boolean) js.executeScript("return jQuery.active
== 0"); // Check if all AJAX requests are complete
```

These common issues and their solutions should help you navigate the complexities of AJAX in automated testing, ensuring that your Selenium WebDriver scripts are robust and reliable.

Best Practices for Reliable AJAX-based Automation

Automation with AJAX-based elements requires a combination of synchronization, robust selectors, and a thorough understanding of how AJAX interacts with the DOM. This section covers best practices for ensuring reliable and consistent results when automating web applications that rely on AJAX.

1. Use Explicit Waits for Synchronization

Explicit waits provide control over the conditions under which your Selenium WebDriver scripts proceed. By waiting for specific events or elements, you can reduce the risk of timing-related issues.

- **Choose Appropriate ExpectedConditions**: Use conditions like `elementToBeClickable`, `visibilityOfElementLocated`, or `presenceOfElementLocated` to synchronize with AJAX-based elements.
- **Set Reasonable Timeouts**: Avoid setting timeouts that are too short, which can lead to false failures, or too long, which can slow down tests. Use a value that accommodates typical AJAX delays.

2. Implement Retry Logic for Stale Elements

AJAX can cause elements to become stale as the DOM changes. Implementing retry logic ensures that your script doesn't fail due to these unexpected changes.

- **Stale Element Handling**: Use try-catch blocks to re-attempt finding elements if a `StaleElementReferenceException` occurs. This approach can be combined with explicit waits to ensure the element has stabilized.

```
WebElement element;
try {
  element = driver.findElement(By.id("ajax-element"));
} catch (StaleElementReferenceException e) {
  // Retry to get a fresh reference
  WebDriverWait wait = new WebDriverWait(driver, 10);
  element =
wait.until(ExpectedConditions.visibilityOfElementLocated(By.id("ajax-elem
ent")));
}
```

3. Use Relative XPath and CSS Selectors

Relative XPath and CSS selectors are more adaptable to changing DOM structures caused by AJAX. This approach reduces the likelihood of encountering issues due to dynamic IDs or attributes.

- **Relative Selectors**: Instead of absolute paths, use relative selectors that navigate through the DOM based on relationships or patterns.

```
WebElement element =
driver.findElement(By.xpath("//div[@class='ajax-container']//button[text(
)='Submit']"));
```

- **Use Unique Attributes**: Locate elements based on unique attributes rather than relying solely on position or ID.

4. Monitor AJAX Requests with Browser Tools

Understanding AJAX behavior in your application can provide valuable insights into timing and synchronization. Use browser developer tools to monitor AJAX requests and adjust your waits accordingly.

- **Network Monitoring**: Tools like Chrome DevTools can help you track AJAX requests, allowing you to identify when elements are expected to be ready.
- **Use JavaScript to Detect AJAX Activity**: JavaScript can be used to check AJAX status, providing additional synchronization options.

```
JavascriptExecutor js = (JavascriptExecutor) driver;
Boolean ajaxComplete = (Boolean) js.executeScript("return jQuery.active
== 0"); // Check if AJAX requests are complete
```

5. Use Page Load Strategies

Selenium WebDriver offers different page load strategies that can help manage AJAX-based delays. Adjusting these strategies can improve synchronization with dynamic content.

- **Set Page Load Strategy**: Use the `eager` strategy to proceed when the DOM is ready but AJAX requests may still be pending, or the `complete` strategy to wait until everything, including AJAX, is finished.

```
// Set eager page load strategy
driver.manage().timeouts().pageLoadStrategy(PageLoadStrategy.EAGER);
```

6. Test on Multiple Scenarios

AJAX behavior can vary depending on user interactions, network conditions, and server response times. Testing across multiple scenarios ensures your automation script is robust and resilient.

- **Test with Different Network Conditions**: Use network throttling to simulate varying conditions and ensure your waits can handle slower responses.
- **Test with Multiple User Flows**: Different user interactions can trigger different AJAX behavior. Ensure your script accounts for all relevant flows.

7. Utilize Implicit Waits Cautiously

While explicit waits are preferred for synchronization, implicit waits can serve as a general safety net. Use them to add a base level of wait time for element searches, but avoid relying solely on implicit waits.

- **Set a Reasonable Implicit Wait**: A short implicit wait can be useful to handle minor delays, but excessive implicit waits can slow down your tests.

```
driver.manage().timeouts().implicitlyWait(5, TimeUnit.SECONDS); // 5
seconds
```

By following these best practices, you can create reliable automation scripts that effectively handle the complexities of AJAX-based web applications. Proper synchronization, robust selectors, and thorough testing are key to ensuring consistent and accurate automation results.

Chapter Summary

This chapter covered essential topics for interacting with AJAX-based elements in automated testing with Selenium WebDriver. AJAX (Asynchronous JavaScript and XML) technology allows web pages to update content without reloading, creating dynamic and interactive experiences. However, these asynchronous updates can pose challenges for automation. Here's a summary of what you learned about finding and handling AJAX-based elements.

Overview of AJAX Technology

- AJAX enables asynchronous communication between the client and server, allowing parts of a web page to update independently without a full page reload.
- This flexibility introduces unpredictability in element rendering times, requiring specific strategies to interact with dynamic content reliably.

Challenges in Locating AJAX-based Elements

- **Asynchronous Loading**: AJAX-based elements might not be available immediately, leading to timing issues in automation scripts.
- **Stale Elements**: As AJAX updates the DOM, existing element references may become invalid, causing `StaleElementReferenceException`.
- **Unpredictable Load Times**: AJAX requests can vary in response times, complicating synchronization with automated tests.
- **Dynamic Identifiers**: AJAX-generated elements often have dynamic attributes, requiring more flexible locator strategies.
- **Timeout Issues**: Automation scripts may encounter `TimeoutException` due to insufficient wait times or complex AJAX operations.

Strategies for Locating AJAX-based Elements

- **Explicit Waits**: Use `WebDriverWait` with `ExpectedConditions` to wait for specific conditions, providing reliable synchronization with AJAX-based elements.
- **Relative XPath and CSS Selectors**: Crafting selectors that adapt to dynamic DOM structures is crucial for locating AJAX-based elements.
- **Custom Waits and Retry Logic**: Implementing retry logic and custom explicit waits can help manage stale elements and asynchronous loading.

Using Waits with AJAX in Selenium WebDriver

- **Implicit Waits**: These waits set a global delay for all element searches, useful for handling minor timing issues.
- **Explicit Waits**: Recommended for AJAX-based scenarios, explicit waits allow you to define specific conditions and timeouts.
- **Combining Implicit and Explicit Waits**: Use implicit waits cautiously as a safety net, with explicit waits providing precise control over synchronization.

Handling Common AJAX Issues in Automation

- **Stale Element Reference**: Implement retry logic to handle `StaleElementReferenceException`.

- **NoSuchElementException**: Use explicit waits to ensure elements are present before interacting with them.
- **TimeoutException**: Adjust explicit wait times to avoid premature failures due to AJAX delays.
- **Dynamic Identifiers**: Use relative XPath and CSS selectors to locate elements in a dynamic environment.
- **Element Visibility Issues**: Ensure elements are visible before interacting with them using explicit waits.

Best Practices for Reliable AJAX-based Automation

- **Explicit Waits for Synchronization**: Explicit waits with specific conditions are critical for reliable interaction with AJAX-based elements.
- **Use Relative Selectors**: Relative XPath and CSS selectors are more adaptable to changing DOM structures.
- **Monitor AJAX Requests**: Use browser developer tools to understand AJAX timing and adjust waits accordingly.
- **Use Page Load Strategies**: Adjusting page load strategies can help manage AJAX-based delays.
- **Test on Multiple Scenarios**: Testing across various scenarios ensures your automation scripts are robust and resilient.

With these key insights, you should be equipped to tackle the challenges posed by AJAX-based elements in automated testing. Implementing the strategies and best practices outlined in this chapter will help ensure your Selenium WebDriver scripts are reliable and effective in dynamic web environments.

Conclusion

Thank you for completing "Conquer Web Element Location with XPath and CSS Selectors." By now, you should have a comprehensive understanding of how to effectively locate elements on a web page using XPath and CSS selectors. You've navigated through the basics and explored advanced techniques to confidently work with a variety of web elements in Selenium WebDriver.

Throughout this journey, you've learned to:

- **Grasp the Fundamentals**: You began by understanding HTML structure and the importance of identifying elements in web development. This foundational knowledge is crucial for the effective use of XPath and CSS selectors.
- **Develop XPath Skills**: You discovered how to construct XPath expressions using various methods, from simple attribute-based selectors to more complex parent-child relationships. You also learned how to manage dynamic elements and use relative and absolute XPath efficiently.
- **Master CSS Selectors**: Building on your XPath knowledge, you delved into the world of CSS selectors. You explored different techniques to select elements based on multiple attributes, classes, and other identifiers. Additionally, you discovered advanced CSS selector techniques for child-node indexing, handling collections, and working with nested structures.
- **Apply Knowledge in Real-World Scenarios**: Lastly, you applied your skills in real-world contexts, focusing on complex web page structures, AJAX-based elements, and interactive user inputs. This section demonstrated how to tackle real challenges encountered in web development and automated testing.

As you close this book, remember that the key to mastering web element location lies in continuous practice and adaptation. The world of web development is constantly evolving, with new frameworks and technologies emerging regularly. By staying updated and experimenting with different scenarios, you can maintain your expertise and remain a valuable asset in the field of test automation and web development.

We hope this book has empowered you to become a Selenium WebDriver element-locating expert. Use your newfound skills to build robust automated tests, create efficient web automation scripts, and explore new opportunities in your career. Remember, the ability to locate web elements with precision is a skill that will serve you well across many domains.

Thank you for choosing this book as your guide to conquering web element location with XPath and CSS selectors. We wish you success in all your automation endeavors, and we look forward to the exciting projects you'll undertake with your enhanced skills. Happy testing!

www.ingramcontent.com/pod-product-compliance
Lightning Source LLC
LaVergne TN
LVHW081752050326
832903LV00027B/1915